I0799784

The Boys From CORBIN

THE BOYS FROM CORBIN

America's Greatest Little Sports Town

by
Gary P. West

Acclaim Press™
MORLEY, MISSOURI

Acclaim Press
— Your Next Great Book —
P.O. Box 238
Morley, MO 63767
(573) 472-9800
www.acclaimpress.com

Book Design: M. Frene Melton
Cover Design: Kimberly M. Paul

Library of Congress Cataloging-in-Publication Data

West, Gary P.
The Boys Grom Corbin: America's Greatest Little Sports Town / by Gary P. West.
pages cm
ISBN 978-1-938905-23-0 (alk. paper) -- ISBN 1-938905-23-7 (alk. paper)
1. Sports--Kentucky--Corbin--History. 2. Football--Kentucky--Corbin--History.
3. Basketball--Kentucky--Corbin--History. 4. Corbin (Ky.)--History. 5. Corbin
(Ky.)--Social life and customs. I. Title.
GV584.5.C67W47 2013
796.097691--dc23
2013007225

First Printing: 2013 Second Printing: 2013 Third Printing: 2016
Printed in the United States of America
10 9 8 7 6 5 4 3

This publication was produced using available information.
The publisher regrets it cannot assume responsibility for errors or omissions.

Contents

Preface

I met Rodger Bird at the University of Kentucky in 1964. He was probably a sophomore, and I was entering my junior year majoring in journalism, hoping someday to be a writer. Rodger was a football player on the verge of becoming an All-American, and hoping someday to play professional football. I was hoping someday to write for a newspaper, never dreaming about a book, much less someone paying money for something I wrote. Perhaps the only thing the two of us had in common was that we both liked football. Rodger played it, and I wrote about it.

And here we are, together again after 50 years, telling the story of a small Kentucky railroad town that has produced more All-State and All-American football and basketball players than any little town in America.

From the very beginning Rodger was under somewhat of a microscope at the Lexington school. He was the last of the four Bird boys from Corbin, and the early prognosis was that he might be the best of them all. But he had to prove it on the field.

Brother Jerry, at 6'6", had been an All-SEC basketball player on Adolph Rupp's team in the early 1950s, and later played in the NBA. Another brother, Calvin, became a gridiron legend of sorts with his unpredictable punt and kick returns, which more times than not bordered on spectacular. He, too, became an All-SEC talent who found a spot on an NFL roster.

Yet another brother Billy, two years older than Rodger, came to the Kentucky program with the highest expectations of all, only to give up the game following his sophomore year. He succumbed to the pressure of being a football player with the last name of Bird and playing for a coach that chased off enough talent to fill an NFL expansion team.

The Bird family wasn't quite through. When Jerry's son Steve came along, there were some that said his football skills might be the best of all. Surely he would go to U.K. and continue the tradition. Not so. As good as he was, there was little interest from the Big Blue, so he headed to Eastern Kentucky University where he became an All-American and followed that into the NFL.

There were few if any families in Kentucky that, athletically, could rival the Birds. But if there was one, incredibly, it came from right there in Corbin. The Selvys.

One cannot write about the Birds or Corbin without writing about Frank Selvy and his NCAA record setting performances. And the fact that he had four brothers that made their way to division one teams only adds to Corbin's legacy.

For this small blue-collar town, often covered with coal dust from the many trains that came in and out daily, there were other great players such as: Roy Kidd, Tommy

Adkins, Bobby Terrell, Jerry Smith, Jesse Grant, Melvin Chandler, Marvin Selvy, Edd Selvy, Curly Selvy, Ted Meadors, Ralph Wilder, Nick Denes, David Chandler, Winton Boone, Ron Boone, Don Turner, Tony Lanham, Fred Rader, Bobby Coleman, and the hundreds of others that were the boys from Corbin.

This is a story about a town in the 1940s, 50s, and into the early 60s that was so dominate on the gridiron and hardwood that few area teams wanted to play them.

What was the phenomenon that occurred in this small town that led to so many really good athletes being churned out? It wasn't the water, as some might think. It was something much deeper, and not easily explained. It happened because Corbin was a town that cared. Its citizens cared about each other, looked out for each other, and even those that didn't play on a Redhound team were Redhounds in spirit.

Just being good enough was never good enough in Corbin. And, like many small towns of that era, high school sports teams were its social life, and with an entire town behind one school and one team, pride became the central driving force. With that pride came "The Boys from Corbin."

If there's a negative about writing a book like this, it is that, unintentionally, someone or some teams will be left out. It would be almost impossible not to overlook an individual or a team that has contributed to the athletic success of Corbin High School. If this has happened, I apologize, but it comes with the territory of writing a book that goes in so many directions. With only a few exceptions, the book concludes with the 1962 teams.

Introduction

Railroaders were a tough lot. From those early days of laying track, it was this courageous group of men who deserve much of the credit for America's westward expansion.

But it was Corbin, and its easy access to coal and timber, that became a vital cog in the industrial upheaval of the country. As the town began to emerge in the 1880s as a "railroad town," along with it came jobs. And jobs meant economic opportunity.

Corbin, by Kentucky historical dates, probably got a late start as a town. And it took the railroad to do it. By any stretch, it is not an old town. Although some of the early day settlers were in and out of the area in the late 1700s into the 1800s, Corbin didn't actually become a settlement until the 1870s. At first it was referred to as Cummins or Lynn Camp. Then local history says that in 1885 the area's first postmaster, James Eaton, was informed that those names were already in use, and that the town needed a new name. Corbin it was. A local minister by the name of James Corbin Floyd, who was liked by many of the locals, was the inspiration.

The Louisville-Nashville Railroad became the key ingredient for anything that happened in Corbin. Once the tracks reached the town it was never the same. When the Civil War ended, L & N began to reconstruct many of the tracks and bridges that had been destroyed during the war, and then look for ways to economically improve its position in Kentucky and Tennessee by laying track, and inching its way into the eastern portion of the state that previously had been underserved when it came to getting those natural resources, coal, timber and iron ore, to market in a more timely manner.

The United States was gearing up to fast-forward into the industrial revolution. The coal and timber available, for the most part previously untapped, would soon make Corbin, and the counties around it, well positioned to do its part in helping to grow the country.

Livingston, Kentucky was as far as the railroad extended at the war's end, and it wasn't until 1883 before L & N took their tracks into Corbin, while at the same time also reaching into Tennessee to the town of Jellico. Three years later, in 1886, L & N stretched its tracks to Pineville. It was at this time that Corbin began to take on its identity as a railroad town. Soon after, Middlesboro was added to the rail network. Then Shawnee, Tennessee came by way of a hook-up with the Norfolk and Western Railroad.

Meanwhile, a roundhouse had been built in Corbin. Soon came a blacksmith shop and an engine house for maintenance as part of the L & N's railroad yard. Now not only were the tracks exporting eastern Kentucky products to the rest of the nation, but passengers were coming in and out of town connecting to trains that would carry them to places many thought they would never be able to visit except in their dreams.

It was exciting times for Corbin as it began to take on the look of a city. A newspaper popped up once there were enough advertisers to financially support it. With increased population came doctors, banks, sawmills, tin shops, cabinet makers, brickyards, grocery stores, dry good stores, and drugstores. The Cumberland Valley division of the Louisville-Nashville Railroad was thriving.

In its own sort of way Corbin was experiencing its "gold rush," and with influx of the outside world came problems. At the top of the list was a shortage of housing to take care of all the workers needed to run a railroad center. Many of the railroaders did not bring their families when they arrived, so to assist in housing them, a YMCA was built. Boarding houses and a couple of hotels sprang up. Quickly certain areas of Corbin became identified as the railroad part of town, not a place for longtime Corbin folks to venture into. These areas became known as Apeyard, Scuffletown, and even Brickbat Hill, and though not very flattering, they nevertheless were true to these days of hard times and hard living.

In the early 1900s the town erected its first streetlights. Allen Dizney, a historian of sorts in Corbin, says those lights went up around 1904. Crudely fashioned streets often became a sea of dirt and mud, eventually giving way to bricks and concrete. "The first street paved here with concrete was Depot Street in 1916," he says. "And it wasn't until 1920 or 1921 that Main Street was paved. Concrete was tried on some of the streets with hills, but there was a problem with it "running" and that caused the streets to have humps in them. Because of that, Gordon Hill was done with bricks." As more and more residents wanted streets paved it fell on them to share the cost of the portion of the street that ran in front of their houses. However, they had several years to pay for it.

The proper city of Corbin officially sits in two counties, Whitley and Knox, with a third county, Laurel, taking in an extended part of the town. However, due to a quirky segment of state law, a Kentucky city is prohibited from being in three counties. Public utilities and tax payments have been issues throughout the town's growth.

The violent reputation Corbin earned in the late nineteenth century, often as a result of a lethal combination of railroad and timber workers and a whole lot of alcohol, led to state soldiers and police being ordered to the town to restore law and order by the governor following the shooting of several law enforcement agents.

In 1921, railroad shop workers went on strike and the town's Hippodrome Theatre became the union headquarters. People from out-of-state moved to Corbin to take the striking workers' jobs. Many, it was said, were from Georgia, and some stayed for 30 years. In the beginning the so-called scabs faced a hostile community. Stores would not sell to them, and it was even told that some of the area doctors refused to provide medical treatment.

Corbin, however, was not experiencing anything that wasn't happening in many towns across, not only Kentucky, but America. Pure and simple, it was the evolution of growing up.

The town's importance and the role it played in the industrial revolution can never be minimized, and the forward thinking and vision its city and county leaders had in working with national railroad officials to push for making Corbin, Kentucky, one of the nation's most active railway hubs, was monumental.

Because of what happened in Corbin, coal and timber from Kentucky, Tennessee, West Virginia, and Virginia, was able to reach the world.

Corbin might be considered one of those "tweener" towns when it comes to its geographical identity in Kentucky. Though it is located in the proximity of the mountains of eastern Kentucky, by some it is not considered a mountain town. The culture that has evolved over the last century and a half has produced several generations of proud blue collar workers who have provided a quality of life that put roofs over their heads, clothes on their backs and food on their tables, in a town that was centered around railroads. For the most part that was the norm for the average family in the area.

In the early part of the 1900s Corbin was reputed to be a tough town. That label it had in common with most of the nearby coal camps of Appalachia. Like coal miners, railroaders worked hard. But when their work day ended or a weekend rolled around, their down time often included visits to a pool hall, which led to arguments, fights and occasionally a killing. It was common for early day workers to carry guns. And, when there are guns, things can happen that are often not good.

Corbin, like several other towns in eastern Kentucky in the early 1900s had acquired a reputation as a "whites only" place to live and work. When the L & N pushed its tracks southeast into Corbin, those in positions of authority had little interest in the political geography of the three counties – Whitley, Knox and Laurel. What they were interested in were the railroads and the lucrative freight business that came with it. Coal cars loaded to the brim headed south to Knoxville and Atlanta, while others chugged north to Cincinnati and beyond. Through it all, Corbin became a very busy place. Its expanding rail yards became a stopover for rail crews and engine repairs. A YMCA was built in 1902 across the street from the ever-growing freight depot, providing overnight lodging for those just passing through in their jobs with the railroads.

Much like frontier towns of the wild, wild west, Corbin, too, had its "economic boon" in the form of saloons, and houses of ill repute. With it all, the prosperous railroads brought something to Corbin in 1920 that many of the residents were not accustomed to, blacks. Records revealed that the 1910 census showed Corbin with a population of 2,800, of which 60 of those were black.

The imported work crews soon increased the black presence in Corbin while meeting the demand of much needed laborers to build railroad facilities, additional yard tracks, and pave dirt streets. The rail yards where these workers ate and slept on train cars were declared off-limits to most of those who lived in Corbin. Most certainly, white families forbid their children to go anywhere near the area. Any crimes committed, regardless of who did it, were usually blamed on the imported black work crews.

It is well documented in newspaper articles and Pulitzer Prize winner Elliot Jaspin's book, *Buried in the Bitter Water...The History of Racial Cleansing in America*, that several Corbinites assembled a raucous group of marauding whites to rid the town of any and all blacks. For sure it was not a proud moment in Corbin's history, but it was a time for some of those permanent white families in Corbin to stand up and be counted. Some stepped up and literally hid black families in their homes until the situation calmed down a bit, and some of those so-called ring leaders of the vigilante group were later successfully prosecuted by the law.

A Corbin newspaper wrote that, "Our name has gone out over the nation with a black spot that can never be removed." It must be pointed out that there are those who believe the racial cleansing of the early 1920s never happened. What did happen was there were a handful of blacks imported via a work crew that was involved in what was considered criminal behavior. It was this crew of blacks and their white bosses who were escorted out of Corbin.

Many residents who once lived there in the mid-40s, through the 50s, and into the 60s have died. Others moved away to find employment when the rail industry declined and the nearby coal mines stopped producing. One thing, though, that never stopped producing was winning Corbin sports teams.

Why are stories still being written and people still talking about teams and players who performed more than fifty years ago? It's because it's part of who we are. It's about an almost indescribable desire to overcome all odds to obtain success. It's about accomplishing something for yourself, your family and your community.

The success of Redhound teams on the football field and basketball court in its own way gave everyone in the town a feeling of pride and success, even if they never played one second, were only a fan, or just read about it in the newspaper. Redhound wins engulfed everyone who lived there, and even those who had moved away. Sports in Corbin meant hope, and if you don't have hope what do you have?

This small town whose economy was fueled by railroad tracks, the trains that ran on them and the coal and timber they carried, was a sports town, one of the greatest in Kentucky history. Over the years Corbin's legendary sports families and the teams they played on have faded a bit, but still the standard many of these teams set are today a benchmark by which teams across Kentucky are measured. The individuals, the teams, and even some of the games they played will be remembered for a lifetime.

The Boys From CORBIN

America's Greatest Little Sports Town

Chapter One

Those Early Years

Unofficially, Corbin's first football team took the field in 1916. Then called the Railroaders, it took seven more years before the team began to play a schedule of any significance.

It would be difficult to imagine a more depressing start for a football team that was destined to become one of the most legendary programs in the history of Kentucky athletics. That first game was at Pineville, in nearby Bell County, and the Corbin team not only lost 142-0, but one of its players, William Cadle, died as a result of an injury during the game. It was probably good that the team only had a three game schedule.

Fortunately, Coach Harold McGregor's teams did get better, and the Kentucky Wesleyan graduate (when the school was located in Winchester) began to build a foundation for a football program that would become the envy of the state. One of his players was Newell Wilder, and the athletic Wilder was said to have been the areas first player to earn a scholarship to play football at the University of Kentucky.

Believe it or not, Corbin came back after the Pineville loss and tied Barbourville 0-0, and won the school's first game ever with a 3-0 win over Barbourville Baptist Institute, a forerunner of Knox Central. Hershell Moore has the distinction of scoring those first-ever points with his game winning field goal. Another footnote was that Bernard Kincaid was the only player on that Corbin team to have ever seen or played in a football game. He had played at Kentucky Military Institute the year before.

Initially Corbin High School colors were purple and gold, but an effort led by Tillie Goodin in 1926 to change not only the school's colors, but also the nickname, was successful. It would be either the Red Devils or the Red Hounds (two words in the beginning). And so it was. The school's new colors were maroon and white, and Corbin teams from then on have been called the Redhounds. In those early days the uniforms consisted mostly of overalls, but in 1926, Corbin High School purchased their first "real" football uniforms.

A.L. Pfammueller followed McGregor as coach. Then came R.L. Brown, followed by Dick Bacon in 1927, who officially coached the first team referred to as the Redhounds.

In 1929 the school embarked on a relationship with a young man fresh out of the University of Illinois. Nick Denes had played with the legendary Red Grange there, and when he arrived in Corbin by way of an L & N passenger train, sports in Kentucky would never be the same.

Not only could Denes coach football, but basketball, baseball, and track. Before his career was over, he became the only coach to win state championships in three different sports in Kentucky. His 1936 Redhound basketball team won the state title, and later at Male High in Louisville, he won championships in football and track.

For sure the hiring of Nick Denes set the standard. What followed was a tradition in football and basketball that has evolved into almost a cult following. Some of the Corbin old timers say it was a win by Denes' football team in only his second season that made the little railroad town realize what could be accomplished.

Denes, being a Midwest boy, scheduled a gridiron game against Dayton Stivers High. The year before, Stivers had not only won the championship of football-rich Ohio, but had also claimed the mythical national title. What a better way, thought Denes, to find out where his team stood than to play the best. With more than 6,000 fans in the stands to see Stivers High play what was referred to as a warm-up game, the Redhounds returned home with a 12-6 win. The Dayton school did not lose another game that season as it claimed its second state title in a row. The Redhound win was a victory that future Corbin generations could build on. And they did.

As good as football has been in Corbin, its basketball also excelled equally, producing some of the best players in Kentucky's history. Once again it was Nick Denes who coached. Though he had never played basketball, he was a coach. He knew by instinct what it took to mold a winning team. Back then a coach had to coach at least two sports, and sometimes three, if he was hired. Denes carried a full teaching load, and any assistant coaches he might have had were volunteers. There wasn't a budget for additional salaries.

In 1936, it was the transfer of the Cluggish brothers from nearby Williamsburg that propelled Corbin into basketball history. Marion Cluggish stood 6'7", and brother Stan 6'4". Together they gave the Redhounds a presence on the hardwood that would be very difficult for opposing teams to deal with.

Corbin put together 18 wins in a row before falling 27-14 to a Benham High team led by future coaching great Spider Thurman. The Redhounds won the district title with a win over Barbourville, and then in the regional championship game turned back Hazel Green for the right to play in the Boys Sweet Sixteen in Alumni Gym on the campus of the University of Kentucky. It was the school's first trip to the tourney.

With the Cluggish brothers leading the way, and strong support from Bill Asher, Wid Ellison, and Charles Sampson, Denes' team upset first Kirksey 27-24, then Henderson 27-17, and then Paris 33-19 before beating Nebo 24-18 for the championship. Marion Cluggish, despite severe bronchitis and lots of bed rest between games, was the tourney MVP and leading scorer with 63 points in four games. Other members of Corbin's first-ever state champion team in any sport were Gordon Gant, Carl Babb, Herschel Nelson, Alford Keck and Robert Sampson.

Marion Cluggish went on to play for Adolph Rupp and the Kentucky Wildcats, and when he graduated he became the first U.K. player to ever play in the NBA when he signed a contract with the New York Knicks.

The 1939 sports season at Corbin ranks among the top when it comes to Redhound success. Ted Meadors, a Corbin High graduate in 1930, and later a Little All-American at Centre College, coached the Redhounds to an unbeaten gridiron season, and Carl Lawson, who had understudied under Denes, coached Corbin's basketball team to a 28-6 mark and a fourth place finish in the State Tournament. The 1938-39 year marked the opening of Edwards Gymnasium, and Louisville St. X came to Corbin to christen the new "palace," which was being hailed as the top round ball facility in eastern Kentucky. St. X won the contest 20-19.

Eighty-eight year-old Allen Dizney's passion for Corbin history has never been questioned. As a community activist, he has for years indulged himself in promoting the town's history as it relates to railroads. His writings and his take on local history, while differing from others on occasion, has been a labor of love.

Dizney's dad had been a conductor on the railroad, and Dizney himself, for a while worked in the railway post office sorting mail. Growing up he took a job at the Hippodrome Theatre as an usher, and sold popcorn. "I could use the extra money," he said.

Dizney was a freshman at Corbin High School in 1939 when Ted Meadors coached the Redhounds to an undefeated season. "I didn't play sports," he said. "I was always so small. In fact I didn't call myself a Redhound because I never played football." But you can bet Dizney was a Redhound in spirit. Upon graduation in 1943, he enlisted in the Army Air Corp, and in order to do so he had to make the weight limit. "I had to drink three quarts of water to make weight. I only weighed 112 pounds at the time."

For several years he wrote a column in the local paper called "Redhound Re-Runs," many of which were recounts of stories he had heard and events he had seen. He recalled a football game Corbin played in Pineville. "There had been a big snow," he recalled. "The football field was covered, but everyone wanted to play. So Coach Denes and the Pineville people got together and decided to line the field with coal dust, which there was plenty of."

He also gave the history of where the term "touchdown" originated. "In the early days anytime a runner crossed the goal line he would have to touch the ball to the ground. That's why they called it a touchdown."

Later on Dizney was a high school football official, and sometimes he would officiate junior high games that Rodger Bird played in. "I picked Rodger up many times by the seat of his pants when he was in junior high," Dizney chuckled. "One time Rodger was on the ground in a pile trying to get a fumble. I said Rodger's got the ball. 'How do you know someone yelled?' I said because his pants are half down. That boy, when he was young, had a hard time keeping those football pants up on the football field."

Nick Denes

At Corbin High School Nick Denes would sometime describe his practices as a Chinese fire drill. "Everybody in town showed up on a good afternoon and wandered around the field helping us," he would declare. "But we had fun, and somehow or other the kids learned enough to win."

To let the multitudes show up at his practice session further points out Denes' inner character, one that permitted him to have the confidence in his own ability. He didn't mind allowing others watching him work. One of those the locals liked to watch was the fleet-footed halfback, Abie Ayers. He was one of Denes' first stars and went on to letter three years at U.K.

Being a former football player from Illinois in the Big Ten gave Denes the self-assurance that he did indeed know football. But basketball was another matter. Talking about his 1936 Corbin High state champions, he was not so bashful or insecure that he didn't mind saying, "I bought a book on coaching basketball and kept one chapter ahead of the kids."

Denes loved to coach and he made winning seem easy, but in the big picture of life, it was his desire to help boys to become good, responsible citizens. Stories abound of him getting boys out of jail and high school dropouts to get back in school. Of course, much of this was about football. He pushed the hot buttons, and more often than not, those he enticed to return were better for it. To Nick Denes this came with the territory as a high school coach. The easy thing for him would be to have done nothing. Who couldn't coach the "good boys?" Who wanted those with problems? Denes did. And the reward was twofold. He got a youngster who could play football, and hopefully turned out to be a good, productive citizen.

Doug Gibson was born in Corbin at Smith Hospital in 1947 and later moved with his family to Elizabethtown, but he had a family story about Denes and an uncle that has been passed down for years.

Apparently some of Denes' players didn't quite see the need to attend classes every day, and Gibson's uncle James was one of them. He played defensive end for the Redhounds, and when Friday rolled around Denes went looking for James. "My dad said almost every Friday afternoon Coach Denes would knock on the door, ask James a few questions and have him sign a sheet of paper stating that this was a make-up test for the classes he had missed that week," Gibson said. "My dad said Denes would tell James to be at the field at 6 o'clock ready to play."

Everywhere Nick Denes coached he left his mark in a positive way. His impact on Redhound sports is legendary, and his eight year football coaching record of 62 wins, 12 losses and 4 ties was significant enough for the Corbin school board to name the stadium in his honor. There might not be another coach in the nation with two stadiums named after him, but Denes achieved that status when Western Kentucky University named their baseball field Nick Denes Field.

In 1937, Denes left Corbin to become the head coach at a junior college. However, after two years at Tennessee Junior College, where he developed Phil Dickens, who would later become the head football coach at Indiana University, Denes moved on to become the freshman coach at Western Kentucky State Teachers College in Bowling Green.

The following year, in 1940, he became an assistant football coach at Male High in Louisville under Paul Jenkins, and in 1948 Denes became the head coach. At Male High Denes never lost a Thanksgiving Day game to Manual when that rivalry was the most bitterly fought game in the entire state.

He won a football title in 1951, to go along with eight track titles, thus making him the only high school coach in Kentucky to claim state championships in three different sports. With today's specialization that record may stand for a long time, because it is rare indeed to coach two different sports, much less three.

In 1954, he retired from football coaching to become Male's director of athletics and concentrated on coaching track. When Denes heard that Western was looking for a new football coach he placed a call to Western President Kelly Thompson to inquire about the job, not for himself, but instead for Male's coach Charlie Kuhn.

"I've got just the right man for you," Denes told the Western president. Thompson listened and Denes kept talking. The more Denes talked the more Thompson became interested in him, not Kuhn, becoming the Hilltoppers' next football coach. He thought Kuhn might be a little young, and besides, Western wanted a coach with a master's degree. Kuhn didn't have one, but Denes did.

So on February 11, 1957, Nicholas George Denes, at the age of 50, reported to the Western campus as the school's head football coach. His first announcement was that Jimmy Feix, a former All-American, and considered Western's greatest football player, would be joining his staff as an assistant following his soon-to-be discharge from the Air Force.

At Western, those who knew Denes felt he was as much of a character as legendary basketball coach Uncle Ed Diddle. The two were friends and found a lot of mutual ground and respect on The Hill.

It was not easy for Denes to generate interest in a sport that was not on the same national level as the Hilltopper basketball program, but he did it anyway. A lesser man would have left. Not saying he was a lesser man than Denes, but Paul "Bear" Bryant decided playing second fiddle to Adolph Rupp was not his thing and left Kentucky to go to Texas A & M.

Under Denes, the Hilltoppers were successful. As only he could, he put together a program that finally won a big one in 1963. Blending his own players with those who vacated the coaching methods of Kentucky coach Charlie Bradshaw and came to Bowling Green to continue their playing days, Denes captured the 1963 Tangerine Bowl in Orlando, Florida, against the Coast Guard Academy, a team coached by Otto Graham, the former Cleveland Brown quarterback.

Graham was the hot topic, even to the point of upstaging his own team. Denes on the other hand, didn't have the national reputation, so most of the media gravitated to

Graham. When the odds makers made the Academy solid favorites to beat Western, he used the lack of respect to play up his "poor little boys from Kentucky."

Western nailed the Coast Guard 27-0, and Denes couldn't help but relish the result. He had played his cards right. He knew he had a great team. Sprinkled with several future NFL players and coaches, he let the actions on the field do his talking. There was plenty of time for talking after the game.

Denes, like many of the so-called small college coaches, would have liked to parlayed his Tangerine Bowl success into a "big school" coaching job, but it never happened. It was much like the situation Roy Kidd found himself in after all of his accomplishments at Eastern. For reasons only those that run those big schools know, an upward coaching move from a successful lessor school to head coach is often very difficult.

Denes was twice Ohio Valley Conference coach-of-the-year, and when he stepped down at Western in 1967, his 36-year combined record for high school and college was an impressive 485-155-14.

Perhaps for the best, Corbin today is less rowdy than in the days Denes was there. A mellower Corbin, one would think, might decrease the so-called town characters. But most agree there is still enough to talk about from the old days. And though Denes might have thought the general citizenry of Corbin were all characters, he left little doubt he was one of them.

The foundation for his future coaching success was built in Corbin. He gave Corbin statewide recognition. When he proved that a football team from a little railroad town could go to the big cities of Louisville and Lexington and win, he gave the town a feeling of pride, confidence and hope...hope that they could do it again. As good as Corbin teams have been over the years, never lose sight that it was Denes who put athletics on the map.

Denes was a people person, he enjoyed them. Talking, listening or just watching, that's what he was all about. Jim Lee Crawford, on December 2, 1975, wrote in the *Corbin Tribune*: "Nick Denes is a folk hero in Corbin. He could have hiked across the Cumberland River without dampening his ankles." And the best thing of all was that Nick was as fond of Corbin as Corbin was of him.

Ted Meadors

No one talks about Corbin history, sports or not, without mentioning Ted Meadors. Considered Corbin's first well-known football player, graduating in 1930, he went on to make a name for himself on the gridiron at Centre College in Danville. Despite weighing only 150-pounds, fifteen pounds more than he weighed at Corbin, he was named Little All-American as a center in the offensive line for the Colonels. National sportswriter Grantland Rice called Meadors "pound for pound the best football player in America."

He came back to Corbin and served as an assistant football coach in 1936, before Denes resigned to become the coach at Tennessee Junior College.

The next year, in 1937, he was named head coach, and his very first team won the Cumberland Valley title. But it was Meadors' '39 squad that is still considered one of the best in Redhound history. The team went undefeated at 9-0 outscoring opponents a staggering 189-9. Dixie Heights out of northern Kentucky fell in the opener 39-7. Then it was Somerset 39-0, Lexington 6-0, Benham 26-0, Loyall 19-0, Middlesboro 7-2, Harlan 26-0, and the final game 7-0 over Danville.

Before the 1941 season, sportswriter, Robert "Bouchie" Cummins wrote this about Meadors' team: "Meadors has whipped his boys into an excellent physical and mental condition, and he has perfected another wang-doodle of an offense, stressing the jitterbug shift. This shift is very tricky and might be a wee bit hard for the other boys to solve right off the bat."

Meadors coached six years from 1937 to 1942 at Corbin before resigning to join the Navy. Even though Ted's last Corbin team finished 2-6 with a 74-0 loss to Danville, he said his record that year had nothing to do with him leaving. It was something he said that he and his wife, Ruth, had planned before the season started.

Returning to Corbin in 1945 after his release from the Navy, he took a job with the Fish and Game Division and Veterans Administration, while at the same time serving as an assistant football coach at Corbin High.

In was in 1949 that Ted was named the first full time athletic director of the Corbin YMCA. And it was here that he left a mark that equaled his football playing days at Centre College and coaching tenure at Corbin High.

Ted would never leave football behind. Over his career he assisted head coaches Ossie Burch, Judge Howard, Moon Conde and Bill Tucker, sometimes paid and sometimes not.

The former Little All-American is considered the "daddy" of two little league sports programs in Corbin. In 1952 he initiated youth baseball, and a year later football was organized.

In the summer of 1956, Ted and Ossie Burch bought the Ford dealership in Richmond, Kentucky. Ted and wife, Ruth, left Corbin, and their son Bill (Yogi) moved in with his grandparents to finish his senior year of high school.

The following year Ted was diagnosed with cancer and soon had a kidney removed. Realizing he needed some downtime, he and Ruth moved back to Corbin. By the time summer was over, though, Ted was ready to do something. Doctors had told him he needed to get lots of sunshine, so he and Ruth headed to Florida in search of a teaching job. "Mom and dad dropped me off in Bowling Green at Western, and they drove down the east coast of Florida, before settling in West Palm Beach," recalled Yogi. "Mom got a job as an elementary teacher, and dad was teaching history at a junior high."

Ted and Ruth felt secure with their son being at Western. After all, their good friend, Nick Denes had recently become the head football coach there, and Yogi would become a part of the Hilltopper team.

A short time later, in 1960, Ted's cancer had returned.

"Dad rarely missed work, but he was unable to continue teaching during the fall semester," offered Yogi. "I spent the summer of '60 with them in Florida before returning for my senior year at Western." In October 1961, at Good Samaritan Hospital in West Palm Beach, Ted Meadors, at the age of 51, was dead. "My father was my hero," says Yogi. "To this day I consider him the finest gentleman I have ever known."

His last deed was what those who knew him would expect. In early October 1960, he wrote a short, but personal note to friends Terry Wyrick and John Bill Black, both Corbin businessmen. He challenged them to maintain their support for the Little League programs. Ted told them his hope was to continue the fine tradition that Corbin has in athletics. Bill Crook, a longtime Corbin sports historian and a local sports columnist, put his ultimate endorsement on Ted's influence. "In my opinion Ted did more for Corbin football than anybody in history," he said.

Chapter Two

THE MAN WHO PUT CORBIN ON THE MAP

Election Day in November 1932 was one of the biggest days in U.S. history. Franklin Delano Roosevelt was elected to his first term as President of the United States of America. And as it turned out, it was to be one of Corbin, Kentucky's biggest days, too. That's the day Franklin Delano Selvy was born. According to the Selvy family tree, he is a fourth cousin, on his mother's side, to Thomas Jefferson. No one is saying Selvy could be President, but by the time 1948 rolled around, he could have beaten Roosevelt in Whitley, Laurel and Knox counties, of which the city of Corbin occupies a little of each.

Born to James and Iva Selvy, Frank was the fourth of ten children. With eight boys and two girls, (Curt, James "Babe," Stella, Frank, Sarah, Edd, David, Don, Marvin, and Charles "Curly"), the Selvys found it difficult to live on the meager income James made as a coal miner. Still he and his wife found ways to provide for their family in a manner that made their children feel as though they were the "haves" as opposed to the "have not's." It was what many Corbin families did at that time.

When Frank was young, his dad became a victim in a mining accident when he became trapped. After a couple of broken bones, at the age of 54, James Selvy decided he could no longer return to the mines. His daily commutes to Straight Creek in Bell County were over. He would now depend on his $90 a month pension to help raise his family. He had been a coal miner for 42 years, since the age of 12.

Before moving to Corbin, the Selvys had lived in Straight Creek. That's where Frank started to school. "I got kicked out of school the first day of first grade," Frank said. "My sister was getting a spanking and I jumped up to help her...kicked the teacher, and my sister and I jumped out the window. My mother sent me to live with relatives in Taswell, Tennessee for a year."

Many of the Selvy brothers were distinguished athletes in Corbin, but Frank was the most famous. And although many have tried to define his life based on one college game he played in 1954, one doesn't have to look far to determine that is not the case.

Basketball Coach Harry Taylor was establishing quite a tradition at Corbin High School. Playing off of the success of the 1936 team that won it all, and the 1939 squad that finished fourth at the state tournament, he had youngsters that actually saw these teams play. They knew what winners looked like and they, too, wanted the same. There had been Marion and Stan Cluggish, Willard Ellison, and Bobby Coleman that left lasting impressions.

In 1949 Frank began to emerge from the shadow of older brother Curt, who in 1947 paced a Redhound team to a 33-2 record and a trip to the Boys Sweet Sixteen where they lost in the opening round to Maysville, the eventual state champions. Many thought Maysville's win was an upset, and considered Corbin one of the very best in the state. Curt, who had great support from Max Mobley, Bobby Sturgill, Dusty Yates, Harold Brooks, and Carl Jones, went on to play at Eastern Kentucky University. Later he toured for several years with the House of David professional team that provided much of the opposition for the original Harlem Globetrotters.

"I remember when Curt returned to Corbin from traveling all over the world speaking about five languages," Frank said. "As years passed he forgot most of them and settled back into speaking basic English." Curt later went on to become one of the most respected sports officials in the state.

Frank lays claim to being the first of the big time Corbin sports stars of the so-called modern era. At age five Frank first began dribbling a basketball, copying what older brother Curt was doing. It was a game he enjoyed early in life, and the Selvy house was just up the street from the YMCA, where much of the kid's recreation at its outdoor basketball courts took place.

Early on, everyone growing up in the Selvy family did something to carry their load. Following Frank's fifth grade of school he went to live in Klondike, Indiana with family to work on a farm, planting and picking tomatoes. He knew then he wanted to do anything but work in the mines like his father had done.

"We were like migrant workers," Frank said. "And I told them I was 16…looked eight, but was actually twelve-years-old. That was the first lie I told in my life. We all stayed in a house owned by a Mr. Klinker. The second lie was when my teacher in Corbin asked me what I got for Christmas. I told her a new coat, pants, just made up stuff. I was embarrassed when everyone else in the class had told what all they got. The truth was I never got anything for Christmas. There was no money in our family for gifts. I felt bad about what I had told her."

Frank worked in Indiana every summer for four years, anything to get away from the possibility of going into those mines. "I didn't want to go close to one," he said. "But I knew I didn't want to farm either after that."

By the time Frank returned to Corbin he had missed two months of school. "It was tough being behind like that," he said. "I was behind in school and in basketball. I never could make the varsity until the second semester of my junior year, and I scored 17 points in my first game. Looking back on it all, I think Ossie Burch talked Coach Taylor into letting me make the team. I also played football my senior year. I was 16, playing against older guys."

It seemed like every kid in Corbin was playing sports. For sure it burned off a lot of energy, while at the same time keeping the boys out of any real trouble. All the while their thoughts were about becoming a Redhound.

They played whatever was in season. In the summer it was baseball, and some even practiced basketball. There were others passing and kicking footballs. The town seemed consumed with athletes, and because of it, when high school basketball and football seasons rolled around, this passion converted into championships.

The 1948 team made a return trip to the State Tournament behind the play of Harold Brooks, Bobby Cathers, Red Anders, and Gobel Jones. But Coach Harry Taylor had several sophomores that gave him reason to believe his Redhounds were going to be good—no, very good—for years to come. Roy Kidd, a three-sport star, Bob Barton, Jerry Brooks and Dick Manor were just waiting their time. But the best sophomore of all didn't even play that year. Frank Selvy broke his right arm in a roller skating fall at the YMCA in late fall, and wound up missing some of the 1948 basketball season.

During the regular season the Redhounds had beaten nearby London twice, but in the opening round of the State Tournament in Louisville at the downtown Armory, the luck-of-the draw pitted the two rivals against each other again. This time London prevailed 66-45 in a shocker.

When the 1949 season began, Frank Selvy was ready to play and so were his seasoned teammates. Harold and Jerry Brooks, Cathers, Kidd, Barton and Tommy Adkins and Sylvester Wright, and a pair of sophomores, Bobby Terrell and Jerry Perkins landed the Redhounds in the Sweet Sixteen for the third straight year with a 27-2 record.

Now all of those shots he had taken at the YMCA courts were paying off. All of a sudden Frank Selvy was good, and more than 60 years later he laughed in remembering when his friend Hayden Ellison would stand under the outside basket and rebound shot after shot for Frank. "To this day I remember Hayden standing there and throwing 'em back to me as he sang 'Hayden, Hayden went a wadin' with a maiden,' then he would make a whistle sound. I'll never forget it."

Two years before, Corbin lost to state champ Maysville, and this year would turn out to be an opening round 53-42 loss to Owensboro and their great star Cliff Hagan, who would go on to win the title. "I modeled my hook shot after his," Frank said. Incidentally the 49' tournament featured three future college All-Americans and NBA stars in Selvy, Hagan and Madisonville's Frank Ramsey.

Over the years, almost all Corbin basketball players also played football (Selvy, too), and because of it one would think it would take several games to regain a hardwood mentality, but not so at Corbin, and it wasn't just the athletes that were interchangeable, so were the coaches. During football season Harry Taylor was Ossie Burch's assistant, and when they took off the pads and put on the shorts, the roles were reversed.

In those days many of the smaller schools throughout Kentucky didn't have football, and didn't require an acclamation period, as they had been practicing together for weeks. So when the 1949 football team finished up their season by playing in the Shrine Bowl at Stoll Field in Lexington on Thanksgiving Day, losing to Dayton High School, they returned home, and the following Tuesday they opened the round ball season.

This Redhound team was loaded. Selvy at 6-foot, and with a hook shot from either side, was peaking for his senior year. Kidd, Brooks and Barton gave Coach Taylor's team a veteran lineup. And with the addition of Bobby Terrell as a starter at forward, an almost unheard of fourth straight trip to the Sweet Sixteen seemed possible. Though the Redhounds were heavy with seniors, Coach Taylor still had a crop of youngsters behind them that would play and were rising stars in their own right. Among them was 6'3" Jerry Bird, C.D. Vermillion and Darrel Storm.

The Redhounds roared out of the gate. A win over a good Louisville Flaget team 64-39 received statewide attention. Then a four point loss to second ranked Clark County, coached by Letcher Norton and led by Linville Puckett and Lewis Snowden, proved to the Corbin team they were among the best basketball teams in all of Kentucky. Selvy and Barton were turning it on and the Redhounds were winning by margins of 60 points or more.

Teammate Bobby Terrell recalls some of Corbin encounters that year with Harlan. "As a small boy I watched their great teams with Wah Wah Jones," he said. "But now here we were beating them by 56 points at home, and then later by 25 at Harlan. In that game their fans gave Frank a big ovation when he made a shot lying on his back. He fell in the foul circle, the ball landed in his hands and he threw it up in the air and it swished the net." That shot may have been a prelude of the other unbelievable shots he would hit in his career.

As the season wound down, the Redhounds were 19-1, with the only loss being to Clark County. Terrell recalls there was a "clamor for us to play" Lexington Lafayette, behind All-Staters Bob Mulcahy and Jim Weiland, who was ranked number one in the state. "A benefit game was arranged on Eastern's floor in Richmond," Terrell said. "They were tough and had a veteran ball club, and gave us a good spanking. We knew if we were going to win the Sweet Sixteen we would have to get past them."

Corbin finished the season 23-2, and Coach Taylor, knowing that his squad had also played football, had had very little time off since the previous August. His practice session eased up as he wanted a team with rested legs going into District tournament play. It worked. With the starters playing only one quarter, Corbin slaughtered Gatliff 119-23 in the opener. The 96 point win was followed by an 84-57 win over Barbourville, 94-37 over Lynn Camp and the finals over Woodbine 80-58.

The 13th Regional in Pineville proved to be about as easy as the District had been. Bob Barton, in the opening game, tied Wah Wah Jones' single game regional scoring record with 29 points in a 76-44 win over Middlesboro. Next came Woodbine, again, and it was 80-58, the identical score as the District. The finals matched the Redhounds against tall and tough Oneida, a team that featured Eddie Mobley and Ray Mills. Mills would later transfer to Clay County and then play for Rupp in Lexington. None of that mattered as Corbin won 58-45. The four seniors, Selvy, Kidd, Barton and Brooks made the all-regional team.

Louisville, Here We Come

The Redhounds were good, but in spite of that, newspapers were playing up the fact that this was their fourth straight trip to the tournament, and they had lost the previous three in the first round.

After checking into team headquarters at the Kentucky Hotel in downtown Louisville, just a short walk to the Jefferson County Armory, the boys did what boys do, checking out the lobby as well as the other teams coming in. Sizing up the opposition, as well as their cheerleaders, was part of the annual ritual, even though they might not have spoken to them.

One newspaper predicted that Corbin might get by their opening game against Dawson Springs, but would fall to Paducah Tilghman in the second round. The lack of respect would work in Corbin's favor.

"The dressing room was all business," recalls Bob Terrell. "We had some information on Dawson Springs and knew they had some capable scorers." Harry Taylor's strategy against the shorter team was to keep them from getting any second shots, dominate the defensive boards and push the ball up fast.

It worked. At halftime the Redhounds were up 43-24 and went on to win 72-50. Barton's 18, followed by Selvy's 15, and Terrell's 13 led the way.

Lafayette and Clark County, meanwhile, advanced with respective wins over Louisville Male and Newport. Remember, these were the two teams Corbin coaches knew they had to keep an eye on.

Terrell recalled that Fairdale's Frosty Able had a big first round game in scoring 33 points in a win over Hindman. Later he and Able were teammates at the University of Louisville playing for Coach Peck Hickman. Able finished his career at Western playing for Ed Diddle.

With Corbin and Paducah Tilghman both advancing, something had to give between the two. The Redhounds at 31-2, and the best record in the state, were playing a team with future Western star Lynn Cole, and future U.K. All-SEC quarterback Bob Hardy.

Corbin jumped out early and at halftime led 35-28, but Tilghman came back in the second half and cut it to two. However, Selvy was on his game as he and his mates pulled away for an easy 69-53 win. Frank led all scorers with 24, Barton and Kidd had 16 apiece, and Terrell's 13 rounded out the top scorers.

With Corbin and Central City rolling into the semifinals, so too did Lafayette and Clark County. The stage was set for a power packed finish, which many felt could be any team's tournament to win.

Four of the legendary coaches in all of basketball crazy Kentucky were set to do battle. Harry Taylor of Corbin, Ralph Carlisle of Lafayette, Letcher Norton at Clark County and Central City's Delmas Gish, were all destined for the Hall of Fame.

It was show time in Louisville. Unlike today's state tournament bracket schedules, in 1950 the semis got underway on a Saturday afternoon instead of Saturday morning. Clark County turned back Central City 59-55 before the Redhounds and Generals got underway close to 3 p.m. that afternoon. Corbin's 10-man roster was down to nine, due to an ankle injury the previous game suffered by Jerry Brooks.

Bob Terrell remembers the game well. "We got off to a horrible start, and we were even grousing among ourselves when we were suddenly down 18-2," Terrell said. "We had never had any disagreements all season, and during a timeout Roy Kidd told us to shut up and play basketball. He brought us back together."

By halftime the Redhounds had cut the lead to 34-28, and in the fourth quarter Terrell recalled his missing a free throw and Selvy making an amazing tip in to cut it to one point with seven minutes left in the game. But the run had taken its toll and the Generals sent the Redhounds down 75-65. Selvy had 16, Barton 15, Terrell 14, Kidd nine, and C.D. Vermillion eight for Corbin.

But there was still more Corbin basketball to be played. Their season was not over. Until 1962, a game to determine third place was played. The game meant little, and often was played by very tired teams who had to come back and play with only a short rest.

It would be Central City and Corbin in the consolation game, and Terrell says, "It was our last game, a game for pride." The Redhounds showed little signs of fatigue, and the loss of reserve Tommy Adkins, with an ankle injury during pre-game warm-ups, didn't seem to be a problem as they jumped out to a 12-2 lead. Corbin led 36-28 at the half, but Central City came roaring back, and in the second half the lead changed hands eight times. With the score tied at 69 and time running out, leave it to Roy Kidd to come up with the play of the tournament when he knocked the bottom out with a near-midcourt shot to give the Redhounds a 71-69 victory and a third place finish.

With Selvy and Barton fouling out, Terrell led all scorers with 21 points. Barton's 17 points and Selvy's 12 gave them both a total of 66 points for the tournament, making them the top scorers. Terrell's 61 points gave him third place.

For the record, the Corbin-Lafayette game had set the state tournament record for total points in a game with 140. Then against Central City those two teams combined to score 140 again. In just five hours Corbin had played in the two highest scoring games in tournament history.

Later that night Lafayette turned back Clark County 55-51 for the title. Finishing 33-3, losing twice to Lafayette and once to Clark County, the Redhounds placed Selvy and Barton on the All-Tournament team, and in the process set a new scoring record with 277 points, 40 more than the previous mark. What a Redhound season it had been!

For the season the team scored 2,634 points for an average of 73.2 per game, while their opponents scored 1,638 points for an average of 45.5. The 27.7 point win margin was unheard of. Individually Selvy had scored 586 points with Barton close behind at 577. Terrell's season total was 400, and their totals were significant in that it marked the first time in school history that a Corbin basketball player would score more than 400 points.

Could it be Five Straight?

Even though Coach Taylor had lost four seniors, all would not be lost for the 1949-50 season as Terrell, Jerry Bird, C.D. Vermillion and Darrel Storm would be returning.

Through it all Frank Selvy had emerged quietly as having the ability to play college ball. As a 6-foot center in high school, he knew if he did it would be at another position. He also knew his high school days at Corbin had prepared him well. Though just a sophomore, during Selvy's senior season, Jerry Bird, a future high school All-American, had proven a worthy practice opponent day-in and day-out during those scrimmages in Edwards Gym.

Most people hit a growth spurt in life. For some it's in junior high, for others it happens between the junior and senior year. For Selvy, his began at about the time he graduated from high school. "I went from being a 6-foot center to all of a sudden 6'2"," said Selvy. "I was only 17-years-old my senior year, but over the summer I grew."

Selvy had a scholarship offer even before the growth spurt. His skills of shooting with either hand and ball handling ability were enough that at least one college coach knew he was a basketball player, and that was Erskine College in Due West, South Carolina. What position he played would be decided later.

As he was adjusting to his "new size," and becoming more self-assured, he began to dominate a game, something he hadn't really done at Corbin High School. He was good all right, but so were his teammates, and there was little need for him to take over a game. He was a team player and that was the mentality he carried into each game.

The great Redhound season and the third place finish at the state tournament had given Selvy enough exposure that all of the summer all-star games came calling. He played for Kentucky, an Ed Diddle coached team, against the best from Ohio, West Virginia, and Indiana, and though he scored only one point against the Hoosiers, even more interest in him grew. "It was common knowledge that Coach Diddle played more of the boys he knew were coming to Western, so I didn't play much that game." It was the in-state East-West All-Star game played in Pikeville that changed the way college recruiters looked at Selvy. All-star games were different. He was smart enough to realize he could use these stages to showcase his talent. And he did.

"I had been scheduled to be the back-up center at the East-West game, but when the guy ahead of me came down with appendicitis I started," Selvy recalled. "I had a great game and was voted MVP, and after that schools like Tennessee, North Carolina, and Eastern Kentucky came around; it changed my career."

And wouldn't you know it, Adolph Rupp even called. They were too late. Nevertheless, Selvy, took a trip to U.K. just to see what it was like. Some of the guys were trying out, just playing around, in the old Alumni gym. "There was a door all of us walked through to get to the floor," Frank laughed. "All of the big guys ducked when they went through it. Heck, I didn't really need to, but I ducked anyway."

What Selvy said next has never appeared in print. "I actually thought I was going to Western Kentucky," he said years later. "Coach Diddle told me he had a scholarship for me, so I wrote him a letter that I wanted to come to Western. I waited but never heard back from him."

Think of the significance of what he said. There had to be a flaw in the U.S. Mail system between Corbin and Bowling Green, because Diddle definitely wanted Selvy. Roy Kidd was with Selvy after the East-West game when he heard Diddle make the offer. Surely Diddle never received that letter.

Had Selvy enrolled at Western he would have teamed with two of the all-time greats there, Tom Marshall and Art Spoelstra. The same what-if could be said if Selvy had gone to U.K. He would have hooked up with Cliff Hagan and Frank Ramsey.

Second guessing is not always a good thing, and in the case of Frank Selvy, for sure it is not. Had he gone to either Kentucky or Western, he may have never been able to develop into the player he became. His talents could have been lost in the proverbial shuffle.

In the big picture it mattered little, because earlier Selvy had piled in a car driven by Corbin Baptist minister Ed "Footsy" French for a six hour ride to Greenville, South Carolina. It was in December and the boys had a few days off for Christmas break.

"Footsy had gone to Furman," Selvy said. "And he wanted some of the Corbin boys to try out for their football team. He drove us down, gave us $35 for food while we were there and we stayed in one of the dorms."

Selvy had no intention of playing football, but Roy Kidd, Carl Oakley, Bob Barton and Sylvester Wright, who were in the car with him, did. His hope was to get a basketball tryout while he was there. In those days it was legal and a common practice for colleges to try out players before offering a scholarship.

After arriving on the Furman campus, French went by Athletic Director Ed Meade's office to let him know he brought the boys from Corbin. Meade walked over to the basketball office, and knowing that head coach Lyles Alley had taken a sabbatical to get his master's degree at Columbia University in New York, he asked assistant coach Melvin Bell to work out a few of the Corbin boys on the court. "Most are here for football," Meade told Bell, "You never know, some of them might be able to help out the basketball team, too."

Bell would be the first at Furman to see a basketball player who would become one of the greatest basketball players to ever play the game. "I came into the gym and Frank was warming up," Bell said. "He must have hit 10 left handed hook shots in a row."

"You a lefty?" Bell asked. 'No sir,' Selvy answered, and then he turned around and hit another 10 right handed. We scrimmaged and it was like watching a thoroughbred pulling away from a quarter horse. He scored any time he wanted."

Bell phoned Coach Alley and told him what he saw. Was it a dream? Had it been real that out of the blue a boy from Corbin, Kentucky, could just show up unannounced and be that good? In Bell's excitement he told Alley they needed to offer Selvy a scholarship. "This Selvy boy will make All-Southern Conference," he said.

Alley, too, was enthused at what his assistant coach told him, but before finalizing anything he wanted to see the boy from Corbin with his own eyes. So back Frank went to Greenville. "It was in the spring," he recalled. "Some of us went back. I got my scholarship for basketball and Barton, Wright and Oakley got football scholarships."

Alley knew that Kentucky hadn't totally given up on Selvy. "If you go there, you'll be just another player," Alley said. "If you come here, I'm going to make you an All-American. "I believed it," Selvy said.

Once school started it didn't take long for word to spread among the 500 students that the freshman basketball team had a special player. While the 1950-51 Furman varsity was going 3-20, Selvy was leading his freshman team to an undefeated season while averaging 25 points.

At Furman, Frank Selvy had become "The Man." His coach, Lyles Alley, knew what he had. The mild-mannered, soft spoken Corbin boy had now grown to 6'4," and in his own words, "could do pretty much what I wanted on the basketball court."

The Furman Palidins were on their way. As a sophomore, and with Selvy leading the way, they finished 18-6 as he averaged 24.6 points. Coach Alley had also landed another good one who was a year behind Selvy. Darrell Floyd, a great scorer, had picked up on the freshman team where Selvy left off.

While Frank was true to his commitment to Furman when he enrolled as a freshman, Coach Alley was equally honest in making the boy from Corbin an All-American.

It was Selvy's junior year that really propelled him into national prominence. Reeling off 12 straight wins to end the season at 21-6, the team had wins over Clemson, Georgia Tech, Virginia Tech, and Davidson. One of the sweetest victories came when they avenged an early season loss to South Carolina with a105-68 thrashing.

The Palidins had scored 100 points or more nine times, and Selvy had averaged a nation-leading 29.5 points an outing. As a sophomore he hung 49 points on Wofford, and then as a junior got them for 45, but it was against Mercer when he scored 63 that gave the first real clue of what might be in store.

Selvy said later, "I could hook with either hand, shoot the fade-away, or I'd fake that and turn and go either way to the basket. I got a lot of points off offensive rebounds, put-backs and three-point plays (not the three-point shot)."

Frank Selvy was an All-American. But to think that Furman was a one man team would be a mistake. Center Neild Gordon had a 52-point game against the College of Charleston, and Floyd had 67 in another game. There were others: Bud Granger, Bobby Thomas, Ken Deardorff, A.D. Barnett, and two other boys from Kentucky, Sylvester Wright from Corbin and Fred Fraley from Wayland.

Fraley had come from the same school that later turned out mountain legend King Kelly Coleman, but his arrival at Furman and becoming a teammate to Frank Selvy took a round-about way. "Football was my sport," Fraley said. "I went to

U.K. as a 6'1", 190 lb. fullback-linebacker to play for Bear Bryant, but after I lost 20-pounds in two weeks I left."

Fraley enrolled at a prep school in Chattanooga, Tennessee where he played basketball. Back at Wayland he had been all-state and played for all-star teams against Indiana and West Virginia.

"I wasn't bad, but I was no Frank Selvy," Fraley said years later. "In Chattanooga I scored 130 points in a four-game tournament and planned on going to Georgia Tech. However, when I found out I couldn't go there because I had gone to U.K. and they were both in the SEC, I went to Furman. Coach Alley took me sight unseen."

Selvy's senior season was looked on with great anticipation. Darrell Floyd was living up to expectations, but make no mistake about it, this was Selvy's team. He scored 50 or more points seven times that season and between 42 and 49 points seven times. (The greatest single game scoring feat in the history of Division I Basketball is detailed later in this chapter.) The Palidins went 20-9 with a schedule heavy with road games that included a season-ending loss to Richmond in the second round of the Southern Conference Tournament. During the season he scored 40 in a loss to Duke, and another 40 in a loss to LaSalle and its All-American, Tom Gola, who had 25-points and 27 rebounds.

In the process he averaged 41.7 points, becoming the first college player to average more than 40 points and score more than 1,000 points in a single season. During his three-year varsity career, Furman was a collective 59-21, beating Duke, South Carolina, Miami (FL), Clemson, Georgia, Georgia Tech, Virginia Tech, and Manhattan. He had become the first player to lead NCAA scoring two years in a row since George Mikan in 1945 and 46.

When the boy from Corbin left Furman, he held 24 major college scoring records and was a two-time first team All-American. That included being named United Press International National Player of the Year, and New York sports writers named Selvy as the most outstanding basketball player to appear in Madison Square Garden. One New York City paper's headline shouted, "Gotham Raves Over Fabulous Frank," after he torched a good Manhattan team for 42 in the Garden.

The 1954 All-American team, in addition to Selvy, was Cliff Hagan, Kentucky; Bob Pettit, LSU; Tom Gola, LaSalle; and Don Schlundt, Indiana.

For the most part, the old Southern Conference was the forerunner of the Atlantic Coast Conference, and years later when Selvy was asked why he went to Furman, his answer was easy. "Why shouldn't I," he answered. "It was in the Southern Conference and it was the best basketball conference in the nation. With West Virginia, Clemson, South Carolina, North Carolina, North Carolina State, Duke, Davidson, George Washington, and William and Mary, just to name a few, it didn't get much better than that."

Legendary Coach Frank McGuire, then at North Carolina, said the Southern Conference was the best conference in the country, and Frank Selvy is the best player in the conference.

Times have changed dramatically from the early 1900s when the Ku Klux Klan ran a train through Whitley County. The two pictures, above and below, were taken at Packard.

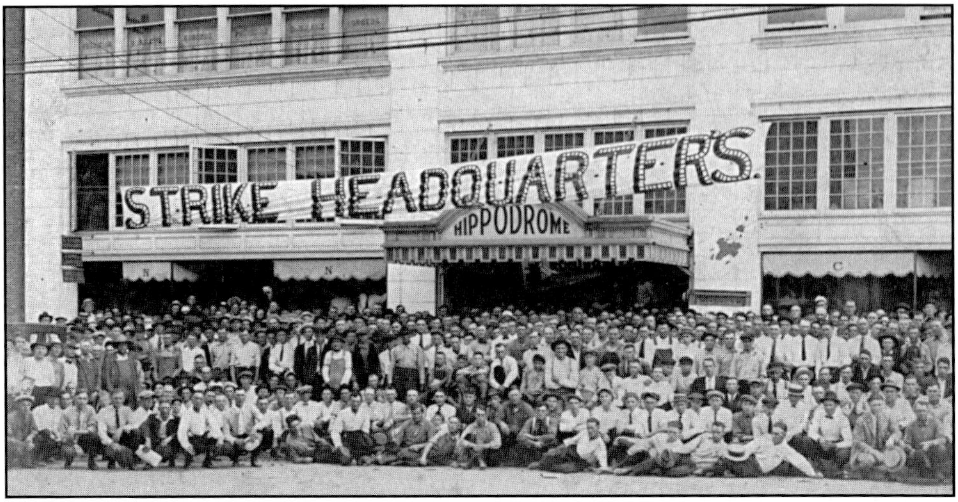

The strike headquarters for the L&N Shop in 1922 was at the Hippodrome Theatre. Here the strikers posed before the meeting. The theatre was located on Main Street in the site now occupied by First National Bank.

Corbin is a railroad town. There is no doubt when you look at this 1927 photo of the Corbin Shop employees.

Picture of the Moonbow Inn at Cumberland Falls in the early 1920s. Later, duPont Lodge at Cumberland Falls State Park would be built nearby.

Corbin was not immune to flooding in the early years.

Railroad YMCA near the railyard in the early 1900s.

The Roundhouse of the L&N Railroad was the center of train activity in 1950. There was a machine shop for locomotive repairs, along with a coal tipple and a great number of coal cars.

Lunch Queen located on Main St. in Corbin in the early 1950s.

Hungry Hound Drive-In Restaurant on the Falls Road in Corbin.

Wing Drive-In on the Falls Road in Corbin.

The original Harland Sanders Court and Café as it looked in 1940. At that time it housed both a restaurant and a motel.

Corbin High graduate David Farmer's painting of the old Pepsi Cola plant on South Main Street.

Lee Petty won the first NASCAR race in Kentucky at the Corbin Speedway in 1954.

Painting of Nick Denes that now hangs in the Ossie Burch Fieldhouse.

Ted Meadors, considered the "father of Little League sports," in Corbin.

Corbin Redhound Basketball in the late 1920s. The coach is Dick Bacon. To his right is Dr. Keith Smith.

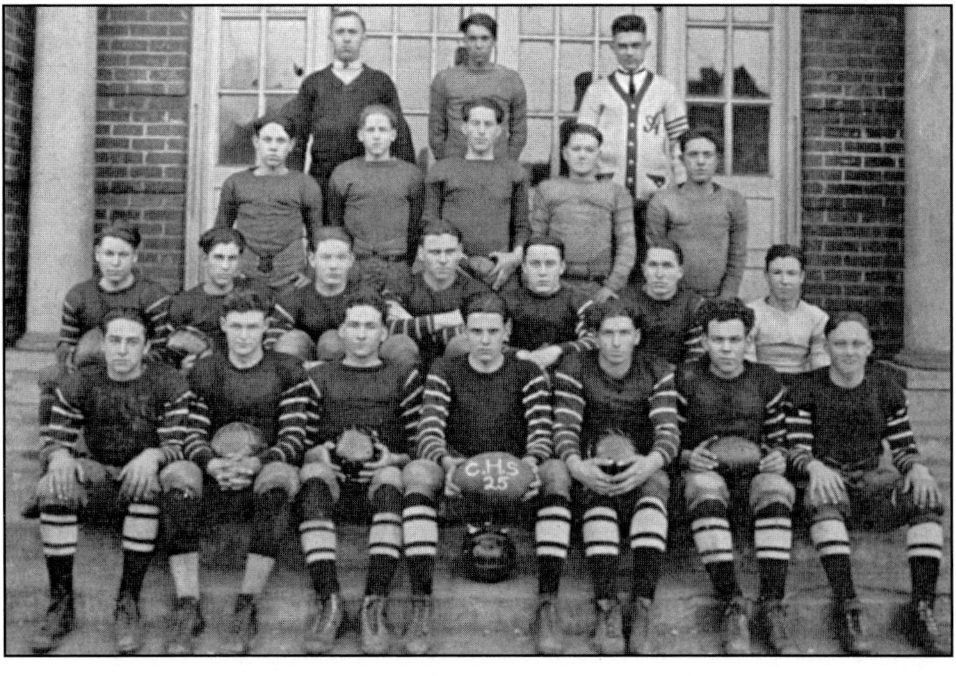

This photo shows the 1925 football team, which included Steely Terrell, Oral Snyder, Jess Burmmett, Harry Taylor, Ted Meadors, Guy Jones, Cloyd Jones, Red Cadle and Coach Howard.

1936 Kentucky State Champions. Front row, from left: Coach Nick Denes and son Billy, Charles Sampson, Stanley Cluggish, Marion Cluggish, Bill Asher, Willard Ellison, Assistant Coach Carl Lawson. Second row: Manager John Rose, Herschel Nelson, Alfred Keck, Carl Babb, Gordon Gant, Robert Sampson. In back are Principal W.E. Burton (left) and Supt. G.W. Campbell.

University of Kentucky Basketball Team, 1937-38. Seated, left to right: Head Coach Adolph Rupp, Harris Walker (Maysville, KY), Robert Davis (Dayton, KY), Ed Gough (Lexington, KY), Charles Combs (Happy, KY), J. Rice Walker (Lexington, KY), Layton Rouse (Ludlow, KY), Harry Denham (Maysville, KY), Ralph Jackowsky (Anderson, IL), and Assistant Coach Paul McBrayer. Standing: Trainer Mann, Elmo Head (Shelbyville, KY), James Goodman (Paris, KY), Fred Curtis (Nashville, TN), Larry Spears (Ceredo, WV), Marion Cluggish (Corbin, KY), Homer Thompson (Jeffersonville, IN), Joseph Hagan (Louisville, KY), Bernard Opper (New York, NY), unknown, and Manager Philip Haring (?). J. Rice Walker, Joseph Hagan and Charles Combs were seniors.

Corbin High School, 1939 Region 13 Champs. Front row, left to right: Quintin Storm, Cecil Meadors, Willard Ellison, Charles Triplett, Pat Kelley, Foster Williams. Middle row: Coach Carl Lawson, Austin Higgins, Bill Belew, Jack Pope, Bobby Coleman, Ernie Prewitt, Assistant Coach Tilmon Goodin. Back row: Manager Gordon Lippert, Russell Peace, Jimmy Cummins, Robert Moberly, Glenn Meadors, Trainer Arlus Gibbs.

From the state champion 1939 Corbin Redhound football team these players let the Hounds to an undefeated season. Pictured from left are Harold Petrey, Rusty Peace, Jimmy Cummins, Bat Vermillion and Bitsy Holman.

Corbin High School, 1947 Region 13 Champs. Front row, left to right: Manager Charles Stuart, Leroy Yates, Harold Brooks, Curtis Selvy, Max Mobley, Bobby Sturgill, Jerry Bryant, Manager Carl Neal. Second row: Bill Brown, James Selvy, Jack Crabtree, Henry Moberly, Dorman Siler. Third row: Charles Eaton, Clarence McNeil, Robert Barton, Carl Jones, Eldred Von Grunigen. Fourth row: Roy Kidd, Robert Cathers, Sylvester Wright. Fifth row: Basketball Coach Harry Taylor, Football Coach Ossie Burch.

Corbin High School, 1948 Region 13 Champs. Front row, kneeling, left to right: Walker, Adkins, Campbell, D. Mobley, Stephens, Terrell, Henderlight, McNeil. Standing: Coach Taylor, Manager Owens, Cathers, Jones, Maner, Siler, B. Mobley, Barton, H. Brooks, Anders, J. Brooks, Kidd, Manager Rutherford, Coach Burch.

Back row, left to right: Coach Carl Jones, Paul Scalf, Frank Selvy, Bobby Terrell, Jack Jones, Wallace Clouse. Front row: Zeke Perkins, Ralph Roaden, Rim Dizney, Joe Ed Scalf.

1949-50 Redhounds. Front row (kneeling), left to right: Robert Barton and Jerry Brooks. Back row (standing): Roy Kidd, Bob Terrell, Frank Selvy and Coach Harry Taylor.

Frank Selvy, 1949-50 at Corbin.

Corbin's fabulous Frank Selvy who earned first team all-american honors while attending Furman University in the 1950s. Selvy led the nation in scoring his senior year with a 41.2 average and set a national record by scoring 100 points in a single game. He played professional basketball for Baltimore, St. Louis and Los Angeles.

Bill "Moon" Conde chats with his team during a rare break in the 1953 winless season.

Above and below:
Frank Selvy at Furman.

Frank Selvy being carried off the floor following scoring 51 points in a win over Georgia Tech on February 11, 1954. Two nights later he scored 100 points against Newberry College.

Frank talks to his mother Iva and sister Stella as dad James keeps an eye on the photographer. Notice the corsage each lady is wearing.

Frank accompanies his parents, James and Iva, to midcourt during the ceremonies of the 100 point game.

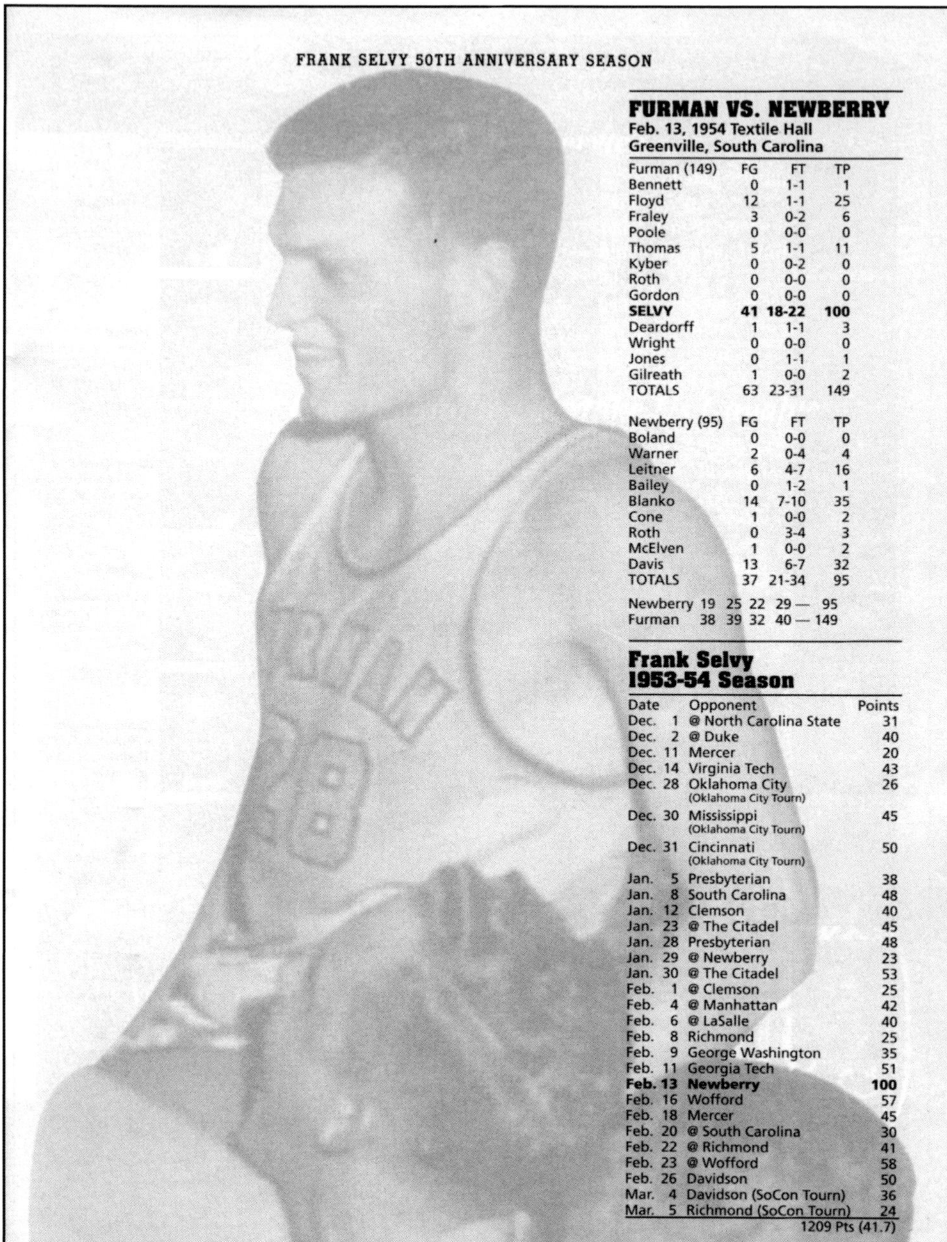

FRANK SELVY 50TH ANNIVERSARY SEASON

FURMAN VS. NEWBERRY

Feb. 13, 1954 Textile Hall
Greenville, South Carolina

Furman (149)	FG	FT	TP
Bennett	0	1-1	1
Floyd	12	1-1	25
Fraley	3	0-2	6
Poole	0	0-0	0
Thomas	5	1-1	11
Kyber	0	0-2	0
Roth	0	0-0	0
Gordon	0	0-0	0
SELVY	**41**	**18-22**	**100**
Deardorff	1	1-1	3
Wright	0	0-0	0
Jones	0	1-1	1
Gilreath	1	0-0	2
TOTALS	63	23-31	149

Newberry (95)	FG	FT	TP
Boland	0	0-0	0
Warner	2	0-4	4
Leitner	6	4-7	16
Bailey	0	1-2	1
Blanko	14	7-10	35
Cone	1	0-0	2
Roth	0	3-4	3
McElven	1	0-0	2
Davis	13	6-7	32
TOTALS	37	21-34	95

Newberry	19	25	22	29 —	95
Furman	38	39	32	40 —	149

Frank Selvy 1953-54 Season

Date	Opponent	Points
Dec. 1	@ North Carolina State	31
Dec. 2	@ Duke	40
Dec. 11	Mercer	20
Dec. 14	Virginia Tech	43
Dec. 28	Oklahoma City (Oklahoma City Tourn)	26
Dec. 30	Mississippi (Oklahoma City Tourn)	45
Dec. 31	Cincinnati (Oklahoma City Tourn)	50
Jan. 5	Presbyterian	38
Jan. 8	South Carolina	48
Jan. 12	Clemson	40
Jan. 23	@ The Citadel	45
Jan. 28	Presbyterian	48
Jan. 29	@ Newberry	23
Jan. 30	@ The Citadel	53
Feb. 1	@ Clemson	25
Feb. 4	@ Manhattan	42
Feb. 6	@ LaSalle	40
Feb. 8	Richmond	25
Feb. 9	George Washington	35
Feb. 11	Georgia Tech	51
Feb. 13	**Newberry**	**100**
Feb. 16	Wofford	57
Feb. 18	Mercer	45
Feb. 20	@ South Carolina	30
Feb. 22	@ Richmond	41
Feb. 23	@ Wofford	58
Feb. 26	Davidson	50
Mar. 4	Davidson (SoCon Tourn)	36
Mar. 5	Richmond (SoCon Tourn)	24
		1209 Pts (41.7)

Page from Furman's recognition publication that honored Frank Selvy's 100 point game in 1954.

Jerry West is often referred to as "the logo." Some say it was this photo of Frank Selvy that was duplicated.

Barbara Banks with her trophy and flowers after Miss Arkansas won the talent competition in the 1956 Miss America contest.

Frank's mother Iva made sure the Corbin star got plenty to eat.

Frank gives pointers to younger brothers at the goal near his home. Left to right: David and Edd, Curly with the ball, and Marvin in pursuit. It is believed this is the same ball used to score 100 points in a game at Furman.

The Selvys. Standing, left to right: Curt, James, Iva and Frank. Sitting: Stella, Don, Curly, Edd, David and Sarah.

Corbin honored its All-American, Frank Selvy, with a parade in the 1950s. He holds a key to the city presented to him by Mayor Robert Daniel.

Mike Selvy (Frank and Barbara's son) stands beside the original backboard from Textile Hall in Greenville, SC where Frank recorded his 100 point game.

Frank's Corbin High School Hall of Fame jersey and plaque. Notice the #11 was the same number he wore as a member of the Los Angeles Lakers.

Frank, Barbara and dog Poopsie with author Gary P. West and wife Deborah at the Selvy home in Hilton Head.

As impressive as he had been on the basketball court, he was just as impressive away from it. At Furman he was senior class president; a member of Blue Key, an academic honorary fraternity; named Who's Who in Colleges and Universities of America; and was named by the school's newspaper, *The Hornet*, as "Student-of-the Year." To further point out just how much he was thought of in Greenville, after he had played his last Furman game, friends and supporters presented Selvy with a new 1954 Ford.

Not long after Selvy's college career had ended on April 26, 1954, he was invited back to Corbin for some big'doins in his honor. A parade down Main Street, a key to the city, followed by a banquet at duPont Lodge were all part of the appreciation and recognition for one of their own.

Governor Lawrence Wetherby came to bestow Selvy a Kentucky Colonel commission. Coaches Harry Taylor and Lyles Alley spoke, telling the audience nothing they didn't already know. Mayor Robert Daniel said a few words, as did Redhound Booster Club President Ted Meadors. The featured speaker for the evening was Tom Siler, nationally recognized sports columnist for the *Knoxville News-Sentinel.* Siler was a Whitley County native, and had closely followed Selvy's career at Furman, often writing about the boy from Corbin. He had come a long way from his high school days and those pre-game meals his mama fixed for him of creamed-wheat with water. "No sugar or milk," he said.

After touring with the College All-Stars against the Globetrotters, Selvy was drafted number one by the National Basketball Association. When he was drafted as the overall number one pick by the Baltimore Bullets, the NBA was not the billion dollar business it is today. His $10,000 salary offer was incredibly the highest ever paid to a rookie coming into the league.

Initially there had been some doubt as to whether he would even play pro ball. Remember, it was a different time and era, and briefly he thought about finding a job in the business world. "Back then the AAU was about as big as the NBA," Selvy said. "I thought about playing for the Phillips Oilers and Peoria Caterpillars. Their offer was $7,500, but it was a guaranteed job."

Two-and-a-half weeks into his first season with the Bullets playing on the road against the Fort Wayne Pistons, the players and coaches were informed that the Bullets had declared bankruptcy. "They came in right after the game and told us," Selvy said. "They also told us we were on our own to get back to Baltimore."

The league did a dispersal draft of the Baltimore players, and again Selvy was picked number one. "It was a re-draft," he said. "And I went to the Milwaukee Hawks. They moved to St. Louis that summer before the next season started.

"I was off to a great start with St. Louis, averaging about 25 points a game when I got drafted into the army." Actually Frank had been an R.O.T.C. student at Furman, and later commissioned as a second lieutenant before going to the Armor School. Later he talked about how he would wear his R.O.T.C. uniform when hitch hiking back to Corbin. "It was easier to catch a ride wearing a military uniform," he said.

Originally stationed at Ft. Knox, Kentucky, he played on a team with Kentuckian Frank Ramsey, who by now had been playing with the Boston Celtics. However, it wasn't long before Selvy received an assignment to Germany.

In the fall of 1957 he was released from the Army. He had been away from the professional game almost three years, so when he re-joined the Hawks he was on the bench. A newspaper reported that Frank told Hawks' owner, Ben Kerner, that he was quitting the team and retiring. He blamed an injured knee he suffered in the army for his decision. Alex Hannum, the coach, had Frank on the bench, and Kerner wanted him playing. The controversy led to Frank's departure from St. Louis. In almost a pass-through trade he went to the Minneapolis Lakers where he played in 12 games. A short time later he was traded to the New York Knicks, and for a brief time he hooked up with another Corbin boy, Jerry Bird. At long last Frank was playing again, averaging 10 points a game.

It was in New York City that Selvy's life changed. This time it was something that had nothing to do with basketball, but it was a result of the game.

Selvy had been a teammate of Bob Pettit's (he finished second to Frank in the college scoring race in 1954) in St. Louis, and it was through the former LSU great that Frank was introduced to Barbara Banks.

Barbara, a former Miss Arkansas from Conway, Arkansas, was living in New York working as a dancer, actress, and performing on the popular Hit Parade weekly television show. Her roommate had gone to college with Pettit, and when his Hawk team came to town he had set up a blind date for Barbara and Frank.

"I had never had a blind date," Barbara said. "I thought, 'Why can't a pro-basketball player get a date on his own?' I was sitting high up in Madison Square Garden that night, and looking down, he looked so short. I was wearing heels and was worried I'd be taller than him, so at half-time I ran back to my apartment, that was only a couple of blocks away and changed shoes. Well, after the game when he came out of the dressing room, I couldn't believe how tall he really was." Barbara, who won the Miss America talent competition in 1956 as a dancer had been in New York City for close to two years, and was a regular on the Steve Allen Show as a result of her friend Bill Dana, the Jose Jiménez character. "He wrote me into 13 of the Allen Shows," she said. "I was also on the Dave Garraway Show several times."

Garraway was one of the Miss America judges along with a young insurance salesman from Owensboro, Kentucky. His name was Wendell Ford and he was selected to be a judge because that year he was the National President of the Jaycees.

"My roommate told me the first night I went out with Frank, 'You're going to marry him.' 'What are you talking about?' I said. We married seven months later in Conway, Arkansas. It was a small wedding."

As a player Selvy's next stop was Minneapolis, which soon became the Los Angeles Lakers. There he joined two of the NBA's biggest stars, Jerry West and Elgin Baylor.

When the boy from Corbin retired from the game in 1964, he left a productive nine year career. Playing in 383 regular season games, plus another 50 in the playoffs, he had averaged almost 11 points and four rebounds, and was an NBA All-Star twice. Along the way he had become a very good golfer. Jerry West, in his autobiography, credits Selvy with introducing him to the game. It wasn't like Frank had grown up playing golf in Corbin or even at Furman, but when he decided to play later, he read a book by Ben Hogan and soon became a scratch golfer.

Frank and his family returned to Greenville where he became an assistant to his old college coach, Lyles Alley, for the next two years. Before the beginning of the 1966-67 season, Alley became the Palidins' athletic director, and Frank became the head coach.

"It was probably a mistake for me to come back and coach," he told reporters after going 44-59 in four years. "I put too much pressure on myself. We made some improvements in a few areas, but I was glad to leave." He had gone 13 and 13 that last season with a season ending loss to William and Mary in the Southern Conference Tournament.

"College coaching is not rewarding and there's not a lot of money in it," he told the local newspaper soon after. "Some people don't think you do a good job unless you win them all."

He then took a job with the nearby St. Joe Paper Company where he worked for 25 years before retirement.

Years later Frank and Barbara's son Mike had this to say, "My dad is the most humble person I've ever known. I was on a kiddie show in Greenville when I was little. They asked me my name, and I said Mike Selvy. They said, 'Oh, your dad scored 100 points in a game.' I said, 'he did?'"

The Game

In Greenville, South Carolina, the night of February 13, 1954, few people in town cared much that Alan Ladd was starring in the movie "Paratrooper" at the local Plaza Theatre, or that Martin & Lewis were laughing it up at the Carolina. What they did care about was Furman's game against Newberry. It was Frank Selvy Night, and although the school's student enrollment was only 500, some 4,000 fans would squeeze into Textile Hall to pay tribute to their living legend.

Two nights before he lit Georgia Tech up for 51 in a 114-67 rout.

That had been the first game Iva and James Selvy had ever seen their son play. They were guests of the News-Piedmont Publishing Company, and for the Selvys it was a whirlwind of activity that involved dinner invitations; tours of Greenville, that included the city's huge textile center; accommodations at the prestigious downtown Poinsett Hotel; and even a corsage for Iva and Frank's two sisters, Stella and Sarah.

"I think I've been missing something," Frank's dad told the newspaper after the Georgia Tech game. "I would like to come again," his mother said. And they did.

Corbin folks were also there. More than 60 had driven some six hours, and 250 miles, to be a part of ceremonies that included Greenville Mayor J. Kenneth Cass presenting a key to Corbin Mayor Robert Daniel. "My City Council is about ready to change the name of Greenville to Selvyville," Cass told Daniel.

Those downtown movies had nothing on what was about to take place in Textile Hall. It was as if someone from Hollywood had scripted it. Frank was presented, prior to the game, a silver bowl with the inscription "Frank D. Selvy, Furman's All-American Basketball Player, 1954."

Every seat was full, and in the balcony it was standing room only. Among the crowd was the Selvy family, who were seeing their son for only the second time play a college game. Also there were five of Frank's younger brothers and two of his sisters, who were to play a "mock" game at halftime.

When referee Lou Bello tossed the ball up for the opening tip, not a single person realized they were about to be a witness to history. Local television station WFBC was broadcasting the game live, making it the first such basketball broadcast in South Carolina, and what they saw that night had not been seen before or since.

Furman had played Newberry earlier in the season and had struggled to win as Selvy scored only 23 points, so when Indian's coach Red Burnette decided not to hold the ball, it fit into Furman's game plan to let Selvy really have his night. "What the heck? We're here to play," the Newberry coach said before the game.

College games were played in four 10-minute quarters back then, and at the end of the first, Frank had 24 points. A Newberry player might have also set a record that night. In the first 2:43 Bobby Bailey fouled out trying to defend Selvy.

At halftime Furman led 77-44, and Selvy had 37 of those points. Sophomore Darrell Floyd, a future All-American who would lead the nation in scoring the next two seasons, had 25.

The television crew from WFBC quickly asked Coach Alley if his team could change to a darker jersey. It seemed that the black and white cameras were having difficulty in separating their silver jerseys from Newberry's white. Frank had scored 37 in the silver and then added 63 more wearing the purple.

At halftime, as one Selvy left the court, seven more came on. The boys, 17-year-old Edd, 12-year-old David, 10-year-old Don, 8-year-old Marvin, and 6-year-old Charles, were coached by their sister Sarah, and to make sure the game went the way it was supposed to, Stella Selvy was the referee. All of the boys wore "Furman" across their purple and white jerseys in honor of Frank.

The halftime opposition that night was a group of local youngsters whose parents were ardent Furman boosters. If a score was kept, no one remembers. The important thing was it was Selvy night.

When Furman returned for the second half, Selvy was the only starter in the lineup. Alley had decided to go the rest of the game with Selvy and four subs. And there was nothing complicated about what he told them, "Feed Frank," he ordered.

There was no resentment or jealousy among his teammates, as they knew what it meant to each of them and their school when Frank had brought them recognition.

Furman needed publicity, and Coach Alley knew how to get it. Just give the ball to the boy from Corbin.

At the end of quarter number three Selvy had 63 points and his team led 109-66. Word had spread across the city about what was happening over at Textile Hall, and anyone who wasn't there wanted to be. Years later it was difficult to find a single person in Greenville or throughout South Carolina who said they weren't there.

Selvy was on fire in the fourth quarter. In somewhat of an understatement, he told reporters after the game that "I really felt good because I knew I was hitting better than usual."

Just seconds into the final quarter he had his 68th point, giving him one more than the entire Newberry team. Then with eight minutes remaining Selvy scored point number 74.

By now the public address announcer had picked up on it, and wanting to make sure that everyone in Textile Hall knew what was happening, even those who couldn't see the count, began giving Selvy's running point total. Suddenly the trip from Corbin for Selvy's friends and family didn't seem so long after all. And the wild crowd didn't have a clue what was to come.

Selvy sank 12 field goals in a row with two of them coming in the final 15 seconds. But it was his last one that climaxed the most phenomenal scoring exhibition by a single player or team in the history of major college basketball.

With only seconds left, and Newberry with the ball, it looked like Selvy would finish with 98 points, but not so fast. Alley quickly yelled for his team to foul. They did and the Newberry player, with the crowd screaming, missed his free throw and Furman rebounded. There was still a prayer.

"They threw the ball to me and I got it near mid-court," Selvy said in describing the final ticks of the clock, as he was guarded by three Newberry defenders. "I did a spin move and let it go." He lofted a shot that may not have been heard around the world, but certainly around Greenville, S.C., and Corbin, Kentucky. With the ball high in the air, the horn sounded just as the ball ripped through the net.

It was the boy from Corbin's 100th point, and Furman exploded into the record books with a 149-95 win. "I never had any doubts about that last shot," he later said.

His 41 field goals in 66 attempts and 18 for 22 from the foul line made for a major college record. He was also proud of his team high 13 rebounds. Could anyone ever dream of scoring 100 points in a single game? Even in a make-believe world it would be hard to imagine.

Was there a reason that Newberry was picked for "Selvy Night," Frank was asked later? "It was sort of close to the end of my senior year," he told reporter Bob Gillespie. "And I think maybe Coach Alley wanted to make sure I scored a lot of points and we won."

After the game Iva Selvy wasn't quite sure what she had just seen her son do. "She asked me why I did that," Frank says. "I think she believed I scored all those points because she was there. And that was okay."

In a bit of a revelation, Frank confessed that for all of these years he had mistakenly thought his 100 point game was the first his parents had seen. "I've been telling it wrong for all of this time," he said. "But, I guess it was the second game. Time can play tricks on you." (Even a *Sports Illustrated* article in December of 2012, recalling the 100 point game, said it was the first time they had seen their son play.)

Against Wofford, the following game, Frank hit for 57 in a 123-102 win. So, for three consecutive games he had scored 51, 100 and 57.

In college basketball, at any level, only three players have scored at least 100 points. Eleven days before Selvy's explosion, Bevo Francis of Division III Rio Grande College (Ohio) tallied 113 points against Hillsdale College (Michigan). The year before, in 1953, against Ashland Junior College (Ohio) he scored 116. But then on November 20, 2012, another Division III player scored 138 points. Jack Taylor led Grinnell College to a 179-104 win over Faith Baptist Bible College (Iowa).

And to only add to the "what-ifs," Coach Alley had recruited Bevo, and Bevo was very interested in coming to Furman. However, the sensational center was married and working to complete his high school education at night school. Academically he was unable to enroll at Furman.

As big and historic as the 100 points were, perhaps the feat has stolen from Frank Selvy all of his other accomplishments, such as leading the NBA in scoring most of his rookie year or making the NBA All-Star team or playing on an NBA championship team in 1958 with the St. Louis Hawks.

One thing, though, the game didn't take from him was his character and presence in life to remain much the same person he was growing up as a young boy in Corbin.

Chapter Three

There Were Others

Roy Kidd

Roy Kidd is for sure a Corbin High School sports legend. When the Redhounds had that incredible run of six straight state basketball tournaments, Kidd played in three of them, starting at guard.

Even though he became better known as the ultra-successful Hall of Fame football coach at Eastern Kentucky University, he honed his athletic skills in basketball, baseball, and football in Corbin in the middle to late 40s.

A first team *Courier-Journal* All-State football player in 1949, Kidd could have played all three of his sports at some of the colleges that recruited him. He drew a lot of attention on the hardwood for just being a teammate of Frank Selvy's, but football and baseball were what he wanted to continue to play.

"Bryant recruited me at Kentucky," he said. "But there I could only play football, and I really wanted to play baseball, too. Three of us, Tommy Adkins, Carl Oakley and I were recruited there. We had all played together at Corbin, but Adkins was the only one who went there. He became captain of the team in 1953."

"I was actually recruited more by Western to play football than Eastern," he continued. "Jack Clayton was the coach there and he had an assistant, Frank Griffin, who recruited me a lot. I will never forget when Selvy and I played in the high school East-West game in Pikeville. Ralph Carlisle coached the West, and John Bill Trivette the East. Frank and I were in our hotel and there was a knock on the door. It was Coach (Ed) Diddle. He came in and told Frank he wanted him to come to Western to play basketball. He told me if I came and played football I could try out for basketball. He told Frank he really wanted him at Western and would give him $80 a month if he came."

Growing up the youngest of seven, four sisters and two brothers, Roy did what most young boys did in his day, played baseball and mowed a few yards. "I usually got 25 cents or 50 cents a yard for a little spending money.

"There were three parts of Corbin back then," he offered, "East Corbin, Central Corbin and South Corbin. I lived in East Corbin, and for the most part we stayed in our own neighborhood."

Roy's dad, Edd, was a train engineer who spent most of his working days hauling coal out of the West Virginia mountains. Although his dad didn't see him play many sports growing up, Roy still has great memories of the two of them catching a train to Cincinnati.

"My dad had a pass to ride the train," said Kidd. "We would leave on a Sunday morning at 3 a.m. to see the Reds play a doubleheader at old Crosley Field. It was so much fun watching the team take batting and infield practice. I was always a big St. Louis Cardinal fan and in particular Stan "The Man" Musial. It was sometime in the 80s, and I ran into him and introduced myself to him. He was quite a guy."

Like a lot of parents, his dad did not want him to play football. "He was afraid I'd get hurt." But Roy went on to be a very good halfback, throwing a pass every now and then. "I think it was those few passes I threw at Corbin that led me to be a college quarterback," he said. "I had never played quarterback until I got to Eastern."

Like so many youngsters growing up in eastern Kentucky, he had been a U.K. basketball fan. "They had Wah Wah Jones, Alex Groza, and Ralph Beard, and I'd listen to some of their games on our radio, which was bigger than some of today's TV's."

In 1949, he got to see another future Wildcat great when Corbin took on Owensboro in the State Basketball Tournament.

"Cliff Hagan was probably the best basketball player I ever played against," he said. "His Owensboro team knocked us out of the tournament. Selvy and Hagan went head-to-head, as both were centers then."

Looking back on it, Kidd says that Corbin coaches Ossie Burch and Ted Meadors probably had the biggest influence on him. And those Redhound games against Louisville football powerhouses Male and Manual he will never forget. Then there was the time Corbin played Kingsport, Tennessee, the number one ranked team in that state. He also recalled the great players in the mountains, like Harlan's Boonie Black, who held the state season scoring record until it was broken by Calvin Bird in 1956, and Middlesboro's Ed Miracle, who became a teammate of his at Eastern.

At Eastern Kentucky State College Kidd was a four-year letter winner in football and baseball. As a record-setting quarterback, he was selected to the All-Ohio Valley Conference team, and in 1953 was named "Little All-American."

His first head coaching job came in 1956 at Madison-Model High School in Richmond. "I was waiting for one of my new assistant coaches to get to town," he said. "I was really scrambling in those early day practices. I wasn't quite sure what offensive and defensive line schemes to use. It just so happened that Ossie Burch and Ted Meadors had bought a Ford dealership in Richmond, so I called Ted, and he came over and really helped me out."

It all worked out, because from 1956 to 1961 his teams were 54-11-1. That first team was 9-0, and Model High put together a 27-game winning streak from 1959 through 1961, and over that span was not scored on in 15 consecutive regular season games.

Kidd's 1960 team finished 11-0, but through a still-hard-to-figure-out ruling, did not receive a spot in the state playoffs. His 1961 team was 13-1, and he was recognized as the state's Coach-of-the Year.

In 1964, Roy Kidd became the head football coach at his alma mater, Eastern Kentucky University, and when he retired in 2002, the boy from Corbin had established a Hall of Fame coaching career.

Here are his accomplishments: Sixteen OVC titles; Grantland Rice Bowl winner; appearances in four straight national championship games, winning in 1979 and 1982, and runner-up in 1980 and 1981; 18 playoff appearances; national record 17 NCAA Division 1-AA playoffs; OVC Coach-of-the Year two times; 37 non-losing seasons; 25 straight seasons with a winning record; coached 55 All-Americans; 41 of his players signed NFL contracts; OVC Hall of Fame; Kentucky Athletics Hall of Fame; at retirement his 314 wins placed him as the sixth all-time winningest football coach in NCAA history; and the school's football stadium is now Roy Kidd Stadium.

In 2003, the boy from Corbin was inducted into the College Football Hall of Fame. Through it all Kidd always kept his eyes out for Corbin boys. He was well aware of the talent that Redhound football produced. And in 1978, he had his eyes on a real bluechipper. And he was a Bird.

Steve Bird, the son of Jerry and Nancy, was something special in Corbin. As an athletic football and basketball star, he fit the mold of...well, of a Bird. Even though Roy had grown up and played basketball with Jerry, he still knew he'd have to recruit Steve because a whole lot of other schools were too.

In the early going U.K. didn't pay much attention to the Corbin star. But when they realized they were missing out on a Bird, they tried to get the youngster to come to Lexington.

"We had him signed," recalled Kidd. "Steve's dad, Jerry, called me and said Steve was really confused about what to do. He said U.K. kept calling and he didn't know what to do. I told Jerry I didn't know what Steve could be confused about. He'd already signed his scholarship, and he was going to play football at Eastern." That should have put the issue to rest, but it didn't.

"Jerry called back and said one of Coach (Fran) Curci's assistants had called Steve again," Kidd continued. "He said Steve didn't know what to do. I told Jerry I wasn't going to release him, and to take Steve out in the backyard and kick his ass. I picked up the phone and called Curci. I told him the next time anyone from his staff called Steve Bird I would turn them into the NCAA. There were no more problems from then on."

In 1981, nearby Kentucky was looking for a new football coach. Jerry Claiborne had just retired and the school was looking for someone who could continue the success of the program. In looking for a coach, all anyone had to do was look no further down the road than Richmond. And sure enough Roy Kidd's name surfaced.

"I was told it was down to me and Bill Curry for the U.K. job," Kidd said years later. But then later my wife told me Jerry Claiborne's wife told her U.K. would never hire someone from Eastern, because it would be beneath them."

Roy Kidd, the boy from Corbin, never missed a beat while becoming a Hall of Fame coach in the shadows of Commonwealth Stadium.

Jerry Bird

When it came to sports, Jerry was the first of the fabulous Birds from Corbin. But it didn't come easy. Jerry was not destined to be a star. In Ruben and Bonnie Bird's family, their oldest son turned out to be the family's trailblazer.

As a small boy, Jerry had helped his dad during the summer on his Honey Krust Bread delivery route throughout the area, and in a typical Corbin-style work ethic, for seven years he delivered the *Corbin Times* newspaper. Beginning to show signs of growth spurts as he entered his freshman year of high school, Jerry was then now expected to play basketball.

The following year he was closing in on 6'6" and started to draw some attention, not only from opposing coaches, but from colleges as well. As his talent began to emerge, he still wasn't good enough to crack the Redhound starting five. These guys were good and Jerry felt good about his progress when Coach Harry Taylor told him he had made the traveling squad.

With Frank Selvy, Bobby Terrell, Roy Kidd, Robert Barton, and Jerry Brooks pacing a Corbin team that had already played in three straight Sweet Sixteen tournaments by the time Jerry arrived, he would have to wait his turn.

In the meantime at practice he went against Selvy every day. "He was a 6'0" pivot man and I was his 6'6" backup," Bird laughed. "But he could play. I learned a lot from him."

Years later Bird laughed in recalling the 1950 State Tournament. That's the one where Roy Kidd threw in one from near mid-court to defeat Central City for third place. "Selvy had fouled out and I had replaced him," said Jerry. "My man had just scored to tie the game. Roy then hit his game winner and came over to me and said, 'I just saved your ass.'"

Now keep in mind that as good as Corbin basketball was, the heart and soul of the town was Redhound football. And Jerry Bird wanted to be a part of that, too. "I went out for the team without telling my dad," says Jerry. "When he found out about it he came home and threw me up against the house and said I wasn't playing football. Coach Taylor couldn't believe it and called my dad. He convinced dad to let me play. I'll never forget it. I was outside and Rodger came running out of the house hollering 'you get to play, you get to play.'"

Bird was tall, quick and fast, and made a nice target for any of the Corbin backs who threw the ball his way. One must realize that if not for the phone call from Coach Taylor, Corbin football history could have been changed forever. Calvin, Billy, Rodger, and Steve Bird might have had to make their name on the basketball court and not the football field.

It was Jerry's younger sister, Nancy Bird Carroll, who perhaps had the best perspective of what it was like growing up with brothers who would one day reach legend-status, at least in Kentucky. "I am two years younger than Jerry and two years older than Calvin," Nancy said. "And it was pretty rough around our house when Jerry wanted to play football and mother and daddy didn't want him to."

Nancy had her take on why her father finally gave in to the kids playing sports. "Daddy was a little man, but he could handle all of the kids," she said. "But when he found out if they played ball they would have a curfew. He really liked that. He knew they'd be home when they needed to be."

The Bird family didn't have their first car until Jerry was a high school junior, and Nancy says it was bought so they could get everybody to school. "I think it was a navy blue 4-door Dodge…don't remember the year," she says. "It seemed like he took the whole neighborhood to school.

"When all of the publicity started about my brothers, we weren't used to it. Heck, they were just my brothers. I remember when Adolph Rupp came to the house. It was like the king had walked in. And when we'd go up to see Jerry play, sometimes I'd be sitting next to Mrs. Rupp. Later on when I'd be introduced to someone they'd say, 'This is the Bird boy's sister.' I didn't really like that. I wanted to be introduced as Nancy Bird."

Even though Jerry became a good enough football player to be offered a scholarship by Paul "Bear" Bryant to U.K., Adolph Rupp informed Bryant and his assistant Charlie McClendon, who had been recruiting Jerry, to back-off. Rupp had his sights on him for basketball only.

Bird had gone from scoring 86 points as a sophomore, to 512 in his junior season. By the time his senior year rolled around lots of colleges came calling. Eastern, Western and Louisville were there. His 23-point average, playing against good competition, opened the door.

"Someone told me they heard where Coach Ed Diddle at Western said he'd trade his whole team for me," laughed Bird years later. "I said they must be pretty bad."

Jerry and several Corbin boys, however, did travel up to the University of Louisville just to check it out. "Some of the guys tried out for football," Jerry recalled. "There was a guy out there throwing them passes that almost knocked them down… turned out to be Johnny Unitas."

But it was Rupp's assistant, Harry Lancaster, who had the inside track from the beginning. "I only considered U.K.," Bird said. In December 1951, he signed the papers to become a Kentucky Wildcat, becoming the first Bird to go to college in Lexington.

He had finished strong at Corbin, scoring 41 points against Hazard, playing in three straight state tournaments, a member of the Kentucky All-Star against Indiana and Ohio, All-State Tourney team, MVP of the 13th region, and his 1,314 career points was a Corbin record at the time. During his years at Corbin his teams posted a 90-10 record.

Jerry began to be invited to several All-Star games. Playing for Coach Ed Diddle against Ohio, he was named the game's Star of Stars. Not long after, he received the same honor playing for a Kentucky team, coached by Pikeville's John Bill Trivette, against a group from West Virginia.

His crowning All-Star accomplishment came when he was named to the annual North-South game played annually in Murray, Kentucky. It was considered THE game at the time, on par today with the McDonalds All-Star game.

Bird not only played in the game, he starred. Although his South team lost 84-70, he led his team with 19 points in outscoring the great Bevo Francis who had 13. Teammates Howie Crittenden from Cuba and Phil Rollins from Wickliffe each had nine. Robin Freeman, a future Ohio State All-American, led the North with 22, points and future NBA Hall of Fame Tom Heinsohn added 10.

Later Chuck Taylor, Converse Rubber Company's internationally known basketball guru, assisted by sports writers and college coaches throughout the nation, named Jerry Bird, along with Bruce Brothers, Freeman, Crittenden, and Heinsohn, to the first five high school All-American team.

Looking back on his high school career, Jerry points to a charity basketball game he participated in after graduating. Somewhat insignificant, it gave him a boost of confidence, as if he needed it. The opposing team featured former 7-foot U.K. All-American Bill Spivey. Bird's team lost 55-54, but the slender 6'6" Redhound held his own, scoring 15 points to Spivey's 19. Each had several blocked shots against the other.

By the time Jerry had finished with the All-Star games, practice sessions and camps, he had been gone from Corbin six weeks. "I was ready to get back home," he said.

Once he arrived in Lexington it didn't take him long to start stockpiling all of the past tales he would hear from the current players, as well as those he picked up on his own. As far back as the 1950s, Rupp's legendary status had already been established. After all, he had coached the Fabulous Five to an NCAA title and an olympic team to a gold medal. Everything the baron of college basketball said was either printed, recorded or filed away to be told later by one of his players.

"*Look* magazine ran a story about Kentucky and printed that (Frank) Ramsey was better than (Cliff) Hagan," recalled Bird. "'You'll never be as good as Hagan,' Coach Rupp told Ramsey. Well, that night Frank went out and scored 30 points."

After his freshman year at U.K., under the tutelage of Harry Lancaster, Jerry was ready to step up and be a contributor on what was to become one of the best teams in Wildcat history.

With Hagan, Ramsey, Bill Evans, Lou Tsioropoulos, Gayle Rose and Phil "Cookie" Grawemeyer as the core, Jerry Bird would become part of a team that would go 25-0. Since Hagan and Ramsey would be ineligible to play in it, the school declined to participate in the NCAA tournament. The year before, the 1952-53 team had been suspended by the NCAA for violations that dated back to the 1950-51 team. In spite of it all, the Helms Athletic Foundation named the '53-'54 team their National Champions.

Four games into the 1953-54 season Jerry Bird knew something was wrong with him physically. "It was something to do with my heart," he said. "I was in the hospital for two weeks and then spent another four weeks in recovery. I got out of the dispensary to take my first semester finals." Jerry, who didn't need to lose weight, had lost a bunch. However, the summer months were good to him, and soon he had regained those pounds.

He then found out that Rupp had recruited a pretty good player out of a Texas junior college. Bob Burrow had the size and skills needed to give the Wildcats a needed boost inside, and his presence would allow Jerry to move out to forward where his quickness would make him more of a scoring threat. The high scoring Kentucky team had four players averaging double figures, with Burrow leading the way at 19 per game. Evans had almost 14, Grawemeyer 13, and Bird 11. Grawemeyer, however, broke his leg and missed the last six games of the year.

All in all it was a good 23-2 year. The real downer, however, had come on January 8, 1955, in Memorial Coliseum when Georgia Tech came to town and snapped Kentucky's 129-home court winning streak. With 12 seconds remaining and the Wildcats up by one, Joe Helms hit a 12-foot jumper for a 59-58 win. The Yellow Jackets also won again later that month in Atlanta. Keep in mind it was the only two conference losses for Kentucky, as Georgia Tech at the time was an SEC member.

After winning the SEC championship, Kentucky fell to Marquette 79-71 in the Eastern Regional. They did defeat Penn State 84-59 the next night in the consolation game played back then. In that era there were only 16 teams that participated in the NCAA Tournament, and out of the SEC only the champion played on.

"I'm not sure," Bird recalled. "But Grawemeyer, Burrow and I were double figure rebounders, and I think we led the nation."

Along the way Jerry was making his own memories when it came to Rupp stories.

"Cookie (Grawemeyer) and I were walking in front of the Fine Arts Building (on campus)," he said. "Coach drove by and saw us…rolled down his window and asked if we wanted a ride. We said no, but while he was still talking to us he side-swiped a couple of cars. Never stopped, just kept going."

Then there was the game against Ole Miss played in Memphis.

"Rupp thought finding bobby pins was good luck," Jerry laughed. "We went to a movie the night before the game and Linville Puckett stopped off at a drug store and bought a bunch of them. He dropped the pens where he knew coach would be walking."

Sure enough, the next night when Rupp came in the dressing room, he said, "Boys we're going to win big, look what I found."

Indeed they did, beating Ole Miss 84-66.

The 1955-56 seasons, Jerry's senior year, was filled with high expectations. After all, Burrow, Gerry Calvert, and Grawemeyer were returning, and incoming sophomore Vernon Hatton was expected to add offensive firepower.

A somewhat disappointing 20-5 record and a second place SEC finish was not what had been expected. Two SEC losses, one to Vanderbilt and the other to Alabama late in the season gave the Crimson Tide the league title. But as so often happened in the Deep South in the 50s, Alabama declined the NCAA bid and Kentucky advanced to the Eastern Region in Iowa City, Iowa. An 84-64 win over Wayne University in the opening round put them against the University of Iowa. A good Hawkeye team with a home crowd behind them won 89-77.

A footnote to the season is worth a look. When the Wildcats lost to Alabama 101-77 on February 25, in Montgomery, Alabama, two nights later in the Louisville Armory they set an SEC record that still stands when they walloped Georgia 143-66. Coach Rupp must have found a few more bobby pins.

Kentucky as a team finished ninth in the Associated Press poll, and Bird had a good year. His 16.2 point average trailed only Burrow's 21.1. Hatton and Calvert averaged in double figures, too. Grawemeyer, however, never quite rounded into form after he breaking his leg the previous season. Jerry Bird was named All-SEC second team.

Jerry had played his last college game. Although it was a loss, he was taken by surprise the next morning at breakfast. "Rupp saw me and jumped up and ran over and hugged me," Bird said. 'Lord, Jerry of all the players, I hate to lose you.' I didn't know where that came from, but I said thank you."

Initially, Jerry was chosen in the third round of the NBA draft in 1956 by the Minneapolis Lakers. It was several years later that the NBA expanded from its then eight teams, so being drafted in the third round was not all that bad. To further put it in perspective, two years before, Cliff Hagan had been drafted in the third round by the Boston Celtics. It was not always a given back then that great college players would play professional basketball. The Industrial League, governed by Amateur Athletic Union rules, was an option. Some teams like the Phillips Oilers, Akron Goodyear and Marathon Oil fielded teams made up of great former college players. The lure was that when their playing days were over, they would move into "executive" type jobs with the companies. Jerry actually became a professional when he signed to play for a team in a 21-game tour against the Harlem Globetrotters.

"They paid me $2,000 plus expenses," he said. "We played all over the country. When I signed I lost my scholarship. I was on my own, food and everything. But it was good money."

Jerry's basketball life was put on hold, however, when he was selected in another draft, this one by the U.S. Army. Because of his ability to play basketball, though, he spent the next two years playing "service ball."

"I played for the 6th Army team in Presidio, California," he said. "We lost in the All-Army tournament to Fort Dix. They had Tom Gola, Si Green, and three Globetrotters."

When Bird was discharged in August 1958, he had been traded to the New York Knicks. "I had to try out to make the team," he offered. "And I did."

At this point in his life, the once-shy skinny boy from Corbin who could have easily padded his high school statistics, but instead was more concerned about what his teammates thought, was now a well-traveled, mature, young man who had established a network of friends all over the country. So when he showed up with the Knicks there were several familiar names, and even some familiar faces. Among them Charlie Tyra, the former U of L All-American, and Art Spoelstra, who had been a scoring machine while playing at Western for Ed Diddle in 1954.

Not long after, Jerry had another new teammate. This one he knew very well. Frank Selvy had been traded to the Knicks from Milwaukee. Who would have ever believed it, two former Redhounds from the railroad town of Corbin, Kentucky, were now playing together in the Big Apple's Madison Square Garden.

For sure Kathleen Britton couldn't believe it. She had moved from Corbin sometime in the 50s to New York City and was working as a hat check girl in one of the night clubs. She had gotten word that a couple of Corbin boys would be playing a basketball game in the Garden. Later she told friends back home how special it was to be there when Jerry Bird and Frank Selvy were introduced to the thousands of fans. "Can you believe it," she said. "Two boys from Corbin." Bird and Selvy had become the third Corbin Redhounds to wear a New York Knicks uniform. Marion Cluggish had played there in 1940-41.

In 1958 Jerry was cut from the Knicks, and still needing nine credit hours to get his degree, he returned to Lexington. He would run into Coach Rupp on campus, and on one occasion his former coach invited him to go have a cup of coffee at the Wildcat Grill, not far from Memorial Coliseum.

"This is some story," Jerry laughed. "My junior year against Georgia Tech I missed a shot Coach Rupp thought I should have made. He called time out, and when I got to the huddle he pinched me, pinched me hard. I never forgot it. Well, when we finished having coffee, I put my arm around him and pinched him. He said, 'Gawddamn, Jerry, what are you doin'?' I asked him if he remembered the Georgia Tech game. He laughed."

There was another day at U.K. Jerry will always remember, and it didn't happen on the basketball court. "Harry (Lancaster) called me in and told me to follow him," Jerry said. "He took me into the equipment room at Memorial Coliseum. There were all of these suits just hanging there. He told me to pick out some and that they had belonged to Bear Bryant. I didn't ask a whole lot of questions, but I think I got ten of them." Does he still have any of them? "Wish I did," he laughed. "I think I gave a couple of them away and probably wore the rest out."

Jerry didn't say it, but he just might have been wearing one of Bear's suits on April 19, 1959, when he married Nancy Howard at Highsplint Coal Company Baptist Church, six miles outside of Evarts, Kentucky. She had been a cheerleader at Cumberland College in Williamsburg and friends with classmate Okeh Craft, who along with her boyfriend Calvin Bird introduced Jerry to Nancy. Clifford Eagle, one of Jerry's best friends in life, served as his best man.

Once Jerry received his degree, he interviewed with Phillips Petroleum Company. He was hired and spent the next several months in their training program in

Indianapolis, Indiana. "As luck would have it, they had an opening in their Corbin office," said Jerry. "So I went back home as a sales rep."

Ten years later Phillips Oil wanted to move Jerry to their Louisville office, but wife Nancy had gone back to Cumberland College to get her degree. "She just lacked a few hours," Bird remembered. "And I didn't want to move, so I resigned."

Luck would arrive again for the Birds, this time in the form of American Greeting Card. Jerry interviewed, was hired, and spent the next 30 years with the company in management before retiring.

Bobby Terrell

Bobby Terrell has left his mark. Not only is he considered one of Corbin's all-time greats in basketball, but he might very well be considered one of its most knowledgeable historians. "If I don't know, I'll find out," he has been heard to say.

Terrell's network includes a stint at Louisville as a basketball player, at Georgetown College playing baseball, and laying claim to playing on the same team with Corbin legends Frank Selvy, Jerry Bird, and Roy Kidd.

But Bobby Terrell brings another element to the table.

Immediately out of college he served three years in the U.S. Marine Corps, and after that he went to work with the Ford Motor Company where he became a top line executive. After thirty years at Ford, he moved to Oklahoma City where he headed up a company that dealt in automotive components and communication equipment. His travels took him worldwide.

In late 1997, the boy from Corbin came back home. "I came back to stay only for a little while," he said. "I was going to play golf, and enjoy the grandchildren and then go on to Hilton Head." Not long after returning, Terrell was at a meeting, and when it was over he had agreed to spearhead fundraising efforts to build the Ossie Burch Fieldhouse. He was the right man to lead the way, because by September 2000 over $1 million had been raised, and the state-of-the-art indoor all-purpose athletic facility was dedicated. Vin and Bill Hoover at Pepsi Cola were very instrumental in the successful project.

It was little wonder that no one wanted Terrell to leave Corbin. He became involved in economic development for the region, and as a community activist, he had the pulse of Corbin.

Bob's dad, Steely Terrell, taught math at Corbin High School, and his mother worked in one of the local law offices. Bob's father was a first cousin to Ida Terrell, who married Nick Denes. "Dad played football here in 1925," Bob said. "And he was mayor in the late 50s before he went to Frankfort to work in the Bert Combs administration."

Along the way Terrell had not only accumulated, but been a part of many stories. At U of L, playing basketball for Peck Hickman, he hit, at the time, the longest shot in the school's history. "It was from the opposite free-throw line," he said. "And I think Marvin Selvy later hit one from even further back to break the record."

Georgetown Coach, Humzey Yessin, talked Bob into transferring from Louisville. He played basketball one more year before signing a contract with Middlesboro, an independent minor league baseball team affiliated with the Reds and Pirates.

In 1955, when Bob graduated from Georgetown (he was inducted into Georgetown's Athletic Hall of Fame in 2004), his first Ford job was in Cincinnati. There, still thinking he wanted to play some more basketball, he hooked up with a team in the city's Norwood Industrial Basketball League.

"I met Bill Spivey and played with him," Terrell said. "Also on the team was Eddie Edwards, a Corbin boy. Eddie had played at Furman, but not at Corbin. He was a senior at Furman when Frank Selvy and Bob Barton were freshman. Furman was so lousy then that Eddie decided to go out for the team. He made it and was even their leading scorer. That year the varsity could never beat the freshman.

"We also had another Corbin boy, Cliff Eagle, who had played basketball and football. We were pretty good...even played some preliminary games for the NBA Cincinnati Royals. Well, Frank was there to play a game one night and saw us Corbin boys on the floor. He couldn't believe it."

Bobby Terrell played in three consecutive high school state tournaments, and perhaps had he not played with some of the "best there ever was," he might be the legend. But many of those who know them say that's exactly what he is...a legend. He was Corbin's leading scorer with 522 points his senior year, and he and Jerry Bird were second team All-State.

"I'm almost embarrassed to say this after all these years," Terrell offered, "but when Frank Selvy and I were kids I was more than able to hold my own against him. I was even a little taller. All of a sudden, though, he got good, really good. He passed all of us."

Edd Selvy

Edd Selvy always wanted to be different. As a youngster growing up in Corbin, he carried himself with a slight cockiness that oozed with confidence. Early in high school he didn't play the traditional sports his older brothers played—football and basketball. He played them on the playground and with his buddies during the summer, but it wasn't until the beginning of his senior year that he decided to play on the high school teams.

By then he had already taken it upon himself to change the spelling of his first name from E-D to E-D-D. "I wanted to do something different," he said. "There were several Ed's, and I wanted my name to be a little different. I don't think my family even realized what I had done." They may not have known about the added D, but Edd's mother, Iva, knew her son wasn't going to be boxing in a local tournament against a visiting team from Knoxville, Tennessee. She would see to that.

"I boxed for a few years in the Corbin YMCA program," Edd remembers. "We had a big match against Knoxville, and mom said no way was I going to box. She locked me in the bedroom, but I crawled out the window and ran as fast as I could to the Y."

Selvy arrived just in time to hear the bell ring for the start of what was to be his match. "They had replaced me," he said. "It was probably a good thing, because the guy that took my place got knocked out in the first round. As I grew older, I got a little wiser and never boxed again."

Like so many youngsters in Corbin, their mother didn't want her sons to play football. Coaches Bill Tucker and Harry Taylor surely had their speeches down pat—speeches intended to persuade protective mothers into letting their sons take the field in order to continue the gridiron tradition in Corbin and become a Redhound warrior. Tucker and Taylor must have been good at it, because most of the time, after a visit with a concerned parent, attitudes and opinions were changed. Edd's mother, too, was against the football thing, but a conversation with the coaches changed her mind.

"I was pretty cocky and knew I could play the game," he recalled. "I had played against these guys in the summer, but I wanted to play quarterback, and I told the coaches that."

In only one year Edd Selvy, the boy from Corbin, had been good enough to make a high school All-American team, been good enough to earn a football scholarship to the University of Kentucky, and even good enough to be a starter as a sophomore. And if all of that wasn't enough, he was just as good in basketball.

"I remember in Corbin, after the basketball season, someone told me they had seen my name in one of the sports magazines, and that I had made high school All-American on the same team with Wilt Chamberlain. I went and got it, and there I was."

Selvy had heard from some 200 colleges, but he only had eyes for U.K. At Kentucky Selvy was a defensive back and punt returner, playing in almost every game as a sophomore. "I enjoyed hitting more than getting hit," he laughed years later.

But with all of Edd's early success things suddenly changed as the season's end came with a game at Tennessee. "I didn't even get in the game," he offered. "We lost and I think if I had played I could have helped us win. I was upset. But I found out later a couple of gentlemen from Corbin had written Coach Collier, questioning him about why I wasn't playing quarterback." By Selvy's own admission he wasn't a college quarterback. "Not a good passer," he said.

"Back then the only coach I could really talk to was Coach Matt Lair, the coach who recruited me. I couldn't ask Collier anything. They knew I was unhappy. Besides that, they reneged on letting me play basketball. Collier said he was afraid I'd get hurt playing basketball."

Not long after, Selvy transferred to Furman to play basketball. "Furman offered my whole family scholarships, including my sisters," he said. "That's how much they thought of Frank and what he meant to the school.

"I never played a game at Furman," he said. "I transferred during the off-season, and before the season I decided to move to Louisville. I had one goal, and that was to marry Sandra (his wife). I was in love."

Back in Louisville he hooked up with Kingman Trailer Company, not only to work, but also to play on their basketball team. "We were good," he said. "Charlie Hampton, an ex-Louisville Central star, and Rudy Montgomery, Charlie Tyra, and sometimes Bob Burrow, Vernon Hatton and John Crigler played for us. Charlie's brother, Freddy Hampton, was our coach."

The team was good enough that the local newspapers reported their games to often include the box scores. "We won the 1958 Kentucky State Amateur Tournament," he said. "We went on and won our region and finally lost in the nationals to Phillip 66 Oilers."

Along the way Edd even considered a shot at pro football. "The Rams called. I even went to a tryout, but decided real quick it wasn't worth $9,000 a year getting my head knocked off by Deacon Jones and Merlin Olsen."

Several years later while working for Leggett and Platt Company, first in sales and then as a division head, he still found that the Selvy name was recognized just about everywhere he went. "It opened doors in the business world," he said. "In New York and Washington, D.C. they'd ask if I was Frank's brother, and I'd laugh and say, 'no, Frank's my brother.'"

Years later there was one more example that the Selvy name was still alive and well. "My youngest daughter Jamie got a letter from Ball State University inquiring about her basketball skills. They thought she was a boy because of her name. They even referenced Frank in the letter," Edd said.

Chapter Four

Another Bird Begins to Fly

"The best there ever was." Those were simple but powerful words often used to describe just how really good our sports stars from days gone by were.

Every school and every town, it seems, has a "the best there ever was," and often it is subject for debate. Not so with Calvin Bird.

Ask anyone who ever saw Calvin take a quarterback-pitch, angle a bit to the outside of the Redhound's left tackle, cut sharply to the right past a couple of diving linebackers, and a split second later in the clear, often untouched, head for the end zone. He might glance over his shoulder at anyone who cared to chase him. Their effort was usually just a formality to show their coach they had tried.

When Corbin sports historian Bill Crook says Calvin "was the best there ever was," you tend to believe him. He's seen most of the modern era Redhounds, and those he hasn't, well, you can be assured he has researched them. Those who saw Bird play for the Corbin Redhounds in the mid-50s say there has never been anything like him, before or since.

Although there had been plenty of good football players and teams in Corbin, make no mistake that it was Calvin Bird and the 1955 team that once and for all put the Redhounds on the football map, not only in Kentucky, but throughout the southeastern part of the United States.

Corbin football was doing fifty years ago what colleges are doing today. Friday night bon-fires and pep rallies before each home game was a given, as was Corbin's marching band, heading up Main Street from the band house with horns blowing and drums beating, their destination Campbell Stadium.

When the Redhounds took the field, usually trotting out single file, they looked more like college players than a high school team from a town of 4,000 people. Their fans adored them, and even the opposition could be seen hesitating during their warm-up to sneak a peek. Home or away, it was a full house. College scouts were there, and though most were there to see Calvin, the talent-rich Corbin team justified a visit from college coaches. They knew if they couldn't get him, they just might land one of the others.

Every major football program in the country was aware of Calvin Bird, the Corbin Comet. At 6'2", 185-pounds, he could run like the wind, throw the ball fifty yards in the air on the run, and had the ability to catch a football as if that's what he was born to do. What college didn't want him?

Older sister Nancy recalled the special relationship she had growing up with Calvin. "We were really close," she says. "Billy and Rodger were so much younger, but Calvin and I hung out in high school." Nancy continued. "Calvin was said to have been the fastest football player in the state, but I could outrun him. When my mother needed to switch him, she would say, 'Nancy, go get Calvin.' I was the only one who could catch him."

There was a trip to Cincinnati for a family picnic that Nancy remembers. "I'm not sure how it all came about, but there was a girl's race, and one of them had never been beaten. Anyway, I beat her, and she was really upset. It's too bad there weren't girls' sports back then, because I would have liked to have played."

For Corbin's sake, it was a good thing older brother Jerry had paved the way for the Bird boys to play football. Not only had his dad been dead-set against it, but his mother had been, too. Calvin recalled that his dad even sawed off the handle from an old broom and told Jerry he'd use it on his rear if he played football. "What helped change dad's feeling about football was when he was given two tickets to a U.K. football game by the bakery where he worked," Calvin said. "He figured he might as well use 'em since they were free."

Years later at a Wildcat lettermen's luncheon in Lexington in 1963, Calvin ran into Ray Correll, a 1953 All-American from Somerset, and told him about his dad seeing him play. "I've always wanted to meet you, so I could thank you for giving me and Rodger the chance to play football," Calvin told Correll. "He was mystified until I told him my dad was so impressed with the way he got downfield and clobbered the punt receivers. My dad listened to the way people in the stands talked about Correll. When he got back to Corbin, that's all he could talk about for weeks. After that I think my daddy would have used the broom stick on me if I hadn't gone out for football."

Even though Jerry had played football it still didn't set well with Bonnie, his mother. Calvin recalled that it didn't help the football playing situation when his mother traveled to Lexington to visit Jerry in the hospital at Good Samaritan his sophomore year at U.K. If injured or sick, that's apparently where all of the Wildcat athletes were sent. On her visits she would see all of those football players with noses broken and all sorts of injuries. "When face masks were allowed a little later, she felt much better about football," laughed Calvin.

As a 14-year-old in 1951, Calvin was a member of the Redhound "pups," a team made up of sixth and seventh graders and coached by Carl Bolton. It didn't take Calvin long to begin his legendary career. As a freshman he broke into the starting lineup as a 162-pound left end. Another freshman, who would also leave his mark on Corbin football, Bill Howard, started at halfback.

The Redhounds were coming off of a 2-8 season, and first year coach Bill "Moon" Conde was determined to implement a program that would separate those who just wanted to have their name on a roster from those who really wanted to play football.

And separate he did. Years later Calvin talked about Conde's arrival. "He was a disciple of Bear Bryant's," he said. "Many of our young men were not prepared for such physical demands from a coach." The season opening lineup had only two seniors, Don Hobbs and Michael Clark; a pair of juniors; and the other seven were freshmen and sophomores.

One of those who stuck around was Bill "Piggy" Howard. "My family lived across the street from Coach Conde," Howard said. "He told me if I could kick the ball over my house, I'd be his punter. I kicked it over and I was his punter."

Conde had chased off most of the upper classmen with his no-nonsense style of coaching, and with only three seniors on his 32-player roster, the success of the season was very questionable.

Before Corbin, Conde had played for Bryant at U.K. One of his teammates had been former Redhound star Tommy Adkins. Conde had also done a WWII tour in the Navy where one of his commanding officers was Harry Lancaster. It was this connection with Lancaster that led Conde to U.K.

Moon Conde's coaching experience before coming to Corbin was at Sidney Lanier High School in Montgomery, Alabama, where he worked with former Wildcat teammate Charlie Bradshaw.

Most people felt that Bryant's coaching style was his and only his, but over the years countless coaches, high school and college, attempted to emulate it.

Conde's first order in pre-season was to take his team to northern Tennessee for a football camp where he would have their full attention. When another trip across the state line took place, it was a sign of things to come.

Corbin fans, at least those who traveled to Morristown, Tennessee, for the season opener that year, saw something they had not seen in a long time. The Redhounds lost 53-0. That night the team picked up only two first downs, rushed for minus yardage, and failed to complete a pass.

In Bryant style, Conde practiced the team the next day, Saturday, in preparation for the home-opener coming up against Lexington Henry Clay. Still the visiting Blue Devils won 26-0.

The following week Corbin did score on a 88-yard kick-off return, but fell at Pineville 29-6. This game marked the first of his career that Calvin Bird's name appeared in a varsity game football story as he caught a 17-yard pass from Ralph Wilder.

Extended practices became the norm. The former hour-and-a half practice turned into two-and-a half. Still nothing helped, though, as Corbin lost 18-6, 48-6, 25-6, 32-6, 25-0, 46-6 and 27-0 over the next seven games.

At the conclusion of the season, Ralph Wilder and Kenneth Cobb were named second team All-Southeastern Kentucky Conference. Calvin and Darrell Hart received honorable mention. Everybody in Corbin was ready for basketball.

Basketball and Football Do Mix

It didn't take long for Calvin Bird, even as a freshman, to find some playing time on a seasoned Redhound basketball team led by Edd Selvy.

In the beginning he was coming off the bench, but before long it was double figure scoring, and a berth on the annual Cumberland Falls Invitational All-Tournament team.

With the season winding down, Calvin saved his best for near the end, as he scored 25 points in leading the Redhounds to an 80-60 win over previously unbeaten Clay County. Edd Selvy scored 24.

In somewhat of an upset, Barbourville turned back Corbin in the 50th district semis 72-71. Calvin fouled out with just two minutes gone in the second half after his team was up by seven at intermission. Edd Selvy was conference Player-of-the-Year, while Darrell Hart made second team, and Calvin honorable mention.

It was a long hot summer in Corbin, waiting for Redhound football. Over the previous two seasons Corbin football teams had lost 16 straight. You read it right, 16! They had lost the last six games of the 1952 season under Coach Judge Howard, and in 1953 they were 0-10 under Conde. When it was over only 16 players had stuck it out with Conde.

But Bill "Moon" Conde was no longer around. Instead, Bill Tucker, who had played high school ball at Louisville Manual and had success while in the Army coaching his team to three All-Army championships, now had the responsibility of turning not only the football team around, but also the town. What had happened was unprecedented. This once proud program's fall had taken its toll on many.

The *Corbin Times* wrote:

> *It's nearly a disgrace to see these past achievements weakened or made cheap in any way. A team must not rely on former victories, but win fame for itself.*
>
> *Corbin fans are disillusioned. They want to be able to speak proudly of the Redhounds. They are looking to the 1954 team to regain the glory which rightfully belongs to Corbin. If this is done, the boys on the team must want to, and want to badly.*

Pressure laid out by the town's newspaper was not taken lightly. But that's the way everyone felt about their beloved Redhounds. The last victory for a Corbin football team was a 20-13 win over Pineville on September 19, 1952.

Bill Tucker knew all about the tradition and all of the wins, but more importantly about all of those losses. He knew he had to do something about the lack of kids playing football, and over the summer he set about to change attitudes. When the season opened he had forty-seven youngsters on the roster ready to play football.

Finally!

"Coach Tucker's approach to football was just as tough as Conde's," Calvin said years later. "But his demeanor was considered much more caring for his young players."

The drought was over as Calvin and David Miller scored two touchdowns each in a 31-0 win over Bell County at home in the first game. What a turn around it was! Although the season's 5-4-1 record was a little light by Redhound standards, it was still good enough to send a clear message that Corbin football was back. An 18-6 win over number one ranked Pineville was the season's highlight. David Chandler's touchdown run put the finishing touch on the final score.

Darrell Hart and Kenneth Cobb were named first team all-conference, while Bird, Edd Selvy, Robert Howard, and Bill Scalf were Redhounds on the second team. Honorable recognition went to David Chandler, David Miller, Morris Garrison, and Ralph Wilder.

Corbin, the town, was already clamoring about next year. Basketball Coach Harry Taylor, who also doubled as the assistant football coach, was doing some chomping-at-the bit, too. He had concerns that several of his key players were also footballers, therefore limiting their pre-season prep time.

He shouldn't have worried. Finishing regular season play at 17-4 with Selvy, Bird, and Paul Engle carrying much of the load, Taylor was more concerned now of getting this team to reach its potential. A berth in the Sweet Sixteen was their finish line. Last year the Redhounds had been knocked out in district play, and Coach Taylor pulled out all stops to avoid a repeat.

He agreed to a March of Dimes double header matchup at Memorial Coliseum on the U.K. campus. He felt that letting his team play on the bigger college floor would prepare them for the state tournament. And besides, it would be a hostile crowd. Their opponent would be Ralph Carlisle's Lafayette Generals led by Doug Shively, son of U.K. Athletic Director Bernie Shively.

Because of their older brothers, the Selvy and Bird names made the Redhounds very marketable. Plus they were good. The Redhounds came away with a 73-70 win over a big city Lafayette school, and were now setting its sights on a Region 13 championship.

True to form, an 88-63 win over Barbourville put Taylor's team back in the regionals after a two year absence. The luck of the draw didn't favor Corbin, however, as their first round opposition would be Clay County on their home court in Manchester.

Coach Spider Thurman had his Clay County team hitting on all cylinders, and they drilled the Redhounds 68-51. The host team went on to beat Cumberland 62-46 for a slot in the Sweet Sixteen. Not only did the Tigers win the game, but Coach Thurman was presented with a new automobile that night. The win gave Clay County back-to-back regional titles.

Sophomore Calvin Bird was named to the all-tournament team.

When the 1955 football season rolled around, the players and the entire town of Corbin could barely contain themselves in anticipation of what this Redhound football team could do. As for Coach Tucker, he was cautious. He had seen what had happened to the basketball team the year before. And, too, it had only been two years since that 0-10 record.

Perhaps one of the reasons for caution was what he had seen that spring in the annual Varsity-Alumni game. It's difficult to believe these games were actually played at full speed, pads and all, but it became a tradition to see some of the former Corbin stars, several of whom were playing in college, come home to prove they still had it. As good as the current Redhounds were projected to be, they lost to the "over-the-hill" Alumni 18-14. Calvin scored both touchdowns for the losing team.

In August of 1955, Tucker packed his team up and headed for a football camp in Doyle, Tennessee. Nine days of conditioning, a full scale scrimmage against Cartersville, Georgia, and a chance for the second year coach to evaluate several possible position changes from the previous year just might be enough to make sure he had all parts moving in the right direction. He was well aware of the talent he had, but the coach knew it could be the little things that made the difference in winning a championship.

The schedule would be tough: Lexington Henry Clay, Louisville Manual, Middlesboro, Pineville, Somerset, and Danville made up the core of the schedule. With seven starters and 13 other lettermen returning, experience was on his side.

Bell County was the first to feel the Redhound bite. Although not as sharp as expected, Corbin won 25-6. Henry Clay, the following week came to Corbin, and unlike the previous game, the Redhounds had a surprisingly easy 33-0 win. The victory was only the third in twelve games against the Blue Devils.

The year before, the *Louisville Courier-Journal* and *Lexington Herald Leader*, had paid little attention to the Redhounds. Occasionally there would be a little lip service to Calvin Bird, perhaps more so because he was Jerry Bird's little brother. But now Calvin and the rest of the Corbin team were making their own way.

It was early, but the authoritative Litkenhous Ratings, a statistical hodge-podge of numbers put together by Dr. Frank Litkenhous to determine where a team ranked in Kentucky, appeared in the *Courier-Journal*, and the Redhounds were ranked seventh. It had been a long time coming, but it looked like they were indeed back.

Next came a 39-0 win at twelfth ranked Pineville that featured a 99-yard Bird punt return for a TD. Quarterback Ralph Wilder began to emerge as a star, too. The left hander could not only pass it long, but could pick up vital short yardage when needed. Halfback David Miller and end Don Turner had become stars on both sides of the ball. Their defensive plays were game changers.

Scoring 97 points and giving up only six, after the third week of the 1955 season Corbin was ranked number one in Kentucky high school football. Now newspapers were not only writing about Calvin, but also Dave Chandler, Bill Scalf, Bobby Morris, Stan Bunch, Gerald Ellison, Bill Howard, Ronnie Riley, Johnny Hoskins, Carl Bible, Tom Steely, Winton Boone, Morris Garrison, and Mel Chandler.

For sure the Redhound program had come a long way in a short time. But if they didn't stay focused it could all be for naught. The top ranked Redhounds now were headed to Louisville to face long time powerhouse Manual, a team ranked number nine.

In somewhat of an irony, the game's two coaches, Bill Tucker and Manual's Bill Jasper, each had connections with the teams they were opposing. Remember that season opening game Moon Conde's team played against Morristown, Tennessee, two years earlier? Corbin fell 53-0 in what was described by one writer as humiliating. The winning coach was Jasper. Corbin's team was number one, and some of those youngsters, who were freshman and sophomores, were now juniors and seniors and loaded for bear.

Coach Tucker had grown up in Louisville and played at Manual, as well as being an assistant coach there. He knew their program and tradition as well as anyone.

But talk was cheap. Both teams had something to prove, mainly to themselves. First, Corbin had not beaten a Louisville team since 1932, and Manual had the pride of...well, just being from Louisville.

A rain drenched duPont Manual Stadium crowd of only 2,500 braved a nasty night even though two of Kentucky's best were battling it out. As might be expected fumbles were crucial. For the game the Redhounds lost two and Manual three. But it was a Manual turnover that is still being talked about fifty-eight years later.

Early in the first quarter, punter Bill "Piggy" Howard dropped back to punt as rain dropped from the sky in sheets. The snap sailed over his head and he was nailed at his own 23 yard line by Manual defenders. With the Crimson Red threatening to score in a 0-0 game, the Redhounds dug in.

It was here that defensive back David Miller made the play he and his teammates will never forget. "I got as close as I could to the line of scrimmage and heard the play," he recalled. "It was going to be an outside pitch from their quarterback. I just stepped in and caught it in the air."

Miller returned the lateral 44 yards to the Manual 35 yard line. No one knew it at the time, but even though Miller's play was early in the game, it turned out to be one of the biggest plays. In the second quarter, Manual was never closer than the Corbin 44, and in the second half failed to cross midfield.

For the first two quarters, the toughest opponent for either team was the driving rain. It wasn't until early in the third that Bird punched it in from just inside the Manual one yard line. Not leaving anything to chance with an extra point kick or pass, quarterback Wilder faked to Bird, tucked it in and fell across the goal line for a 7-0 Corbin lead that turned out to be the final score.

Corbin returned home to face archrival Middlesboro, and the Yellow Jackets managed to cross midfield only once in the entire game in a 46-0 loss. It was the most lopsided Corbin win since coach Ted Meadors' team won 44-0.

Barbourville was next. And it was not pretty unless you were a Redhound. Scoring 11 touchdowns, five by Bird, Corbin won 76-0. Miller scored three times as well as adding six extra points. Wilder scored twice and Ronnie Riley once.

Even though Corbin was running roughshod through their schedule with a perfect 6-0, when the weekly Litkenhous Ratings were released Corbin had been replaced at the top by Paducah Tilghman, who had defeated Owensboro 47-0 the previous Friday night.

A sidebar to it all was the number of points Bird was racking up. His 86 points through six games earned him top scorer in Kentucky, 12 points ahead of Shelbyville's

Sammy West. As Bird's notoriety began to grow, for sure the opposition would try to put the brakes on him.

Somerset was always tough, but they had never seen a Redhound team like this. As good as Bird was in a 45-6 win for Corbin, Wilder was even better. The lefty passed for four touchdowns, ran 43 yards for another, and added three extra points. Don Turner was on the receiving end of two of Wilder's throws, as was Bird, who also added a 23 yard score.

By now some sportswriters were calling Bill Tucker's team "one of the finest high school teams ever produced in Kentucky prep circles," especially after they pounded eleventh ranked Danville 34-20 at Corbin. The loss snapped a twenty-three game Admiral win streak. The state record for consecutive wins was held by Ashland. From 1928 to 1932, the Tomcats won thirty-five.

In the modern era of keeping football records, Corbin had never beaten Williamsburg (not including the late 20s) in three tries going into the '55 season. The year before, Corbin lost 13-6 with practically the same team minus Edd Selvy. Bird, Wilder, Miller and Howard, Corbin's leading scorers during the '54 season were held scoreless by Williamsburg a year ago.

But times they were a changing. Now averaging just over 40 points a game, and with a halfback on schedule to break the state single season scoring mark, Williamsburg, with a 7-1 record, could be in big trouble. And they were. The Redhounds blasted their neighbors 61-6.

Knox Central was the next to fall, 56-0. Bird flashed for 20 points, giving him a state record 149, breaking Cumberland's Ronnie Cain's total of 145 set the previous season.

Corbin's regular season was over. At 10-0 they had matched Ted Meadors' 1939 record as the school's only two unbeaten, untied teams.

Early in the season, you can bet Redhound fans started thinking about winning it all. For them to do that they would have to advance to the Recreation Bowl, played annually in Mt. Sterling.

The Bowl's selection tabbed number one Corbin against an 8-1 Newport Public ranked seventh in the state according to the Lit Ratings.

The game was a war with Corbin winning 27-21 and scoring the winning touchdown with only 1:20 left in the game. Newport Public came right back and was at the Corbin nine-yard line when the game ended. Fullback Bill Howard was named the game's Star of Stars. Bird had scored 14 points and ended the season with a new record of 163. For the season, Corbin as a team had scored an incredible 450 points while giving up only 59. As would be expected, the celebration began and individual honors for Coach Bill Tucker and his team began to pile up.

A banquet in duPont Lodge (named in honor of the same family that is connected to duPont Manual High School in Louisville) at Cumberland Falls State Park, sponsored by the school's Quarterback Club, featured the appearance of former Redhound coach Nick Denes, who many say is responsible for getting it all going at Corbin. Denes served as master-of-ceremonies that night, and his presence reinforced that Corbin High School still appreciated what he had done for the school back in the 30s.

While introducing the primary speaker for the event, Denes couldn't help but tell of his first meeting with Blanton Collier, now the head football coach at U.K. "It was on the basketball court," Denes told the audience, "At the 1936 state basketball tournament, and we beat Blanton's Paris team in the semi-finals." Corbin went on, of course, to win it all that year, but it might make for a good trivia question someday. What two Kentucky legendary football coaches faced off in the State Basketball Tournament?

The night belonged to the Redhound players and their coaches. Captains Dave Chandler, David Miller and Bill Scalf received the 1955 state championship trophy from Chamber of Commerce president Tom Catron, and then passed it on to the already-named team captains for next year, Calvin Bird, Bill Howard and Tom Steely.

The school received from Carson Mullins a life-size mural depicting the entire team and one of Coach Tucker and the cheerleaders. Ralph Reasor, representing the local Kiwanis Club, recognized Bob Howard with the Leadership Trophy; Don Turner received the Rotary Club's Scholastic Trophy from Foley Ruggles; Lions Club member Jack Finley gave the Sportsmanship Trophy to David Miller.

Corbin players on the SEKC All-Conference team was a given when it came to awards, as was Coach-of-the-Year, Tucker. Bird, Chandler, Turner, Steely, Scalf, and Wilder were all first team; Garrison and Ellison, second team; and David Miller, Bill Howard, and Bob Howard received honorable mention. Miller could have easily been named to the first team, and no one would have complained.

When the *Courier-Journal* named its 33rd All-State team, Calvin Bird, just a junior, was the top vote getter and honorary captain of the elite team. No other Redhound made the second team, but all-state honorable mention was a different story. Turner, Wilder, Bill Howard, Chandler, Scalf and Steely were recognized. Again, Miller was noticeably missing.

The *Paducah Sun-Democrat* had its own ranking of all-state teams. They even listed separate offensive and defensive teams. Calvin Bird was, as expected, the top vote getter, and was named to both units. Corbin teammate Don Turner was named first team defensive end.

In spite of Corbin's success and its 11-0 record, Tucker and Henderson's Don Shelton shared most of the state's Coach-of-the-Year honors. His team had gone 10-0.

A footnote to the unbeaten season: Although it was unofficial, remember the team did lose a game. The Hounds lost to the Alumni. "I hate to say it, but they beat us that year," Calvin said. "They were tough guys, some of them in the Army, and they could still play. On one of my runs I was tackled by Big Eye Hughes, and he bit me on my leg. It wasn't a hard bite, but a bite. I asked him why he did it and he said because he wanted to."

Basketball Time

Although Harry Taylor's Redhounds had been somewhat of a disappointment the previous two years, big things were expected out of a twenty-one game schedule. Bird was back, and 6'2" Don Turner looked like he was ready to pick up some of the scoring load. Center Eldon Poynter and Crittenden County transfer Keith Lockhart were expected to contribute.

As usual, in small high schools like Corbin, the athletes were interchangeable when it came to sports. It was common to see the same kids playing football, basketball, baseball, and track. By all appearances it didn't take long for the Hounds to adjust from football. A 70-36 win over Lynn Camp, followed by a 57-39 victory over Williamsburg jump-started the Redhounds. Next to fall were Barbourville and Hazel Green, but then a good London team, on their home floor, handed Corbin their first loss of the season, 61-59.

In late December, the Redhounds participated in the prestigious Louisville Invitational Tournament. An opening round 64-52 win over Louisville Shawnee was followed by a 78-63 pounding at the hands of Louisville Valley.

Berea won the championship game big, 77-54, over Louisville Manual. Bird made the All-LIT team along with future college basketball stars Don Mills (Kentucky), John Turner (Louisville), Corky Withrow (Georgetown/St. Louis Cardinals baseball), Darrell Bicknell (Western) and Winfred Thompson (Kentucky Wesleyan).

It was up and down over the next few games. They had a one point loss to Pineville, a 59-48 thumping by Clay County, followed by a win over Barbourville and a get-even 87-60 win over rival Clay County. In the win over the Tigers, Turner had 29 and Monty Lobb, 26. The Hounds followed that win with a get-even 85-55 win over London, a team they had lost to earlier. Bird had 33, and Turner 26.

In a 100-57 win over Middlesboro, Calvin Bird scored a career high 42 points and Tom Stapleton had 29 for the Yellow Jackets. Harvey Yeary for the first time appeared in Middlesboro's starting lineup against Corbin. He later changed his name to Lee Majors, the actor. (Yeary took his last name from Johnny Majors, the great UT tailback.)

Throughout the season Bird and Turner had been on a team with strong support from Lockhart and Lobb, closing out the season with an 88-62 win over defending state champion Hazard. Calvin Bird for the second straight time scored 42 points.

The Redhounds breezed through district play and into the regionals where, you guessed it, they drew always tough Clay County in the first round. But this time it was different. The Redhounds won 65-54. They then turned back Black Star 68-58 behind Turner's 30 points. Now Harry Taylor had his Hounds in position to get to the "show" in Lexington as they prepared to face Bell County.

Bird's 28 points and Turner's 21 were not enough though, as Bell County advanced 68-59. One of Bell County's stars was John Brock, who later went on to be Kentucky's Superintendent of Education. Brock said that his claim to fame, however, came in the 1956 state tournament when he "held" Wayland's King Kelly Coleman to 68 points in the consolation game.

With the season over for Corbin, Turner was named the SEKC Player-of-the-Year. Bird finished second in the voting. The *Paducah Sun Democrat* named Bird All-State second team, while the *Courier Journal* had him on their third team. Don Turner was honorable mention.

Not quite done with sports for this season, Bird had some track team obligations. His specialties were the 100 and 220 dashes, and he did not disappoint. Winning the conference and regional titles in both events, he advanced to the state meet in Lexington. "I got to state and false started in both events and was disqualified," recalled Bird. "I didn't have a whole lot of experience with starting blocks."

The Last Year at Corbin

With Calvin's senior season at hand, not only did the town people know this would be their last chance to cheer on the greatest football player in Corbin history, but so did his classmates, teachers, school principal, H.A. Howard, and superintendent G.W. Campbell, for whom the football field had been named.

The cheerleaders, Janie Thomas, Penny Tucker, Shelby Thurston, and twins, Pat and Jo Satterfield, were anticipating another football season just like the year before…a state championship. They would definitely have something to cheer about. Or would they?

With just three starters back from a 11-0 team, it would be very interesting to see if last year's squad depth would be talented enough to step in and continue the Redhound's success. With guard Tom Steely and back Bill Howard, both seasoned veterans, returning, would they be enough to continue the best football to come along in Kentucky in many a year?

If the 47-6 opening game win over Bell County was any indication, no one needed to worry. Bird's five touchdowns' and quarterback Tony Lanham's four scoring passes, may have sent a message that Corbin football is here to stay. Corbin was once again rated number one in the state, ahead of Manual, Male, Newport Public, St. X, Flaget, Pikeville, Dixie Heights, Danville, and Caldwell County.

Next Henry Clay fell 42-6. With Bird scoring three times, and with Lanham settling into the quarterback roll, the Redhounds were looking good. Backs Bill Howard and Ronnie Riley were keeping the defense honest, so Bird couldn't be keyed on every play. Plus, the outside speed of Winton Boone and Harold Queary gave Lanham another option to throw deep.

Pineville was the next to fall, 66-6. Bird upped his season point total to 75, to go along with Lanham's nine touchdown passes.

Calvin Bird had established throughout his prep career that he was a fabulous runner, could kick extra points, and make jarring tackles. But in the big picture of his game, it was his pass catching ability that often went unnoticed, to everyone except Ralph Wilder the year before, and now Lanham. Coming out of the backfield and catching a pass near the sideline, and then doing his thing, was something for Redhound fans to see when this Bird was in full flight.

Seven thousand fans turned out at Manual Stadium to see number one Corbin against the fifth ranked Crimson. Corbin had won last year's game there, 7-0, in a driving rainstorm that eventually chased away most of the crowd. Not this year.

Even before the opening kickoff, a bit of a battle erupted near midfield when the Redhounds took the field wearing their maroon uniforms. Manual had planned to wear red, the only color varsity uniform they had.

Bill Jasper, the Crimson coach, insisted he had an agreement with Corbin on what color uniforms each would wear, and that his team would wear red and Corbin white. He accused Coach Tucker of deliberately bringing only the maroon colors to upset his team just before kickoff. Tucker denied the accusation and Manual changed into white junior varsity jerseys.

There might have been another reason for the confusion. Tucker had not even been expected to coach in the game. As a member of the Kentucky National Guard, his unit had been on call to active duty to deal with a racial disturbance in Clay, Kentucky.

For the record, newspaper clippings revealed that the year before at Manual, Corbin did in fact wear white jerseys and Manual red. However, for the most part, it is generally accepted that the home team will always dress in light colored uniforms unless a previous agreement has been reached.

So much for the jersey debacle. Manual won the game 27-6 with Bird scoring Corbin's only TD. The Redhound loss snapped an eighteen game winning streak that dated back to October 22, 1954. It was reported to be state's longest streak of games without a loss.

It should be pointed out that during the days before modern technology, record keeping, statistics, and even scores were sometime reported incorrectly or not at all. To say the system was loose would be an understatement. An example: It was believed that Calvin Bird had broken the state individual scoring record the year before. But then it was reported that Harlan's Hugh "Boonie" Black had scored 238 points back in 1950.

The *Harlan Daily Enterprise*, after checking its files, reported that writer Clarence Green said that after Harlan's eleventh game of the season in the Flood Bowl played at Pikeville against Lynn Camp, Black had scored 238 points during the season. However, at the pace he was scoring, even after only six points against Manual, Bird, many thought, could still surpass that record.

Three touchdowns in a close 19-16 win over Middlesboro gave him 98 points. In a pre-game story, it was pointed out that one of Middlesboro's best players was all-conference end Harvey Yeary.

In a 66-0 pounding of Barbourville, Calvin tallied another 30 points, two on runs and three more from Tony Lanham passes.

Five more touchdowns came Bird's way in a 39-0 win over Somerset at Campbell Field. Lanham continued his hot passing with three scoring passes, and Winton Boone began to emerge as a Redhound star, both receiving and extra point kicking.

Roy Kidd tosses a pass during a Redhound practice, altough he says he never actually played quarterback in high school.

Roy Kidd

Roy Kidd's painting hanging in the Ossie Burch Fieldhouse.

Bob Barton

Tommy Adkins, 1949-50

Robert Barton, 1949-50

Jerry Brooks, 1949-50

Frank Jervis, 1949-50

Roy Kidd, 1949-50

Jerry "Zeke" Perkins, 1949-50

Wendal Rutherford, 1949-50

Darrel Storm, 1949-50

Bobby Terrell, senior, 1950-51

C.D. Vermillion, 1950-51

Bob Johnson (left), Carl Oakley, 1949-50

South Ward Wildcats. Front row: Jack Coffee, Kenneth Freeman, Michael Mink, Arthur Bingham, Kenny Wells, Don Underwood, Terry Woolum, Rodger Bird. Second row: Eddie Reeves, David Hamblin, Dewayne Hart, Gerald Rice, Pete Martin, Bill Woolum, E.R. Hopper. Back row: Coach Clifford Eagle, Claude Poynter, Bill Bird, Huey Parker, Bobbie Hart, Jim Underwood, Hampton Wright, Norman Hamblin, Jim Cobb, Coach Nick Diachenko.

East Ward Green Wave. Front row: Frank Greer, Jim Wilder, Lanny Myers, Jack Watkins, Willard McBurney, Gerald Hounchell, Charles Wells, Dan McCowan. Second row: Bobby Watkins, Bill Ramsey, Theo Martin, A.B. McCowan, Nelson Miller, Terry Smith, Tom Vanlandingham, Jerry Smith, Glenn Sasser, Malcolm Pace, Coach Ed White.

Central Red Devils. Front row: Richard Wilder, Harold Ellison, Dennis Akers, Pat Green, Kenneth Bryant, Phil Henderlight. Second row: Mike Bias, Jerry Green, O.L. Lynch, Duane Martin, Lowell Wyatt, Bill White, Bobby White. Back row: Coack Dick Vermillion, Bernard Bunch, Glenn Hill, Kirk Helton, Brooks Morgan, Fred Rader, Larry Jervis, Doyle Barnett.

Central Gold Nuggets. Front row: Charles Hammons, Richard Davis, Roy Houser, Phil Henderlight, Ralph Hodge, Mike Morton, David Farmer. Back row: Coach Jack Vermillion, Harold Whitson, John Culver, James Turrentine, Harold Queary, Harry Estridge, Melvin Chandler, Don Adkins, Coach Red Anders.

Corbin's 1951 sixth, seventh and eighth grade football team. Front row, left to right: Mickey Terrell, Don McCowan, Jerl Ellison, Bill Meadows, Winton Boone, Mickey Green, David Miller, Bobby Stewart, Buddy Poynter. Back row: Shively Barnett, Bobby Farmer, Wayne Hart, Bill Bunch, David Chandler, Lonnie Cornelius, Lee Carter, Calvin Bird, Don Anders, Ralph Wilder, Larry Gilbert, Ronnie Riley.

The 1952 Freshmen Football Redhound "Pups" of Corbin High School. Front row: Jim Harrison, Gerald Ellison, Don Turner, Larry Monday, A.C. Gibbs, Jim Pace. Second row: David Miller, John Hoskins, Jerry McKeehan, Bobby Stewart, Delford Jones, Eddie Hodge, Mickey Green, Vance Bacon. Third row: Coach Carl Bolton, Clay Rice, Max Mathis, Eddie White, Bob Howard, Stan Bunch, Lonnie Cornelius, David Chandler.

1952 Terrell-Reasor Boys League Champs. First row: Fred Davis, Jerry Wells, David Hamblin, Bill Meadors, Norman Hamblin, Gerald Rice, Rodney Barton, Bill Woolum. Second row: Manager Bobby Terrell, Paul Thacker, Shannon Sparks, Ray Ballou, Larry Sampson, John Hoskins, David Miller.

Back row, left to right: Johnny Hoskins (class 1956), Mike Morton, (class 1961), Bill Meadors, (class 1957), Larry Jervis (class 1958). Kneeling: Johnny Gibbs (class 1962).

One of Corbin's early basketball teams plays in Edwards Gymnasium.

Above and below: *Corbin fans and cheerleaders, 1952.*

Jerry Bird, Corbin High School Junior, 1950-51.

Corbin High School, 1949 Region 13 Champs. Kneeling, left to right: Joe Ed Scalf and James Owens, Managers. First row: Robert Cathers, Phil Henderlight, Robert Terrell, Frank Selvy, Robert Barton, Harold Brooks, Jerry Brooks, Sylvester Wright, Tommy Adkins. Second row: Coach Harry Taylor, Jimmy Walker, Jerome Lawson, David Karr, Foster Hamlin, James Saylor, Dual Mobley, Robert Huddleston, Dick Maner, Dan Farris, Jerry Perkins, Coach Ossie Burch.

Corbin High School, 1950 Region 13 Champs. Left to right, kneeling: Storm, Vermillion, Perkins, Adkins, Brooks, Bird, Selvy, Barton, Terrell, Kidd.

1950 Tournament

First Round — Campbellsville 69, Bush 49; Central City 60, Tompkinsville 51; Maysville 56, Owensboro 40; Clark County 58, Newport 47; Fairdale 53, Hindman 49; Lafayette 63, Male 41; Paducah Tilghman 61, Pikeville 59; Corbin 72, Dawson 50.

Quarter-Finals — Central City 45, Campbellsville 41; Clark County 52, Maysville 43; Lafayette 73, Fairdale 53; Corbin 69, Tilghman 53.

Semi-Finals — Clark County 59, Central City 55; Lafayette 75, Corbin 65.

Final — Lafayette 55, Clark County 51. For third place—Corbin 71, Central City 69.

(Championship Game)

Lafayette (55)	fg.	ft.	pf.	Clark Co. (51)	fg.	ft.	pf.
Mulcahy f	5	0	4	Wells f	6	2	0
Weiland f	3	1	2	Pelfrey f	8	1	3
Langston f	0	0	0	Snowden c	5	3	1
Adams c	3	0	3	Rogers g	1	1	4
Hutchens g	7	3	1	L. Puckett g	1	2	1
Hadden g	7	1	5				
Sharp g	0	0	0				
Totals	25	5	15	Totals	21	9	9

Half-time Score: Lafayette 30, Clark County 24.

Free throws missed: Lafayette—Weiland 4, Hutchens; Clark County—Wells 2, Snowden 3, Rogers, L. Puckett 2.

Officials—Vincent Zachem, Lus Oxley, Bob Forsythe, Travis Combs.

All-Tournament Team — Bob Mulcahy, Jim Weiland, and Bobby Adams, Lafayette; Linville Puckett, Clark County; Frank Selvey and Bob Barton, Corbin; Forest Able, Fairdale; Joe Mack Howard, Central City; George Cooke, Maysville; Lynn Cole, Tilghman.

Corbin High School, 1951 Region 13 Champs. Front row, left to right: Clark, Jervis, LeForce, Bolton, Wesley. Second row: Coach Harry Taylor, Eagle, Storm, Perkins, Dillman, Bird, Terrell, Vermillion, Howard, Assistant Coach Howard. Back row: Adkins, Gilliam, Whitus, Byrley, Crawford, Myers, Cunningham, Wyatt, Lewis.

Corbin High School, 1952 Region 13 Champs. Back row: Coach Harry Taylor, Eagle, Vermillion, Hart, Selvy, Taylor, Lewis, Assistant Coach C.R. Howard. Front row: Byrley, McHargue, Bird, Gilliam, Harklewood, Storm.

Jerry Bird goes up against U.K. All-American Bill Spivey in a charity game in Edwards Gym.

Jerry Bird accepts 13th Region MVP trophy in 1952 as Coach Harry Taylor looks on.

All-American High School five named by Chuck Taylor at North-South classic. Left to right: T. Heinsohn (Union City, NJ), R. Freeman (Hughes, Cincinnati, OH), Bruce Brothers (Quincy, IL), Chuck Taylor, Jerry Bird (Corbin, KY), Howie Crittenden (Cuba, KY). Players are holding certificates.

Jerry Bird talks to younger brother Calvin (right) and Edd Selvy before a Redhound game.

The 1952 Kentucky All-Stars lost to Indiana 86-82. Front row, left to right: Curt Moffett (Louisville Manual), Linville Puckett (Winchester), Jerry Bird (Corbin), John Mustain (Bowling Green), Phil Rollins (Wickliffe). Back row: Coach Ed Diddle, Jimmy Tolliver (Whitesburg), Billy Bibb (Owensboro), Phil Grawemeyer (Louisville Manual), John Price (Bowling Green), Dick Keffer (Hazard), Assistant Coach Ted Hornback.

Jerry Bird as a Redhound pass catcher.

Jerry Bird, University of Kentucky, 1953-56.

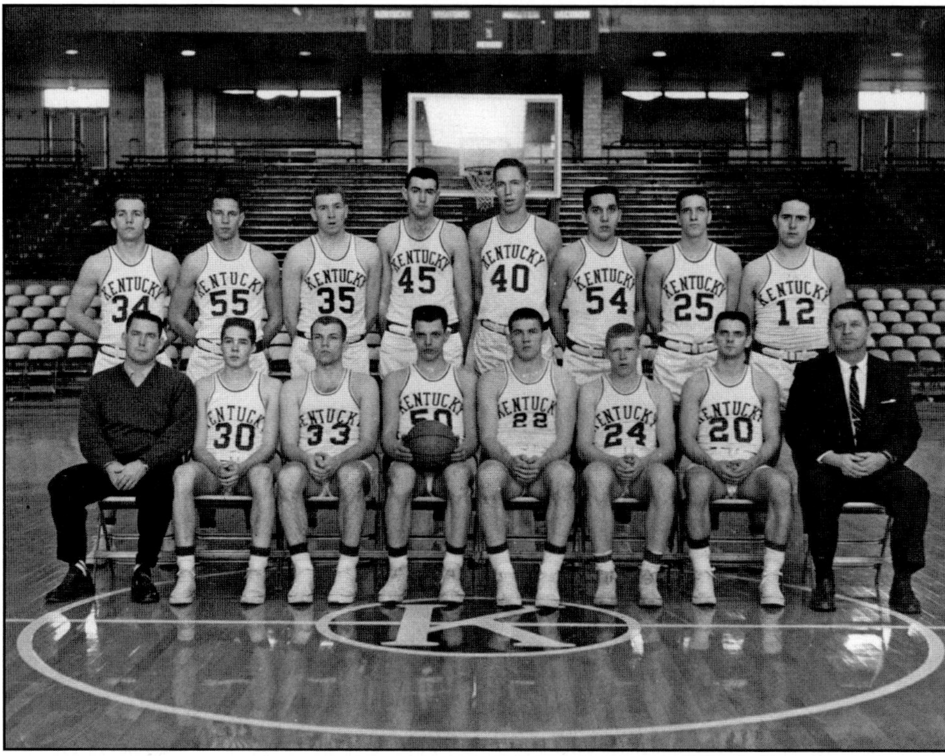

Calvin Bird (#22) on "picture day" as a member of the Kentucky freshman basketball team.

Adolph Rupp and team are all smiles before the 1954-55 season. Left to right: Gayle Rose, Jerry Bird, Bob Burrow, Phil Grawemeyer, Billy Evans and Linville Puckett.

FRANK SELVY and JERRY BIRD – HIGH SCHOOL AND PROFESSIONAL TEAMMATES

Looking Over the 1958-59 Knickerbockers

(Continued from Page 7)

RON SOBIE—24, 6-3, 195, DePaul. Sobie was headed for a sensational soph season last year. He was averaging 15.6 points in his first nine games, but ruptured a blood vessel in his foot, Dec. 16, and sat out seven straight. There was a reinjury and on Feb. 25, after a month of limited service, he went on the disabled list for the rest of the season. Despite his troubles, Ron, whose correct name is Sobieszczyk, wound up with an 11.5 average on 630 points in 55 games. His best evening was in St. Louis, Dec. 8, when he hit 11 field goals and 10 for 10 from the foul line for 32 points. Sobie scored 1,222 points in college, which is more than any other DePaul athlete scored in three years, including the great George Mikan.

KENNY SEARS—25, 6-9, 195, Santa Clara. Sears' 1,342 points last year made him the Knicks' top scorer and ninth in the league. He also was runner-up to Naulls in club rebounding with 785, 14 fewer than his fellow Californian's total, but he was tops in time played with 2,685 minutes. Boasting a remarkably high .439 percentage for an outside shot, his team highs included most points for a single game of 38 against Boston, in the Garden; field goals, 15 (tied by Naulls) also against the Celtics; free throws at home, 16 of 18, and rebounds at home, 24, also against Boston. His 38 points is runner-up to Braun's 47 as an all-time Knick high for one game. A standout in the East-West game, he also averaged double figures against every rival. He's unmarried.

FRANK SELVY -- 26, 6-3, 180, Furman. Came to the Knicks from the St. Louis Hawks in exchange for New York's second draft pick in 1959. Rejoined St. Louis after a two year Army hitch, spending part of last season with the Hawks before he was sent to Minneapolis and returned when the campaign ended. First pick in the 1954 draft by the Baltimore Bullets, who later disbanded. Selvy then became a member of the Milwaukee Hawks and enjoyed a great rookie year with an average of 19 points per game. He ranked fifth in the league. All-American at Furman University. Climax of his career was the 1953-54 season when he averaged 41.7 points a game, scored 100 points against Newberry College, was the leading vote getter in the AP All-American balloting, chosen UP "Player of the Year," and named the best visiting player to appear in the Garden by New York sportswriters.

JERRY BIRD – 23, 6-6, 210, Kentucky. First season with the Knicks, in service past two years. He played at Kentucky from 1953-56. Lives in Corbin, Ky. All-State two years at Corbin High, named to 1951 All-American high school team. Started every game as a junior at Kentucky in 1954-55. Wildcats second best scorer as senior with 421 points for a 16.2 average. Played on unbeaten 1954 Kentucky team, along with Cliff Hagan, now with the St. Louis Hawks, and Frank Ramsey of the Boston Celtics. Agile for his size, score well with hooks and jump shots. Originally drafted by Minneapolis Lakers, as their third choice, in 1956. Lakers assigned him to the Knicks.

MIKE FARMER—22, 6-8, 210, San Francisco. The Knicks top draft pick of 1958. Generally considered the best defensive player in collegiate ranks last winter, Mike was a much-sought NBA prospect. He was named to the All-American team, voted the most valuable player in the West Coast Athletic Conference and selected as the "Player of the Year" by the Northern California sportswriters. In the course of leading San Francisco to a 25-2 record last season, he set a West Coast Athletic Conference mark of 29 consecutive free throws and missed only 11 the entire year. He is well coordinated and scores with one-hand jumps from the outside. Over a three-year period with the Dons, he tossed in 868 points and had a field goal percentage of .371. He's married and the father of two girls.

Knicks All-Time Scoring Records

(TEAM, ONE GAME)

Points—142, vs. Minneapolis in MSG, Dec. 31, 1957.

Points, Half—72, at Philadelphia, Feb. 17, 1957 (2nd half); vs. Minneapolis in MSG, Dec. 31, 1957 (2nd half).

Points, Quarter—45, vs. Boston in MSG, March 19, 1955 (2nd quarter).

Field Goals—51, vs. Minneapolis in 69th Regt. Armory, Feb. 16, 1957.

Free Throws—51 (of 64) vs. Baltimore in MSG, March 26, 1949.

Rebounds—94, vs. St. Louis in 69th Regt. Armory, Jan. 14, 1956.

Assists—38, vs. Minneapolis in Boston, Feb. 9, 1955.

Personal Fouls—48, at Syracuse, March 26, 1950.

Jerry Bird and Frank Selvy's "double" as high school and NBA teammates is a rarity.

Jerry Bird, New York Knickerbocker, 1958-59.

New York Knicks. Pictured are Guy Sparrow, Ron Sobie, Carl Braun, Richie Guerin, Jerry Bird, Pete Brennan, Willie Naulls, Mike Farmer, Charlie Tyra, Ray Felex, Art Spoelstra, Kenny Sears. Fuzz Levane, Coach.

1959 New York Knickerbockers. Pictured left to right: Willie Naulls and wife, Head Coach Fuzzy Levane and wife, Don Howard (trainer) and wife, Jerry Bird, Assistant Coach Red Holtzman and wife, Carl Braun and wife, Charlie Tyra and wife.

Left to right: Billy Bird, Nancy Bird and Rodger Bird holding niece Eva Lou, sister Shirley's daughter.

Jerry Bird, wife Nancy and son Steve.

The Birds. Left to right, standing: Jerry, Calvin, Billy and Rodger. Sitting: Ruben, Bonnie and Nancy.

Ruben and Bonnie Bird

Ruben Bird has his hands full with one of his son's many trophies.

Calvin Bird in 1951.

Jerry, Calvin, Billy and Rodger Bird.

CORBIN FINISHES FOURTH IN SEK TRACK MEET, BIRD TAKES TWO FIRST

Corbin faired exceptionally well last week in the Southeastern Kentucky Conference track meet held on the campus of Union College at Barbourville despite the lack of a training season.

The Redhound thinlies finished fouth in the six team scores capturing two first in the individual performances and one team first. The thinlies were directed by Assistant football coach, Joe Lankford.

The championship went to Bell County's Bobcats for the second straight year. They compiled a team total of 35 1-3 points. Finishing behind them and the team point totals were Knox Central 26½; Middlesboro 21½; Corbin 18; Barbourville 16 2-3; and Williamsburg 15.

Calvin Bird was the main reason for the 'hounds fine showing. He grabbed off the 100-yard dash in a time of 10.5 and the 200-yard event in 23.1. He teamed with Ralph Wilder, Harold Queary and Bobby Wyatt in the 880 yard relay.

Finishing behind Bird in the 100 yard event were Bird, Williamsburg; and Present Saylor, Bell County. Second and third in the 220-dash were Shelton, Knox Central and Saylor, Bell County.

Middlesboro and Barbourville were second and third behind Corbin in the 880 relay.

Bird joined Tony Harris of Barbourville as the only individual to grab off two first places.

The other results in the various events were:

High hurdles—Harris, Barbourville; Mays Williamsburg; Hampton, Pineville, 16.5.

Mile-Routh, Middlesboro; Brock and Barnett, Bell County, 5:14.8.

The Corbin High Redhounds will wind up what is considered their mosts successful athletic year in the history of the school to date when it sends its first entries to the state track meet in Lexington. Front row, left to right: Billy Howard, Bobby Wyatt, Calvin Bird, Harold Queary. Standing: Tom Steely, manager, Joe Lankford, coach and Don Williams, manager.

1953 Redhounds. Bottom row, left to right: Gerald Wilson, Winton Boone, Bob Green, Fred Davis, Bob Wyatt, Bill Howard, Jimmy Harrison, David Miller, Tom Steely, Don McCowan, Bill Meadows. Middle row: John Hoskins, Eddie Hodge, Muriel Barnett, Ken Cobb, Ronnie Riley, Calvin Bird, Arlan Prewitt, Lonnie Cornelius, Ralph Wilder, Mike Clark, Bob McBurney. Back row: Don Mullins, Buster Scalf, Roy Joyner, Eddie White, Bob Howard, Morris Garrison, David Chandler, Don Hobbs, Carl Bible, Darrell Hart.

The 1955 Kentucky Football Champions. First row, left to right: Tony Lanham, Gerald Ellison, Ralph Wilder, Bill Howard, Ronnie Riley, Calvin Bird, Harold Queary, Bob Howard. Second row: A.B. McCowan, David Chandler, Curtis Bailey, Tom Steely, Bobby Green, Vernon Wilder, Bobby Wyatt, Johnny Hoskins. Third row: David Miller, Bill Meadors, Charles Poynter, Charles Alsip, Don Turner, Winton Boone, Bobby McBurney, Melvin Chandler. Fourth row: Manager Bruce Hodge, Carl Bible, Bill Scalf, Melvin Howard, Don Williams, George Jones, Morris Garrison, Stan Bunch, Gail Phillips, Manager Eddie Hodge. Coaches are pictured below.

Assistant Coach
Harry Taylor

Head Coach
Bill Tucker

Assistant Coach
Ted Meadors

Bird, Hughes, Justice Brothers Head All-State

By JOHNNY CARRICO

Kentucky's top scorer, a repeater and the first brother act in the history of the all-star arrays are the flavorful ingredients of the 33d Courier-Journal All-State high school football team.

Calvin Bird of Corbin, whose 157 points wrote the season high in the Bluegrass state, is the honorary captain of the "dream" club since he polled the majority of the votes of the coaches, sportswriters, sportscasters and officials who named the team.

The repeater is Lowell Hughes, Prestonsburg's precocious quarterback who led the balloting last year as a junior. The brothers, first ever named the same year since the all-State selections were initiated in 1923, are Everett and H. L. Justice of Pikeville.

Benham's Kirk Named

Also named among Kentucky's eleven best were end Jerry Kirk of Benham, tackles Wayne Perry of Franklin-Simpson and Don McAllister of St. Xavier, guards Don Adkisson of Harlan and Ray Hammond of Caldwell County, center Pascal Benson of Henderson and halfback Mike Hemmer of Manual.

Bird, who led Corbin to a perfect season (11 straight wins including a bowl victory) and a state championship, is the only underclassman on the team. He is a junior.

Highlights Are Listed

The all-state unit has good size, the line averaging a hefty 192 pounds and the backs 181.2. Overall they scale 188.1 pounds per station which makes the '55 crew rank with some of the heavier teams of past years. They probably are older as a group than any team chosen since the 20-year age limit was introduced. Three are 19-year-olds and there is one 20-year-old (Adkisson).

All-State Grid Team

Pos.	Name	School	Age	Wt.	Ht.	Yr.
E	Everett Justice	Pikeville	19	175	6-1	Sr.
E	Jerry Kirk	Benham	17	174	6-2	Sr.
T	Wayne Perry	Franklin-Simpson	19	195	6-3	Sr.
T	Don McAllister	St. Xavier	17	216	6-2	Sr.
G	Don Adkisson	Harlan	20	185	5-10	Sr.
G	Ray Hammond	Caldwell Co.	19	195	6-1	Sr.
C	Pascal Benson	Henderson	17	204	6-0	Sr.
B	Calvin Bird	Corbin	17	185	6-0	Jr.
B	Lowell Hughes	Prestonsburg	17	185	6-1½	Sr.
B	H. L. Justice	Pikeville	17	185	6-1	Jr.
B	Mike Hemmer	Manual	17	170	6-0	Sr.

Second Team	Third Team
E—Bob Hovious, Bowling Green.	E—Carl Kimmel, Eastern.
E—Dick Mueller, St. Xavier.	E—Don Lewis, Cov'gton Holmes.
T—Paul Schmitt, Flaget.	T—Leroy Berry, Sturgis.
T—Bruce Miracle, Bell County.	T—Bill Clements, Shelbyville.
G—Charles Newton, Bowling G.	G—Fayette Crutcher, Frankfort.
G—Don Wilbourn, Manual.	G—Don Dixius, Bellevue.
C—Dick Young, Atherton.	C—John Green, Madison.
B—Robert Meade, Whitesburg.	B—Lester Morris, Mayfield.
B—Billy Richards, Frank.-Simp.	B—Vernon Rehm, Shawnee.
B—"Sonny" Watkins, Hend'son.	B—Wayne Kelley, Caldwell Co.
B—Charles Burton, Harrodsb'g.	B—Glenn Ed Shaw, Paducah.

Bird also is an outstandin[g] [b]asketballer, scoring better than [?]00 points the past two seasons. [A] great runner, he has quick [c]hange of pace and good speed. . . . **Hughes** won four grid let[t]ers and three basketball monograms. In four years he completed 225 of 347 passes for 3,482 [y]ards and 36 touchdowns. A [y]ounger brother of John Delmar [H]ughes who was a selection in ['5]1 and '52. He scored 46 touchdowns in his prep career and [k]icked 46 extra points. A total [o]f 31 colleges, including Duke [a]nd Texas A. & M., pursued him [b]ut he signed with Kentucky this [w]eek.

Hemmer is Manual's first selection since "Bunky" Gruner [i]n 1949. A halfback, he has both [s]peed and power, was a regular [f]or three years with the Crimsons. . . . **H. L. Justice's** 121 [p]oints was the highest in the [B]ig Sandy area. A fine breakaway runner, 11 of his 19 touchdowns were 70 yards or longer. [P]layed both offense and defense, [a]lso lettered in basketball.

Kirk is the first player from [B]enham to make the squad in [?] years (last selection was ["S]pider" Thurman in '36). He [le]d balloting for the All-Cumberland Valley Conference team, [w]as a line-backer on defense. [T]he 174-pounder caught six T.D. [pa]sses, also has lettered in bas[ke]tball, baseball and track. An [ab]ove average student and presi[de]nt of the student council, he [pl]ays with the concert band in [th]e spring.

Perry is the first All-Stater in Franklin-Simpson history. "Fast for his size, strong blocker, aggressive tackler" is the way scouting reports read on him. Perry has been a football and basketball regular for three years and represented his region in the shot put at the state track meet the past two years. Plays both offense and defense and was all-W.K.C. Sought by U.K., Tennessee, Vanderbilt, Murray and Western.

McAllister is the quarry of Kentucky, Indiana and Vanderbilt, and Notre Dame has shown interest in him. A whale of a downfield blocker, moves exceptionally well for his 216 pounds. "The best tackle at St. X. in 20 years," is his coach's description of him. Injuries dogged him all through his career but failed to curb his fierce spirit. He is an A student.

Adkisson, who signed with U.K. last week, could be the Wildcats' prize yearling this fall. Plays both offense and defense, missed the last three games when he became overage. . . . This fall he blocked four punts, scored two touchdowns. He lettered five years in football, also sings in the glee club.

Hammond is only the third Princeton player to receive the accolade and the first since the name, Caldwell County, was substituted. His speed made him a good pulling guard and he was excellent at trapping. A shot putter, he also is a basketball regular. Played as an eighth-grader and won four letters in football. Vandy, Alabama and Kentucky have him on their list.

Everett Justice tallied nine touchdowns and three extra points for the Panthers during their perfect season. Caught ten TD passes as a junior and scored six on end-around plays this season. Plays both offense and defense, has earned three football and two basketball letters.

Benson is the seventh Henderson player to be chosen and the first since "Shorty" Jamerson in 1946. State basketball tournament followers will recall him from the '55 meet when he helped the Hens take third place in the state. Held down the Henderson center slot for three years, also has won three letters in baseball. A tremendous tackler, he shone on defense although he is a fine blocker and diagnoses plays well. Kentucky, Murray, Western and Louisville want him.

Coaches of the All-State players are Clayton Powers (the Justices), Charles Davis (Kirk), Jim Ownby (Perry), Johnny Meihaus (McAllister), Joe Gilly (Adkisson), Fred Clayton (Hammond), Don Shelton (Benson), Billy Tucker (Bird), Robert Wallace (Hughes), Bill Jasper (Hemmer).

Henderson's Shelton Voted Coach of Year

Bird of Corbin Player of Year

Corbin, Ky., Dec. 10 (AP)—The Paducah Sun-Democrat, in its Sunday edition, has announced its all-state high school football team and football coach of the year.

The team was named from a poll made from coaches throughout Kentucky.

Calvin Bird, junior halfback from Corbin, was voted player of the year. Bird was followed in voting by Mike Hemmer, Louisville Manual, and Don Adkisson, Harlan. Both Hemmer and Adkisson made the all-state team's defensive and offensive units as guards.

Named coach of the year was Don Shelton, who took his Henderson City squad to 10 straight wins and no losses for a West Kentucky Conference Championship last season.

Corbin was ranked as the number one football team with an 11-0 record. It was followed by Paducah Tilghman, Henderson, Louisville Male, Louisville St. Xavier, Newport Public, Dixie Heights, Louisville Manual

Six Redhounds On First Team Captained By Back Calvin Bird

The Corbin High School Redhounds dominate the 1955 All-South Eastern Kentucky Conference football team by placing six men on the first team, two on the second while three others were in the honorable mention list.

The Williamsburg Yellow Jackets placed two, Bell County two along with Lynn Camp, Pineville and Knox Central's one each on the 13-man squad, which saw ties for two positions.

Williamsburg led the second team choices with three placements while Corbin had two along with Knox Central and Middlesboro. Bell County and Lynn Camp placed one each on the secong squad.

The Redhounds dominated the all-Conference selections as they did all their opponents in the 1955 campaign climaxed by a comeback victory over Newport Public in the Recreation Bowl at Mt. Sterling Friday night for their 11th victory of the year.

Corbin's Calvin Bird is automatically captain of the all conference squad. He drew the SEKC "most valuable player" honor on the strength of his total votes which surpassed the other 12 making the first eleven. Bird scored 13 points Friday night to run his years total 163 points.

The Corbin halfback will be long remembered by his SEKC opponents for his long runs, from scrimmage, punt returns and pass catching.

His team mates joined him on the all-star eleven are ends Don Turner, David Chandler, tackle Bill Scalf, guard Tom Steely, and quarterback Ralph Wilder.

The choices from Williamsburg were Freshman guard Elmer Patrick and senior fullback Charles Stanfield who was tied for the position by Lynn Camp's Leroy Jackson.

Bell County's contributions were in tackle Bruce Miracle and end Claude Cheek. The latter was tied with Corbin's Turner for the flank position, which gave the All-SEKC 13 men.

Knox Central's pivotman Bruce Hensley and Pineville's backfield star W. A Denney complete the star eleven.

The all-Star's have eight seniors, three juniors a sophomore and freshman. Pineville's Denney is a Sophomore, Patrick the freshman, Corbin Steely, Bird and Bell's Cheek are junior's

The second team had only two under classmen. They are Williamsburg quarterback Donnie Rains and Bell County's sophomore signal caller Carlo Miracle. The All Conference Team.

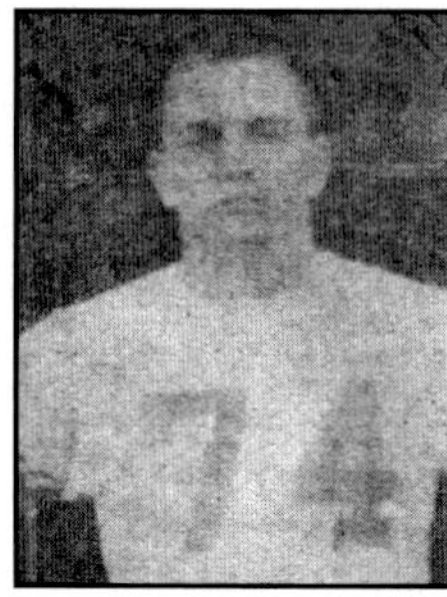

Bruce Miracle
Bell County Tackle

Leroy Jackson
Lynn Camp Back

Charles Stanfield
Williamsburg Fullback

Elmer Patrick
Williamsburg Guard

FIRST TEAM

NAME—	SCHOOL—	POSITION
David Chandler	Corbin	End
Don Turner	Corbin (Tie)	End
Claude Cheek	Bell County (Tie)	End
Bruce Miracle	Bell County	Tackle
Bill Scalf	Corbin	Tackle
Elmer Patrick	Williamsburg	Guard
Tom Steely	Corbin	Guard
Bruce Hensley	Knox Central	Center
Calvin Bird	Corbin	Back
Ralph Wilder	Corbin	Back
W. A. Denney	Pineville	Back
Charles Standfield	Williamsburg (Tie)	Back
Leroy Jackson	Lynn Camp (Tie)	Back

SECOND TEAM

Harrell Campbell	Knox Central	End
Jimmy Hinel	Middlesboro	End
Eddie Boyd	Williamsburg	Tackle
Morris Garrison	Corbin	Tackle
John Burch	Middlesboro	Guard
Gerald Ellison	Corbin	Guard
Robert Saylor	Williamsburg	Center
Buddy Martin	Knox Central	Back
Donnie Rains	Williamsburg	Back
Jack Taylor	Lynn Camp	Back
Carlo Miracle	Bell County	Back

HONORABLE MENTION

ENDS — Murph Slusher, Bell County; Raymond Sutton, Williamsburg.

TACKLES — Doug Roper, Pineville; J C. Carnes, Knox Central; John Mason, Pineville; Ronnie Sharpe, Middlesboro.

CENTER — Robert Howard, Corbin.

BACKS — Jack McCowan, Lynn Camp; Bernard Beach, Middlesboro; Roger Burch, Knox Central; H. E. Uhl, Middlesboro; Harry Siler, Williamsburg; Billy Howard, Corbin; David Miller, Corbin; Billy Joe Hampton, Pineville; Hugh Ed Howard, Middlesboro; Tony Harris, Barbourville.

Paducah Sun-Democrat
March 25, 1956 —13-

1956 All-State

	Player, School	Class	Ht.	Votes
1.	Corky Withrow, Central City	12	6-4	301
2.	Don Mills, Berea	12	6-7½	294
3.	Kelly Coleman, Wayland	12	6-2½	292
4.	Martin Holland, Heath	12	6-8	147
5.	Roger Newman, Greenville	12	6-4	141
6.	John Turner, Newport Public	12	6-3	132
7.	Byron Pinson, Henderson	12	6-2½	108
8.	Mickey Kelly, Flaget	12	6-1	106
9.	E. A. Couch, Carr Creek	12	6-1	97
10.	David Denton, College High	12	6-3	96

Second Team Player, School, Votes	Third Team Player, School, Votes
Bill Lickert, Lafayette (94)	Rex Story, Mayfield (73)
Calvin Bird, Corbin (90)	Ronnie Bridewell, Newport (61)
Harry Todd, Earlington (89)	Dickie Baugh, Somerset (59)
Ken Cornelius, Mt. Vernon (88)	Bobby Shepherd, Carr Creek (50)
Lowell Hughes, Prestonsburg (86)	Wally Johnson, Butler Co. (48)
Ken Meyer, Montgomery Co. (83)	Fred Hynson, Henry Clay (48)
Dave Eakins, Henderson (81)	Jerry Vest, Sedalia (47)
Herby Kays, Shelbyville (78)	Don Parsons, Lily (43)
Freddie Luigs, Tilghman (76)	Charles Osborne, Flat Gap (42)
Darrell Bicknell, Berea (76)	Ned Jennings, Nicholas Co. (42)

All-State Cage Squad

Second Team Player and School	Player	School	Age	Ht.	Year	Third Team Player and School
Kenneth Meyer, Montgomery County.	Kelly Coleman,	Wayland	17	6-3	Sr.	George Carroll, Ashland.
Dave Denton, College High.	Corky Withrow,	Central City	17	6-4	Sr.	Darrell Bicknell, Berea.
Charles Osborne, Flat Gap.	Don Mills,	Berea	18	6-7	Sr.	David Eakins, Henderson City.
Bob Shepherd, Carr Creek.	Roger Newman,	Greenville	17	6-4	Sr.	Don Parsons, Lily.
Ken Cornelius, Mt. Vernon.	Billy Ray Lickert,	Lafayette	17	6-3½	Jr.	Herbie Kays, Shelbyville.
Mickey Kelly, Flaget.	Lowell Hughes,	Prestonsburg	17	6-1½	Sr.	J. D. Kiser, Olive Hill.
Fred Hynson, Henry Clay.	Martin Holland,	Heath	17	6-8	Sr.	Pascal Benson, Henderson City.
E. A. Couch, Carr Creek.	John Turner,	Newport Public	16	6-4	Jr.	Calvin Bird, Corbin.
Ralph Davis, Vanceburg.	Byron Pinson,	Henderson City	18	6-2½	Sr.	Jim Self, Manual.
Rudy Moser, Dixon.	Harry Todd,	Earlington	17	6-7	Soph.	Freddie Maggard, Carr Creek.

Honorable Mention

FIRST REGION—Robert Hall, North Marshall; Gene Herndon, Almo; Gene Hobbs, Fancy Farm; Ed Jones, Benton; Charles Lamb, New Concord; Jim Tucker, Wingo.

SECOND—Jerry Bozarth, Lyon; Bobby Bradley and John Camp, Todd; Louis Croft, Crofton; Ronnie Johnson, Lacy; Roger Junker, South Christian; Dorris Thomas, Hopkinsville; J. B. Thompson, Livingston County; Tommy Wring, Crittenden County.

THIRD—Barry Gager, Holy Name; Mary Kirkendoll, Owensboro; Bill Martin, Owensboro Catholic; Bobby Martin, Holy Name; Rudy Moser, Dixon; Ronnie Newman, Henderson County.

FOURTH—Pusey Carter, Leitchfield; Robie Harper, Hughes-Kirk; Alan Herron, Clarkson.

FIFTH—Roger Davis, Lewisburg; Bobby Donoho, Alvaton; Willard Hanes, Warren County; Leon Higginbotham, Park City; Kelly Hudson, Richardsville; Luther Kelsey, Allen County; Jim Riley, Russellville; Charles White; Warren County; John Wilhite, Bowling Green.

SIXTH—Darrell Florence, Hodgenville; Billy Lawler, Munfordville; McQueary, Adair County; Mossbarger, Glendale; Rautter, Ft. Knox; Richardson, Lynnvale; Bobby Simpson, Greensburg Arnold Taylor, Cub Run; Denny Vaughn, Memorial; Will Profitt, Caverna.

SEVENTH—Benny Howell, Male; Jimmy Jeans, Valley; Terry Leitchfield, Manual; John Laurent, Eastern; Jimmy Mitchell, Valley; Jimmy Self, Manual; Jerry Watkins, Valley; Dave Weber, Holy Trinity.

EIGHTH—Eckler, Carrollton; Froman Frye, Bagdad; Horine, Oldham County; Smith, Taylorsville; Bobby Swindler, Shelbyville.

NINTH—Paul Carr, Newport Catholic; Louis Crigler, Boone County; Stacey, Dixie Heights; Charlie Utz, Boone County.

TENTH—Jackie Allison, Maysville; Al Bane, Tollesboro; Bill Jackson, Fleming County; McMillan, Scott County; Joe Patterson, Harrison County; Allen Smith, Maysville.

ELEVENTH—W. R. Brown, University; Shannon Johnson, Irvine; Dickie Russell and Bobby Stratton, Anderson.

TWELFTH—Doug Brickey, Stanford; Mark Day, Danville; David Mahan, Junction City; Bobby Morris, Monticello; J. D. Popplewell, Russell County; Jimmy Poynter, Danville; Noel White, Danville.

THIRTEENTH—Glen Campbell, Clay County; Ray Canady, Barbourville; Jack Johnson, Bell County; Dickie Parsons, Harlan; Don Turner, Corbin; Don Stapleton, Middlesboro; Slusher, Lone Jack; Jack Webb, Pineville; Monty Yobb, Corbin.

FOURTEENTH—Barnett, Cordia; Combs, Buckhorn; Davis, Hazard; Maggard, Carr Creek; Sexton, Whitesburg; Strong, Combs Memorial; Williams, Hindman.

FIFTEENTH—Adams, Van Lear; T. Adkins, Pikeville; Curry Wheelwright; B. Hall, Paintsville; Horn, Inez; Thompson, Martin; Vanney, Belfry.

SIXTEENTH—George Carroll, Ashland; Buck Crank, Orangeburg; Ralph Davis, Vanceburg; Rex English, Carter; Bert Greene, Olive Hill; Jim Hall, Clark County; J. D. Kiser, Olive Hill; Bob Kouns, South Portsmouth; Stull, Owingsville.

COACH—Orlando Wyman, South Hopkins; Delmas Gish, Central City; Ralph Dorsey, Caverna; Gene Kenny, Flaget; Evan Settle, Shelbyville; Rice Mountjoy, Boone County; Fred Reese, Bourbon Vocational; Elmer Gilb, Henry Clay; Chuck Mrazovich, Russell County; Pear Combs, Hindman; Jack Fultz, Olive Hill

Right: *Calvin Bird (right) takes a "handoff" from Corbin quarterback Tony Lanham as the two attended the UK-Vanderbilt game.*

Below: *Calvin Bird (cuffed jeans) was featured in the Louisville Courier-Journal in 1956 showing him as a Corbin High student.*

Photo of East team in the annual East-West high school all-star game in Lexington. Calvin Bird (#31) and Tom Steely (#62) represented Corbin. Note the signature at the top middle. It ready Harvey "Ralph" Yeary. Number 86 in the photo later became Lee Majors. Below is the back of photo with more signatures.

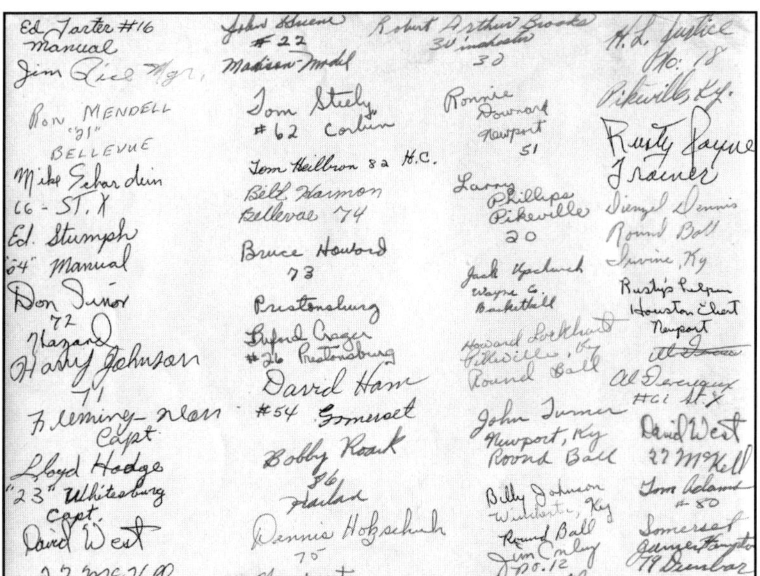

1957 East-West High School All-American East football team starters. Linemen, front row, left to right: Tom Adams (Somerset), Harry Johnson (Fleming-Neon), Al Devereaux (St. Xavier), Ronnie Downard (Newport), Tom Steely (Corbin), Don Sinor (Hazard), Harvey Yeary (Middlesboro). Back row: Head Coach Johnny Meihaus, Larry Phillips (Pikeville), Lloyd Hodge (Whitesburg), Jim Conley (Paintsville), Calvin Bird (Corbin), Assistant Coach Bill Kleier (Shawnee) and Assistant Coach Walt Green (Middlesboro/Corbin).

1957 East-West High School All-American West football team starters. Linemen, front row, left to right: John Kappas (Dixie Heights), Albin Appleby (Madisonville), Jerry Sheehan (Trinity), Floyd Weaver (Covington Holmes), Jim Yarbrough (Morganfield), Gerald Poynter (Owensboro), George Berry (Sturgis). Back row: Head Coach Bill Wellborn (Madisonville), John Kuchenbrod (Flaget), Tom Rodgers (Madisonville), Charlie Sturgeon (Owensboro), Ronnie Lewis (Sturgis), Assistant Coach Jim Ownby (Franklin-Simpson), Assistant Coach Bill Shannon (Dixie Heights).

CALVIN BIRD, TOM STEELY NAMED STARTERS BY JOHNNY MEIHAUS

Middlesboro Star Also Gets Starting Berth For East

LEXINGTON, Ky. (AP) — Coaches for Saturday night's East - West High School All-Star football and basketball games yesterday announced their probably starting lineups.

Basketball Coach Roy Doc Adams said his West starters probably will include four Louisvillians — Terry Litchfield of Manual, John Laurent of Eastern and Clyde Dudley and Bob Carpenter, both of Central — and Dave Eakins of Henderson.

East Coach John Bill Trivette plans to start Billy Ray Lickert, Lexington Lafayette; Howard Lockhart, Pikeville; Bobby Jones, Maysville; Bobby Slusher, Lone Jack; and John Turner, Newport Public.

East football Coach John Meihaus announced a lineup headed by halfback Calvin Bird of Corbin, calling him "the best high school back I've seen in a long time."

With Bird in the backfield will be halfback Larry Phillips, Pikeville; quarterback Jim Conley, Paintsville; and fullback Lloyd Hodge, Whitesburg.

Linemen wil be ends Tom Adams of Somerset and Harvey Yeary of Middlesboro; tackles Donny Day Sinor of Hazard and Harry Johnson of Fleming-Neon; guards Al Devereaux of Louisville St. Xavier and Tom Steely of Corbin; and center Ronnie Downard of Newport.

Coach Bill Welborn of the West will counter with a big line and a star-studded backfield of quarterback Tom Rodgers of Madisonville, fullback Charlie Sturgeon of Owensboro and halfbacks Ronnie Lewis of Sturgis and John Kuchenbrod of Louisville Flaget.

The linemen are ends John Kappas of Dixie Heights and Gerald Poynter of Owensboro; guards Jerry Sheehan of Louisville Trinity and Jim Yarbrough of Morganfield; and center Lloyd Weave rof Covington Holmes.

Welborn, hard-hit by injuries, reported no new mishaps but said he still was doubtful whether halfbacks Petie Bryant of Henderson and Harold Craig of Valley would be able to play.

The Corbin Daily Tribune, Kentucky and Monroe Sts., Corbin, Ky.
Page Two Friday, August 9, 1957

PRESSBOX PARAGRAPHS

By JIM LEE CRAWFORD

Tommy Steely has won a starting berth in the East-West All-Star game tomorrow night. The Corbin guard will be teamed up with Al Devereaux of Louisville St. Xavier. Tommy has always been one of those unsung hero type of players. Although I wasn't in Corbin too much when Tommy was playing, I'm sure he's never turned in a bad performance. He's not the kind of boy to do that. But, because Tommy wasn't a back or an exceptionally large lineman, he probably didn't get the recognition he should have. He's a natural leader and a fierce competitor, and these are two of the most important traits a ballplayer can have. I'm sure Tommy will be a valuable addition to some college team.

* * * *

Southeastern Kentucky is pretty well represented on both the East football and basketball teams. Of course, there is Calvin Bird who East head coach Johnny Meihaus called "the best high school back I've seen in a long time." Besides Bird and Steely, one of Middlesboro's stars, Harvey Yeary, will be starting at end. Donny Sinor of Hazard is a starting tackle, and Tom Adams of neighboring Somerset will open the game at end. As far as basketball is concerned, Lone Jack's Bobby Slusher will be a starter. Slusher will be running in fast company tomorrow night because other starters on the East team include Billy Ray Lickert of Lafayette, Bobby Jones of Maysville, and John Turner of Newport Public.

* * * *

WCTT will broadcast the football game. Final arrangements were confirmed yesterday. Kenneth Turner and Archie Wyatt will be on hand for the play by play at about 9 p.m. for the folks who can't go to Lexington.

* * * *

Belk-Simpson and Corbin Deposit tangled in the Pony League finals this afternoon. Belks smacked Weed Laundry 6-2 in the opening game of the playoff Wednesday afternoon. In the nightcap Corbin Deposit sw... Dr. Pepper 6-1. First National will play Seven-Up in ... tomorrow afternoon. The Bankers sc... the Lions Club in a semi-final mat... Seven-Up drew a bye into the final... 7-5 in the opening round Tuesday.

Pressbox Pickups

By BILLY THOMPSON

Third Member Of Bird Family Named To High School All-America Team—

Chalk up another remarkable feat for the Bird family of Corbin. Jerry Bird was named to the All-America high school basketball team a few years ago and his brother, Calvin, was named to the All-America high school football team picked by Wigwam.

Now the third boy of the Bird family—Billy Morris Bird—has been named on the All-America football team. Three members of one family selected to All-America ratings. We'll call that a record until someone comes along with four members from one family.

In fact, it may be that the Bird family will have four All-Americas before too long. Roger Paul Bird, who will be a junior at Corbin High next fall, is a whale of a football player—and may make the All-America rating.

Mr. and Mrs. Ruben Bird are to be congratulated for having three All-America high school sons. Many parents feel mighty proud if they have three who are athletes and you can imagine how Mr. and Mrs. Bird must feel with three All-Americas.

Calvin will be a senior halfback at the University of Kentucky this fall while brother Billy will be a freshman gridster at UK. Brother Jerry formerly played basketball at the University.

Coach Taylor, Winton Boone #10, Bobby Morris #5, Calvin Bird #12 (senior year), Charles Littrell, Charles Poynter #7, and David Wells #6. Courtesy of Shirley Hall.

A poster of a charity basketball game played in Elizabethtown in 1967. A group of former U.K. basketball and football stars played a team made up of former area stars. Calvin Bird, working in E'town, organized the game.

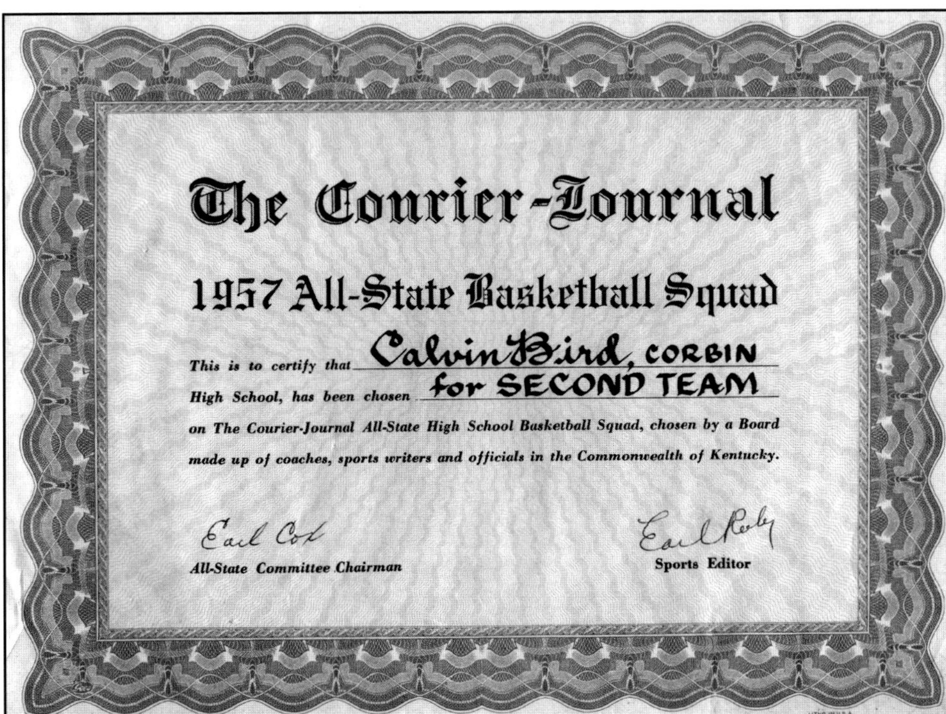

The Courier-Journal

1957 All-State Basketball Squad

This is to certify that Calvin Bird, CORBIN *High School, has been chosen* for SECOND TEAM *on The Courier-Journal All-State High School Basketball Squad, chosen by a Board made up of coaches, sports writers and officials in the Commonwealth of Kentucky.*

Earl Cox
All-State Committee Chairman

Earl Ruby
Sports Editor

Calvin Bird was selected as a Playboy Magazine All-American and invited to the Chicago Playboy Club. Here he tries out the drums.

Calvin Bird with teammates at the Playboy Club. That's Calvin with the white socks.

At U.K. Left to right: Dickie Mueller, Calvin Bird, Coach Blanton Collier and Bobby Cravens.

U.K. athletic trainer Rusty Payne helps Calvin Bird to the sidelines.

Calvin Bird is greeted upon his arrival in Hawaii for the 1960 Hula Bowl.

Calvin Bird during practice for the Hula Bowl in Hawaii following graduation from UK.

Calvin Bird hauls one in against the Vols.

Calvin Bird (#21) heads for the goal line against Tennessee.

Calvin Bird with San Diego Chargers.

Melvin (left) and David Chandler, July 31, 1949.

Cruisin' time in Corbin for Melvin and David Chandler.

The new underpass in Corbin, 1930s. The first car to pass through the underpass officially was Otto Yeary.

Artist David Farmer recreated the underpass as it would have appeared in 1959 following a 20-0 win over U.T. Every Vol fan driving back to Knoxville had to drive through the Highway 25 underpass.

Left to right: Majorette Patsy Stugill, Drum Major Bill Partin, Majorette Peggy Sturgill.

Band Sponsor Carolyn Sue Day

1955 Cheerleaders. Jo and Pat Satterfield, Janie Thomas, Penny Tucker and Shelby Thurston.

At U.K., one of the most impressive collegiate staff ever assembled was this 1959 group. Left to right: Ed Rutledge, Howard Schnellenberger, Ermal Allen, Blanton Collier, Don Shula, John North, Bob Cummings and Bill Arnsparger.

Scenes from football camp held by Coach Bill Tucker at Sparta, Tennessee, Summer 1955. At right are Ralph Wilder, Moe Green and Johnny Hoskins. Below are Ronnie Riley and David Miller.

Scenes from football camp held by Coach Bill Tucker at Sparta, Tennessee, Summer 1955. At left are Gail Phillips, Stanley Bunch and Don Turner. Below are Winton Boone, Gail Phillips and Carl Bible.

Princess McBurney

The Corbin Youth Center was organized and dedicated April 18, 1952. Princess McBurney (center) was the supervisor of the center from 1952 to 1968. The first location was at the old bowling alley on Depot Street. After a year the Youth Center moved to the corner of Fifth and Main Streets. In 1957 it was given a home over City Hall.

Calvin and Rodger Bird with Princess McBurney.

Left: *Dick Vermillion with Princess McBurney.*

Below: *Princess McBurney*

Billy Bird with wife Tommie, son Bill Jr. and daughter Angela.

Billy playing with Bill Jr. and Angela.

Billy Bird with little brother Rodger.

Billy Bird

Billy Bird in high school.

The Bird brothers were a fireball backfield. Billy #21, Rodger #22.

It's the Birds, son Rodger, father Ruben and son Bill, pictured in a moment of exuberence after son Bill rolled up 66 points for the Corbin Redhounds. The points broke his brother Calvin's single game total of 49 points set in 1955 in a 54-7 win over Barbourville. Bill scored ten touchdowns and six extra points. Rodger scored a touchdown and extra point in the game. Calvin scored eight touchdowns and an extra point in the 49-point total against Barbourville.

Head football coach Walt Green, Rodger Bird (sophmore) and Bill Bird (senior) preparing for Danville game, 1959.

Billy Bird in football action, 1961 at U.K.

Kentucky vs Kansas State, 1961. Billy Bird (#21) on 40 yard touchdown run from line of scrimmage.

U.K.: With help from sophomores it could be the best season in years

ARE you a hunch player? If you are, you might consider this: the only time other than this season that Kentucky opened the football season against a major non-conference opponent, the Wildcats had their best record under Coach Blanton Collier.

That was in 1954, Collier's first season. The Cats opened against Maryland. Although they lost 20-0—and were beaten the following week by Mississippi 28-9—they ended with a 7-3 record.

Except for 1958, when U. K. opened against minor-league Hawaii, the remainder of the season openers have been against Southeastern Conference opponents.

Last night at Lexington, the Wildcats opened against Miami of Florida—a major independent opponent. This is what Collier has been seeking for some time: a tough opener against a non-S.E.C. foe. He hopes thus to be sharpened for S.E.C. play—Mississippi is at Lexington this Saturday night—and, if he has lost, to minimize the demoralizing effect a season's opening defeat might have on his team.

The reasoning is that a team that opens against an S.E.C. foe and loses immediately is placed behind the eight-ball in its quest for the conference championship. A young team might take this harder than a veteran one, and it's a young U. K. squad that opened the grid campaign last night.

The squad, when this was written, was composed of 31 sophomores, 19 juniors and nine seniors. This number included 17 lettermen, only five of whom U. K. rates as starters of last season. These are junior end Dave Gash of Louisville Shawnee (oddly, All-S.E.C. junior end Tom Hutchinson of New Albany, Ind., didn't start a game in playing 207:30 minutes of a possible 600); tackles Bob Butler of Madisonville, a senior, and Junior Hawthorne of Pomeroy, Ohio, a junior; senior guard Jerry Dickerson of South Point, Ohio, and senior center Irvin Goode of Florence, who played at Boone County.

Because of the squad's youth, it requires experienced depth. The backfield is an example of U. K.'s needs at most positions.

The Cats appear to have a good starting unit in the backfield, but after the first four Collier is attempting to find reserve strength. During pre-season practice, the backfield lined up this way and, barring bad luck, should be operational for U. K. in early season, at least:

Junior Jerry Woolum of Richmond Madison-Model High at quarterback; senior Bill Ransdell of Elizabethtown at left half, junior Gary "Jock" Steward of Henshaw, who played at Morganfield High, at right half, and senior Gary Cochran of Etowah, Tenn., who played at Fort Thomas Highlands High, at fullback.

The hunch, though, is that Kentucky may have its best season since Collier first took over. That hunch is based mostly on help from sophomores, as last season when the record was 5-4-1, but 5-1-1 in the last seven games. *Larry Boeck*

Pictured above, members of the University of Kentucky Wildcats 1961 football team. Front row, left to right: Assistant Coach Ed Rutledge, Joe Marajo, Don Carson, Joe Brandel, Doug O'Brien, Jim Hill, Jon Jurgens, Gary Cochran, Dave Chapman, Irv Goode, Mel Chandler (#60), Bill Ransdell, Jerry Dickerson, Bob Butler, Wayne Dixon, Tommy Simpson, Junior Hawthorne, and Assistant Coach George Boone. Second row: Assistant Coach Ermal Allen, Assistant Coach Norm Deeb, Karl Crandall, Billy Bird (#21), Bob Farrell, Marshall Johnson, John Mutchler, Dennis Schrecker, Herschel Turner, Tommy Brush, Howard Dunnebacke, Jerry Woolum, Clarkie Mayfield, Gary Steward, Chris Georgehead, Bob Waddle, Bob Kasid, Ken Bocard, Perky Bryant,

FRONT ROW

Assistant Coach Ed Rutledge.
76—Tackle Joe Moraja, Springfield, Ky.
23—Halfback Don Carson, Oneida, Tenn.
77—Tackle Joe Brandel, Hamilton, Ohio
78—Tackle Doug O'Brien, South Attleboro, Mass.
61—Guard Jim Hill, Neon, Ky.
66—Guard Jon Jurgens, Newport, Ky.
41—Fullback Gary Cochran, Etowah, Tenn.
24—Halfback Dave Chapman, Richmond, Ind.
55—Center Irv Goode, Florence, Ky.
60—Guard Mel Chandler, Corbin, Ky.
28—Halfback Bill Ransdell, Elizabethtown, Ky.
62—Guard Jerry Dickerson, South Point, Ohio
75—Tackle Bob Butler, Madisonville, Ky.
72—Tackle Wayne Dixon, East Point, Ky.
88—End Tommy Simpson, Lebanon, Ky.
71—Tackle Junior Hawthorne, Pomeroy, Ohio.
Assistant Coach George Boone.

SECOND ROW

Assistant Coach Ermal Allen.
Assistant Coach Norm Deeb.
31—End Karl Crandall, Millersburg, Ohio.
21—Halfback Billy Bird, Corbin, Ky.
57—Center Bob Farrell, Cincinnati.
63—Guard Marshall Johnson, Lancaster, Ky.
50—Center John Mutchler, Paducah, Ky.
81—End Dennis Schrecker, Louisville.
70—Tackle Herschel Turner, Alexandria, Ky.
73—Tackle Tommy Brush, Jenkins, Ky.
42—Fullback Howard Dunnebacke, Oak Ridge.
17—Quarterback Jerry Woolum, Richmond, Ky.
26—Halfback Clark Mayfield, Alva, Ky.
20—Halfback Gary Steward, Henshaw, Ky.
52—Guard Chris Georgehead, Louisville.
38—Guard Bob Waddle, Somerset, Ky. (has left).
25—Halfback Bob Kosid, Glenview, Ill.
40—Fullback Ken Bocard, Ashland, Ky.
43—Fullback Perky Bryant, Evarts, Ky.
Assistant Coach Bill Arnsparger.

THIRD ROW

Student Coach Harry Johnson.
Student Coach Mike Coyle.
22—Halfback Darrell Cox, Miami, Fla.
56—Center Mark Thompson, Franklin, Ky.
67—Guard Ken Willits, Miami, Fla.
15—Quarterback Louis Owen, Nashville.
49—Guard Ray Heffington, Cadiz, Ky.
68—Guard Larry Schad, New Albany, Ind.
80—End Tom Hutchinson, New Albany, Ind.
16—Quarterback John Rampulla, N. Miami, Fla.
74—Tackle Bill Baker, Louisville (has left).
65—Guard Frank Sakal, Aliquippa, Pa.
83—End Jim Jarrett, Charleston, W. Va.
46—Fullback Vince Semary, Cleveland.
82—End Jerry Shepherd, Louisville.
12—Quarterback Shelby Lee, Miami, Fla.
18—Quarterback Benny Monroe, Athens, Tenn.
Assistant Coach John North.
Student Coach Leeman Bennett.
Head Coach Blanton Collier.

FOURTH ROW

Assistant Coach Joe Shannon.
51—Center Steve McGee, Ashland, Ky.
85—End Dan Haley, Pineville, Ky.
69—Guard Gary Myers, Knoxville (has left).
64—Guard Bobby Lee, Ashland, Ky.
34—Halfback Neil James, Cleveland.
27—Halfback Duane Schwartz, Louisville.
14—Quarterback Elmer Jackson, Danville, Ky.
33—Halfback John Helmers, Owensboro, Ky.
44—Fullback Bill McManigal, Lexington, Ky.
47—Tackle Clark Maples, Murfreesboro, Tenn.
48—Tackle Phil Martin, North Canton, Ohio.
32—Halfback Denny Cardwell, Louisville.
84—End Dan Reveiro, Miami, Fla.
Assistant Coach George Sengel.
Assistant Coach Chuck Knox.
Not present when photo was taken was end Dave Gash, Louisville.

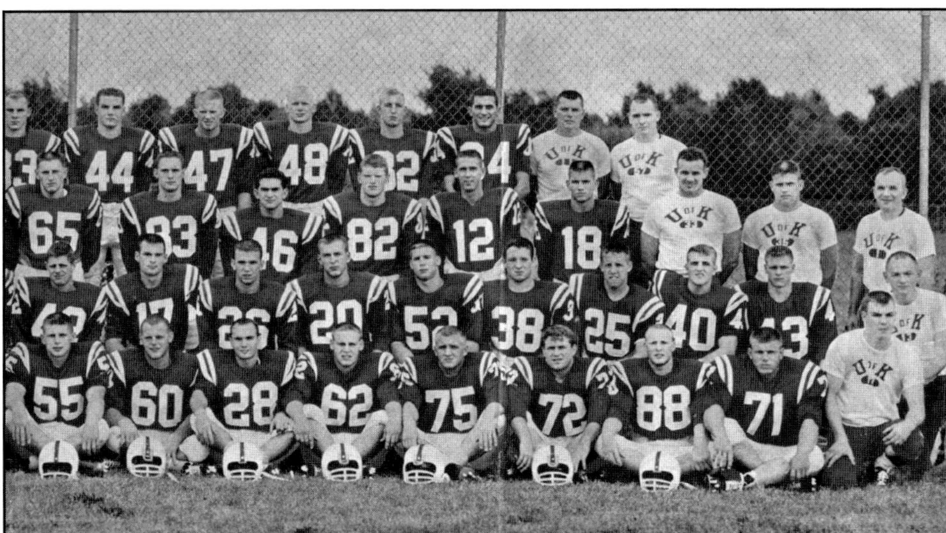

and Assistant Coach Bill Arnsparger. Third row: Student Coach Harry Johnson, Student Coach Mike Coyle, Darrell Cox, Mark Thompson, Ken Willits, Louis Owen, Ray Heffington, Larry Schad, Tom Hutchinson, John Rampulla, Bill Baker, Frank Sokal, Jim Jarrett, Vince Semary, Jerry Shepherd, Shelby Lee, Benny Monroe, Assistant Coach John North, Student Coach Leeman Bennett, Head Coach Blanton Collier. Fourth row: Assistant Coach Joe Shannon, Steve McGee, Dan Haley, Gary Myers, Bobby Lee, Neil James, Duane Schwartz, Elmer Jackson, John Helmers, Bill McManigal, Clark Maples, Phil Martin, Denny Cardwell, Dan Reveiro, Assistant Coach George Sengel, and Assistant Coach Chuck Knox. Not pictured: Dave Gash.

David Farmer was friends with classmates who played basketball at Corbin. He often heard the stories and under the name of "Swenney" came up with various cartoons.

With the Hounds at 6-1 and Bird running his point total to 158, his more-than 22 points a game was almost unheard of in football.

For Corbin, Danville never seemed to be an easy game, and on October 17, 1956, it would be no different. Late in the third quarter Danville trailed 28-6 with what appeared little hope. However, over the next fifteen minutes the Admirals scored three times before losing 28-26. Bird and Riley did most of the damage early, scoring three and one touchdown respectively. Winton Boone, however, left the game with a broken arm.

In a crazy-weather snafu, a violent rainstorm cancelled the Friday night Corbin-Williamsburg tilt, and it was re-scheduled for the following Tuesday night. It probably wouldn't have mattered what night the game was played, as Corbin won 26-6. Ronnie Riley had three interceptions for the game.

Next Knox Central came to town, and what a night it was! Scoring every time he carried the ball, Bird registered a state record 49 points in a 54-7 win. In spite of having four scores nullified, his eight touchdowns and one extra point gave the high flying Bird 240 points, setting a new individual point standard. And he still had two games remaining.

The Corbin-Pikeville game would be tough. Early in the season the Pike County school had been ranked as high as number three in the state, but Calvin's three TD's overcame Pikeville's Max Butcher's opening kickoff eighty-yard score.

For the second year in a row Corbin would be playing in the Recreation Bowl in Mt. Sterling. A 27-21 win last year over Newport Public gave the Redhounds the state title. There would also be another northern Kentucky team standing in Corbin's way, this time Dixie Heights.

Bird's 258 season points were only six less than the entire Dixie Heights team, who had lost only to Newport Public during the season. But their defense had given up only 66 points in ten games.

But a repeat win in the Recreation Bowl was not to be.

Dixie Heights' defense prevailed and their ground game held Corbin and Bird in check for a 26-7 win. His 48-yard run and Boone's extra point kick was it.

And so, the career of Calvin Bird had ended. Anyone who ever saw him play said was the best there ever was.

His 264 season points were believed to be a national record, and for his prep career at Corbin he had totaled 453 points.

Where to Now?

Many believed it was a given that Calvin would play football for the University of Kentucky. That's where older brother Jerry had gone to school. But not so fast my friend. Just because U.K. Coach Blanton Collier had spoken at last year's state championship banquet in Corbin didn't mean it was an automatic. It's difficult to imagine, but rumors during the season were out that the Wildcats weren't that interested in the Corbin Comet. Not so, said Collier. "I told him last year at the banquet how much I wanted him in Lexington." Jerry Bird wanted him at U.K., too. So did his mother and father, Ruben and Bonnie. And so did his coach, Bill Tucker, who had played at U.K.

No matter how good a football player you are or think you are, when you get personal visits, phone calls, and letters from the likes of Tennessee's Bowden Wyatt, LSU's Paul Dietzel, Texas A & M's Bear Bryant, it is cause for pause.

Calvin was in New Orleans as Dietzel's guest, sitting on the Tiger's bench watching them wallop Tulane. And there he was, if you can even think it, in Knoxville, sitting behind Coach Wyatt on the Volunteer's bench watching them play—you guessed it—the Kentucky Wildcats.

Several other schools thought they might have a distant chance, so it was common to see coaches in the Campbell Field stands from North Carolina, Vanderbilt, South Carolina, Indiana, Clemson, Louisville, and Xavier just to name a few.

Jerry Bird called Calvin, even wrote him a letter urging him not to make his signing decision too soon.

Jerry's handwritten letter from Fort Leonardwood, Missouri, while in the Army:

> *I suppose everyone in town is telling you where to go. There is a lot of things that a person has to consider, but the most important one is for a person to be well satisfied with the college that he picks. You don't only play football in college.*
>
> *Calvin, I would like to see you play for Kentucky, but if you don't want to go there, it would be better for you to go where you will be satisfied.*

Jerry continued:

> *Calvin, don't sign until after Christmas or even later. I will be home and I will help you out; I will go any place you want me to, and I think I can help you out. We won't let anybody shoot you the bull.*
>
> *As Ever, Jerry*

Jerry Bird's words were sincere. It was a tone of encouragement and brotherly love, just wanting to make sure Calvin wasn't taken advantage of. Others, too, wrote the Corbin senior. Some said go to U.K., some said U.T., one even warned about the abusive language used by Coach Bryant at Texas A & M. The writer said he knew first hand, having played for him at Kentucky for three years. He went on to say he played his last year under Blanton Collier, and wrote of how the coach had made football fun again.

"Tennessee recruited me just as hard for basketball as they did football," Bird said. "My dad really liked one of the assistant coaches, but he didn't like Bowden Wyatt at all, especially after the night he showed up at our house and had been drinking. Dad told me to forget U.T."

"Bear Bryant even called me the night before I was to report to Lexington and told me I could still come to Texas A & M," he continued. "But my dad had made up his mind where I was going. He said I wasn't leaving the state."

Calvin was thinking about it all, and by the time the team's post-season banquet rolled around he had made his decision. Or had he?

With most of the recruiting pressure coming from Tennessee, it was easy to see why fans and coaches at Kentucky were concerned.

As the packed crowd of Corbin boosters arrived at duPont Lodge at Cumberland Falls State Park, there was a never-before-excitement in the air. Blanton Collier once again was the featured speaker, and Nick Denes was back, too. After the usual pleasantries, introductions, some motivational words from Collier, and all of the civic club's awards, the U.K. coach employing his best effort told the crowd, and particularly Calvin Bird, that Corbin boys do well in Lexington.

"Edd Selvy could be a regular next fall if he wants the job bad enough," he said. "Selvy has the natural ability, and if he is willing to work, he'll be my regular halfback next year."

Four other former Corbin players, junior Jack Martin, and freshmen Morris Garrison, Don Turner and David Chandler, playing for Kentucky, were also complimented.

Collier's words were spoken with confidence, as well they should have been. Shortly before the banquet began, the coach sat down with Calvin to watch him sign Wildcat scholarship papers. Watching it all were Bill Tucker, U.K. assistant Dominic Fucci and, of course, Calvin's mother and father. Calvin Bird was a Kentucky Wildcat!

Everyone was writing about Bird, including two other boys from Corbin. Dean Eagle, a 1930 Corbin High School graduate, who later became sports editor for the *Louisville Times*, and Marvin Gaye, for years a writer of note with the *Times* and *Courier-Journal*. Both had worked for the *Corbin Times-Tribune* before moving to Louisville.

One writer ran into U.K. athletic Director Bernie Shively the year before at the Recreation Bowl. Shively said it was then when he saw Bird run in for the winning touchdown against Newport Public that "this one play convinced me that Calvin deserved a grant-in-aid to Kentucky." But what about all those points, all those years, all those yards, all those wins? Interesting...one play?

Courier-Journal sports writer Earl Cox had done a full blown article with pictures of Calvin, his family, classmates, and teammates. Soon after the banquet, Collier phoned Cox. "Calvin wanted me to call you to tell you he is going to Kentucky." Almost lost in it all was the post season All-SEKC team. Five Redhounds made first team: Calvin Bird, Tom Steely, Charles Poynter, George Jones, and Don Williams. Middlesboro's Harvey Yeary also made the first team.

Winton Boone was named to the second team, while Harold Queary, Bill Meadors, Bill Howard, Ronnie Riley and Bobby Wyatt were named honorable mention. Where was Tony Lanham? His absence was noticeable.

It was sort of ho-hum when Calvin was once again named captain of the all-state team. But it wasn't over. *Scholastic Magazine* and *Wigwam Wiseman of America* named him to their All-American teams.

What was over at Corbin was Calvin Bird, and in a surprise move Coach Tucker resigned to become the head coach at Mayfield in far western Kentucky. School officials were quick, however, to hire Middlesboro Coach Walt Green. No surprises here. He knew the conference and he knew Corbin football.

Time for Basketball, Again

As incredible as it sounds, there were those who thought Calvin's best sport was basketball.

Off to a roaring start individually, the team unfortunately was up and down early. Calvin's 28 against Lone Jack, 32 against Lynn Camp, 37 against London was a preview of what was to come.

And then came the night. The night he scored more points on the hardwood than he had on the gridiron. His previous scoring record went out the window when he scored 61 points in a 94-52 win over Williamsburg. His points came on 17 field goals and 26 of 35 free throws. But it still wasn't the 13th Region record. That belonged to Harlan's great Wallace "Wah Wah" Jones in the mid-40s when he tallied 64 against Artemus.

In the meantime, a rumor was circulating that Calvin might wind up at Ohio State. His signed grant-in-aid with Kentucky meant Kentucky was the only SEC school for whom he would be eligible to play. Any other school was still an option.

"Woody Hays (Ohio State coach) wanted me," recalled Calvin. "And I actually visited the school. I can't remember who it was, but someone in the Corbin area had been a graduate from there and he drove me up there. It was a long drive."

In those so-called basketball off nights, Calvin's teammates picked up some of the slack. Bobby Morris, Winton Boone, and even little brother Billy Bird, just a sophomore, stepped up. Early in the season Coach Taylor told local writer Jim Lee Crawford that "Billy will probably be the best athlete in the Bird family."

There weren't any more 60 pointers, but Calvin still rang up 30 pointers on a regular basis.

The Hounds lost to Middlesboro twice. The first time 69-47, with Calvin getting 23, and then 67-65. In that game Calvin had 30, and his opponent Harvey Yeary had 20.

In a game of big scorers, Middlesboro's Jack Johnson scored 51 to Calvin's 30, as the Yellow Jackets prevailed 89-81. A sidebar to the basketball game is that Johnson, an end in football, had signed with U.T., while Bird was headed to U.K.

The Redhounds barely finished the season 500 heading into district play. Still they managed to make it to the regionals by losing to Williamsburg in the district finals 71-69. The winner and runner up qualified for regional play.

Like so many times before, Clay County and Coach Spider Thurman turned back Corbin in the 13th Region finals 44-42. As inconsistent as they had been that season, Corbin came within three points of reaching the Sweet Sixteen.

Calvin closed out his high school basketball career with 18 points. Bird, Winton Boone, and Morris were named to the All-Regional team. For the third consecutive year Calvin was named SEKC Player-of-the Year.

Although the football/basketball star had averaged 33 points a game, he only received second team honors on the All-State team. For the Birds and Corbin basketball, Jerry had been the first ever to average more than 20 points, and now Calvin had become the first to average more than 30.

The next outing for Bird would be the prestigious East-West football game at Stoll Field on the U.K. campus, and in that game his East team fell to the West squad 13-0. Two future U.K. teammates, Tom Rodgers from Madisonville, who ran for a TD and passed for another, and Owensboro's Charlie Sturgeon paced the winners.

Harvey Yeary was a teammate of Calvin's on the East All-Star team, and on the official game program that Calvin kept for a souvenir, the now-Lee Majors signed, writing "to one helluva runner, Harvey Yeary."

"Lee and I were real good friends in the old days" said Calvin. "He would spend the night with me, and mom would fix breakfast. He originally went to Indiana to play football, but then transferred to Eastern. I ran into him a few times in later years, and I could tell Hollywood had really changed him. He wasn't the same person."

(Several attempts were made to contact Lee Majors. Calls to Los Angeles publicity agencies produced only more agents to call. Finally an e-mail address turned up. A message was sent to him telling him about this book and asking for a quote or two. A simple response came back stating that Lee was unavailable for an interview.)

It is interesting to note that Calvin Bird's #66 football jersey was the same number that King Kelly Coleman had worn playing basketball for the Wayland Wasps, another mountain school. Both, in their respective sports, are considered among the all-time greats.

On, On U. of K.

As Calvin Bird headed for the University of Kentucky, some were saying he had been the greatest high school football player in Kentucky history. However, being a great prep performer didn't always translate into something special at the next level. In his case, his size, speed, natural instincts and all of that God-given talent, plus his love of the game, gave him a tremendous advantage of picking up in Lexington where he had left off in Corbin. No one needed to worry.

Playing for the Kitten freshman team in an abbreviated schedule in 1957, his coaches thought he was phenomenal. Posting a per-carry rushing average of 11.2 and leading his team in scoring, pass receiving, kickoff returns and total offense, he disappointed no one. In a win over Vanderbilt he rushed eight times for 196 yards and two TDs, and on top of it all he had to give it a try, so he played that season on Harry Lancaster's freshmen Wildcat basketball team.

He had done more than was expected of him. Calvin, in the very first game of his varsity career, scored four touchdowns and booted an extra point in a 51-0 win over Hawaii in Louisville. The kicking thing was not new for him, as he had done that now and then back at Corbin. The reason he didn't do it on a regular basis is that he was often winded following one of his long touchdown gallops.

His 25-points had set an individual scoring record for modern-era football at Kentucky. The following week Calvin scored once in a 13-0 win over Georgia Tech.

Next came Ole Miss and a 27-6 loss for the Wildcats, followed by a 8-0 shutout at the hands of Auburn, and then a 32-7 loss to LSU behind All-American Billy Cannon. Georgia then defeated the Wildcats 28-0. Finally after four straight SEC losses, Mississippi State fell 33-12 in an upset. It was Calvin's three touchdowns, one by air and two by land and two extra point kicks that were the difference.

Vandy and Kentucky battled to a 0-0 tie before the Wildcats defeated Xavier 20-6.

Against Tennessee to close out the season, both teams battled 0-0 in the first half. Calvin, however, put the Vols on the scoreboard first when he was trapped on a punt return in his own end zone for a safety to put U.T. on top 2-0. In that same period, defensive back Jerry Eisaman, ripped the ball away from a Vol ball carrier to set up a Bird TD run, and a 6-2 Kentucky win. It marked the fourth win in the last five games for Kentucky. It was also a game where Bird scored all of the points for both teams.

Perhaps the most excited person in Stoll Field that afternoon was Kentucky Governor A.B. "Happy" Chandler. Sitting on the Wildcat bench throughout the game, immediately after hugging Collier he declared a statewide holiday for the following Wednesday, and issued an invitation for the Wildcats to play in the inaugural Blue Grass Bowl December 13 in Louisville. "We'll see if the boys want to go," Collier offered. "I want to go, but I don't want to unless the players want to play one more." With a 5-4-1 record, the team voted not to play.

For his efforts, though only starting four games, Calvin was voted SEC Sophomore of the Year, after leading the conference in receptions with 21 for 373 yards and four TDs. His 65 points, coming on ten touchdowns and five point-after kicks ranked him second in conference scoring behind only Billy Cannon. He ranked seventh in the nation in scoring. The boy from Corbin had passed the test.

"When I got back to Wildcat Manor after the game, there were some flowers in the lobby area for me," said Calvin. "There wasn't a note as to who sent them or anything. I thought it was someone making fun of me because I'd gotten trapped for a safety, so I just threw the damn flowers out in the front yard. A few days later I get a call that Coach Rupp wanted to see me. I went over to his office and he told me he had sent me some flowers to let me know how much he thought of me. He said, 'I can't give you money, or a car or anything, so I sent you flowers. But I heard some story about you throwing those flowers away, and I don't appreciate it.'"

Though Rupp sent flowers, there were a few other perks along the way. "I was taken care of with some basic needs, but not what could have happened at some other schools," Calvin said. "My dad could have had a couple new cars, but he said 'what would I do with two new cars?'"

Okeh Bird, Calvin's wife, recalled on occasion someone would slip a few bills in Calvin's hand. "We were married, the finances were low, and every now and then it helped," she said.

The 1959 season brought hope. Collier was beginning to feel the pressure of not being able to match the success Bryant had had before him. It was his 4-1 record against Tennessee that, so far, had kept the wolves at bay.

But the season was not to be. Losing 14-12 to Georgia Tech and 16-0 to Ole Miss was not the start Collier expected. A 32-7 win over Detroit meant very little to a team that made its reputation in the SEC.

Powerful Auburn was next and walloped the Wildcats 33-0. This was followed by another shutout at the hands of LSU, 9-0. The defending national champions of coach Paul Dietzel managed only eighty offensive yards, and All-American Billy Cannon netted only 11. In a real oddity, fellow SEC coaches voted Collier SEC Coach of the Week honors in the loss.

The season was five games old and already Kentucky had been blanked three times. Georgia then measured the Wildcats 14-7, before Kentucky turned in one of their best remembered games of the season against Miami (Fla.). The Wildcats were penalized 148 yards but still beat the Hurricanes, who had a quarterback named Fran Curci, 22-3. Bird was flying again, this time with a 55 yard punt return for a score in the first period, and then in the fourth he scored again on a 30 yard run. Over the next two outings it was an 11-6 loss to Vandy and a 49-0 win over Xavier.

Although Collier and his Wildcats appeared to have the Vols' number as they headed into the final game of the season, at 3-6 nothing was a sure thing. In a game that will be talked about for as long as the Wildcats and Vols play each other, Calvin Bird turned in a game for the ages.

Remember the date, November 21, 1959, at Stoll Field, Lexington, Kentucky.

Tennessee coming into the game was 5-2-1, but had taken a 37-7 thrashing from Ole Miss the previous week. An expected win over Kentucky and Vanderbilt would put them in line for a possible bowl bid, and take a little of the heat off of their coach, Bowden Wyatt, who had finished 4-6 the year before.

"I had injured my shoulder the week before against Xavier and Coach Shula (Don Shula, assistant coach) had a special brace made for me," Calvin said. "I only played about forty percent of the game, but it seemed like every time I touched the ball something good happened."

His first TD came on a three yard sweep on a pitch from quarterback Lowell Hughes in the first quarter, and after his extra point kick Bird led U.T. 7-0. He scored again in the quarter from one yard out, but that one yard turned into an actual 25 yard jaunt as only Bird could do it. As the Wildcat crowd moaned, he retreated back to the twelve until he saw an opening. Then he weaved in and out past Vol defenders into the end zone. A winded Bird failed on his extra point attempt. Kentucky led 13-0.

A second quarter Bird fumble was his only blemish in the game. "Even though I was doing good things, Coach Shula kept chewing me out every time I'd come to the sideline," Bird recalled.

But the boy from Corbin wasn't done. Always a scoring threat on kick returns, in the third quarter he did not disappoint. Gathering in a U.T. punt at his own 38, he darted for the sideline, cut back to his right and was gone. Sixty-two yards, behind some great blocking, he sprinted into the end zone untouched. Completely unexpectedly, he tossed the ball into the bleachers, something he had never done before.

"Coach Shula was waiting for me on the goal line and ordered me out of the game," Bird said. "Jimmy Johns came in and kicked the extra point." With 12:26 left in the third, the game was over as the Wildcats led 20-0. Calvin had scored 19 of those points.

Earlier, in the fourth quarter, Kentucky tackle George Boone and Vol tackle Ken Frost had been ejected for fighting, and when the final horn sounded there was a brief flurry of fisticuffs among a couple of the players. A newspaper report also said that "during the game, state troopers captured a U.K. fan—he appeared to be a student—who tried to steal Smokey, the Vol mascot hound dog." Apparently, keeping the traditional beer keg that annually goes to the winner wasn't enough.

As you imagine, when the game ended the delirious Kentucky fans converged onto the field to tear down the goal post while the Wildcat players gave Coach Collier a traditional victory ride on their shoulders. Once again Gov. Chandler declared the following Wednesday Kentucky Wildcat Day across Kentucky.

The next morning Coach Shula arrived at Wildcat Manor, where the varsity footballers lived, to check on the team, and especially to see how Calvin was doing. "He asked me to go to breakfast," remembered Bird. "He wanted me to know why he had been chewing me out so much even though I had been playing well. "He asked me how much I was thinking about my shoulder. I told him I wasn't. He said the chewing I was getting was taking my mind off the injury. I heard later he did that with that fullback Larry Czonka they had when he coached the Miami Dolphins. Coach Shula was special. He even had me to watch his cocker spaniel one time while he was away."

There were those who thought the win was a job saver for Collier, who in their opinion had not carried on the success of Bear Bryant. According to newspaper articles, though, U.K. President Frank Dickey was having none of that, and in spite of a 4-6 record, while winning only one SEC game, extended Collier's contact through the 1964 season.

To add a little more pain to Tennessee's misery on their long bus ride back to Knoxville, they had to pass right through the heart of Corbin on Highway 25, and wouldn't you know it, someone had painted on the overpass that every bus and car had to pass under, "Bird 20-Tenn 0."

The Final Curtain Call

Bird had had a fantastic season. He started every game, led the team in about every category, ranked third nationally in kickoff returns, eleventh in punt returns, and third in the conference in both receiving and scoring (55).

The September 1960 issue of *Playboy Magazine* released its first "Pigskin Preview" that featured their All-American team. And there was Corbin's very own Calvin Bird. He, along with the other 10 honorees, was flown to Chicago for a magazine photo shoot and, of course, to Heff's Playboy Club. The team consisted of some of the great names in all of football: Bill Brown, Illinois; Ken Rice, Auburn; E.J. Holub, Texas Tech; Tom Brown, Minnesota; Marlin and Mike McKeever, USC; Bob Lilly, TCU; Dick Thornton, Northwestern; Fred Mautino, Syracuse; and Ernie Davis, Syracuse, who he roomed with for the three days they were there. A few second team members listed in the magazine included Mike Ditka, Pittsburgh; Lance Alworth, Arkansas; Pat Dye, Georgia; and Earl Faison, Indiana.

Here's what Anson Mount, a national sportswriter had to say in his *Playboy* article about Calvin and the Wildcats: "The Kentucky Wildcats are annually a gridiron puzzle. Usually they take the bitterness out of a losing season by clobbering Tennessee in the final game. Despite the presence of Calvin Bird, the best halfback in that part of the country, Kentucky again looks just good enough to drop some close ones to the best teams in the SEC."

Calvin didn't have a whole lot of time to let the win over U.T. soak in because he had other things on his mind. Exactly one week from the day he had scored those 19 points in a win over Tennessee, he and sweetheart Okeh Lee Craft were married on November 28 at the Cumberland Methodist Church.

According to Calvin, Collier was not pleased about the marriage. Most coaches of that era didn't want any outside distraction, and often they set rules to that effect. Calvin already had other teammates who were married. Rupp was also one who thought along those same lines, but he too had exceptions.

But soon Calvin had something else to worry about. "I came down with yellow jaundice," he said, "And I probably shouldn't have played at all."

After a disastrous 0-3 start for the 1960 season, losing competitive games to Georgia Tech 23-13, Ole Miss 21-6, and Auburn 10-7, the Wildcats notched their first win by blasting Marshall 55-0. They followed that up with a 3-0 win over LSU on a Clarkie Mayfield field goal, and then lost in a squeaker to Fran Tarkenton and his Georgia team, 17-13 at Stoll Field. Next came three shut out wins, 20-0 over Florida State, 27-0 over Vandy and 49-0 over Xavier. A couple of sophomores, quarterback Jerry Woolum and end Tom Hutchinson, were putting up good numbers, and going into the final game against U.T. the defense had held five of their nine opponents scoreless.

"I was not on real good terms with Blanton most of the year," Calvin said years later. "And he didn't start me at Tennessee. But the situation got sort of desperate and he finally put me in." In the waning minutes of the game it took another Clarkie Mayfield field goal to salvage a 10-10 tie.

Calvin Bird's season and career were over at the University of Kentucky. The boy from Corbin had never lost to Tennessee. "I was really upset the way it ended," he said. "I didn't go back with the team. My wife drove us to Corbin.

Statically speaking it was not what Calvin wanted during his last year, but still he led the team in kickoff returns, all-purpose yards, and tied in scoring with Hutchinson and Bill Ransdell at 30 points each.

Though his collegiate career was over he still had some football to play. He was named to several post season all-star games. First he played in the All-American Bowl where he was voted outstanding back, and then he participated in the Hula Bowl in Hawaii.

"In the Hula Bowl I was on the same team with Fran Tarkenton, Mike Ditka, Tommy Mason, Earl Fiason, and Tom Matte," he said. "Tarkenton nor I started, but he threw the first touchdown to me and we went on to win 14-0 over the West."

He was also on the winning team in two other all-star games.

The Los Angeles Chargers (before they moved to San Diego) of the American Football League drafted Bird in the sixth round and the Cleveland Browns of the NFL selected him in the 17th round.

"By the time I had signed with the Chargers they were in San Diego," Bird recalled. "I was only there during the exhibition season before I was released. Then I signed a contract with Cleveland, but after I found out Collier was their coach I didn't care too much about playing for them. Cleveland later sold my contract to the New York Jets, but by that time I had been out of football for so long I decided not to play."

Working then with General Telephone in Lexington for the next few years, he became a weekend scout for Al Davis, the coach and owner of the Oakland Raiders in the AFL. "I was flying somewhere every weekend during the football season," he said. "One of those games took me to Birmingham to see Alabama and U.T. After the game I was in the airport and ran into Bear. We talked and I told him what I was doing and heading back to Lexington. He said he was traveling to see a recruit and would be flying over Lexington and they'd drop me off there. I couldn't believe it when we landed in Lexington in that big red Alabama plane."

The Bear and Calvin crossed paths again. "Okeh and I had moved to Alabama, and I wanted to take my boys to see Kentucky play Alabama in basketball. Tickets weren't a problem for basketball, but I still drove over to Tuscaloosa to get them," Calvin recalled. "I think it was 1970 or 71. Kevin was eight and Jamie nine, and I wanted them to meet Coach Rupp." When Bird walked into the gym to buy tickets, guess who he saw.

"Coach Bryant saw me and hollered 'Calvin Bird'. He took me to the ticket office and gave me four tickets. We went to the game, and after it was over I took my boys to the dressing room and Coach Rupp invited us in. He was so gracious, and then Coach Bryant walked in. We all talked for a few minutes. It was a special moment for sure, two of the greatest coaches of all time standing there together meeting my boys."

Rupp and Bryant very well might have had their differences when Bear was at Kentucky leading the way for his departure to Texas A & M, but if they did, it never became public. The closest that Rupp came to saying anything against football coaches was done tongue-in-cheek.

"People have been saying for years that I'm jealous of football coaches," Baron Adolph said. "I may as well confess that I am. Every time a football coach wins a game a mob of people hoist him on their shoulders and ride him off the field. I've won 608 games and not a man has put a hand on me. But I found out why. Those husky people who carry the football coaches are fourth stringers—on scholarships—and their job is to carry the coach off—if he wins."

In August 1997, Calvin's #21 was retired and a facsimile of it hangs in Commonwealth Stadium. And on September 10, 2005, the boy from Corbin, along with 87 other Wildcat athletes, was inducted into the Charter Class of the University of Kentucky Hall of Fame.

Chapter Five

More Than Just the Athletes

As respected as all of the athletes and coaches were throughout the ages of Redhound sports, for the most part they had to share the spotlight with Princess McBurney.

It was Princess who had the pulse of Corbin's youth like no other person. As the director of the local Youth Center, she was a caretaker, friend, confidant, and even an angel and savior to many.

Jessie Phillips was one of those kids. The younger sister of football player Gail Phillips, Jessie learned the lessons of life about goodness, respect and sportsmanship from Princess.

Jessie, along with her mother, Wilhelmina, and brother moved to Corbin in the summer of 1953. The year before, her dad, a coal mine foreman died in a car accident in Man, West Virginia.

"My mother didn't want to stay there anymore," said Jessie. "She was 39, Gail 17, and I was seven when we moved to a house at 112 ½ Popular Street. We rented from Mrs. Reed. We lived downstairs and she was upstairs."

Like so many in Corbin, mothers, like the fathers, worked, especially if they were single moms with a family. Jessie's mother, who went by the name of Billie in Corbin, soon found a job working for Flossie Eubanks at the Hungry Hound Restaurant for 50 cents an hour.

"For a while my mother also worked as a waitress at the Wilbur Hotel at the same time," says Jessie. "She made 20 cents an hour plus tips. And people didn't tip much back then. She would work breakfast and lunch, and walk home until it was time to walk back to the hotel for dinner. After the dinner shift she'd take a taxi home instead of that long walk. It was a lot to do for 20 cents an hour, but that's what people did back then. Our mother made sure we got a high school diploma and a graduation ring."

With working parents, the kids in Corbin, back in the 50s, were considered fortunate to have Princess at the Youth Center and Ted and Ruth Meadors at the YMCA to help turn lives around and fill up idle hours.

It was not unusual for Princess McBurney to step up on behalf of Corbin kids who were on the verge of running afoul of the law, even going to the local police and city leaders, speaking up for kids headed the wrong way in life. For sure she made an impact in Corbin, and the respect she earned has placed her alongside all of the great teams, players and coaches in Corbin history.

A Vocal Redhound

Don Estep wasn't a basketball or football star at Corbin. As a matter of fact he didn't play at all. Still he is a Redhound, and possibly the most vocal in Corbin history.

He wasn't there on May 8, 1947, either, when radio station WCTT signed on the air, but he wasn't far behind. He couldn't remember a time he didn't follow sports, and with very little television, radio and newspapers were pretty much the only way. Unless you were there.

"When I was in the sixth grade I lived only a couple of blocks from Edwards Gym, and my parents would let me go to the basketball games on my own," Don said. "I never asked for any money to buy a ticket, and they never questioned me as to how I got into the games. They must have thought admission was free."

No, the games weren't free, but where there's a will there's a way, and Don and a couple of buddies figured it out. "We would wait at the back of the gym until somebody opened the restroom door," he explained. "And then we would scamper in. The restroom was where the men went to smoke, and they delighted in letting us in the game."

Estep's memories perhaps parallel many young boys growing up in the 40s and 50s, but in Corbin it all seemed so different.

"Our neighborhood gang of boys lived and died with every game," he continued. We had our heroes, and mine was Bob "Country" Cathers. We made a basketball court on a piece of land next to my house." The land had been used as a garden. It was triangular in shape and the furrows left over from rows of corn made it very difficult to dribble a basketball. Adding another challenge, the new court was next to a creek.

"One of my friend's dad worked at a lumber yard and he got us enough lumber to make a backboard," Estep said. "And our goal was a big lard can." The boys used liquid shoe polish to inscribe the numbers of their heroes on their T-shirts, and to make their fantasy games even more realistic, took their names. "We played on that court every day," remembers Estep.

There were enough sports heroes to go around. Corbin football was improving, and Coach Harry Taylor's basketball teams were in the middle of what turned out to be six consecutive trips to the state basketball tournament.

Estep wanted to see more than just home games as he grew older, so by the time he was a freshman he would hang out in front of Edwards Gym in search of a ride to the game. "At that time the players were taken to the games by volunteers in cars," Don says. "Baker Reasor always drove Coach Taylor, and when he had some extra room he'd motion for me to get in."

Later Estep became the basketball team manager along with Phil Taylor, the coach's son. Not only did it guarantee him a ride to the games, but also a good seat. Don makes no apologies when he says Calvin Bird, a classmate, was a major influence in his life. "It wasn't just me, but the whole town," he says. "He was a really great guy, too."

Bird, like Bob Terrell, Frank Selvy, Jerry Bird, Roy Kidd, Bob Barton, and those before him made it easy to be a fan. "He averaged about 32 points in basketball, and ran for all those touchdowns. He inspired everyone in Corbin," Don said. "He is the best football player I ever saw in high school."

Getting to away football games while in high school presented Estep and his friends with a small challenge, but nothing they couldn't overcome with their thumbs. "We'd hitchhike," recalled Estep. "Jerry Green and I hitch-hiked to the Corbin-Manual game in Louisville in 1955. That's the one Calvin scored the only touchdown of the game. I had a sister in Louisville where we spent the night, and we hitchhiked back the next day."

When it came time for Don to go to college his choice was easy. "Calvin inspired me so much that I went to U.K. with the intention of watching him play," he said. Going to a college because Calvin Bird went there turned out to be a defining moment in Don Estep's life, because it was at U.K. where he became interested in radio broadcasting, and sometime worked with veteran broadcaster Claude Sullivan.

I did the play-by-play on the University's station, WBKY, for Kentucky's home games in football and basketball," he said. "I was the first person to ever replace Cawood Ledford on WHAS. It was in December 1960, and Kentucky was playing Alabama. I was preparing my broadcast for the University's station when Sports Information Director Ken Kuhn approached me and asked if I would fill in for Cawood because he was stranded in a snow storm in Frankfort."

WHAS was the all-powerful 100,000 watt radio station in Louisville that broadcast Kentucky sports, and at the time Ledford had not yet become a legend. What an opportunity for the 22-year-old Estep! He knew his verbal description of the Wildcats would be projected that night to almost three-fourths of the United States.

"I looked at my color man and told him the school's broadcast was his, and that I'm doing the game for WHAS," he laughed. "It was the thrill of a lifetime, and I still have the audio tape of that game." The boy from Corbin was on his way.

Don returned to Corbin after U.K., and soon became the voice of the Redhounds for the next thirty years on WCTT. In 1990, Don moved over to do games on the local cable TV outlet and hooked up with Corbin sports historian Bill Crook as his color man. "People were so crazy about Corbin football," he laughed. "Heck, I had twenty-two sponsors, and there were more commercials than game."

Some twenty-five years ago, after being in the newspaper business in nearby London, Estep and businessman Terry Forcht started a weekly paper in Corbin, the *News-Journal.*

As a newspaper publisher/editor he has not lost his passion for Redhound sports, and one of the paper's most popular columns is the one written by old friend Bill Crook. Crook takes readers back to the days of yesteryear, before the days of cable television, Google, Facebook, and all of the other distractions that have taken away from a simpler life, back to when the Redhounds were "the best there ever was."

Estep recalled a few years ago looking through his 1957 Corbin yearbook and finding names and faces of 17 athletes who received scholarships to college. "Eight went to U.K., two to Western, and one each to Georgia Tech, Eastern, U.T., Furman, Iowa Wesleyan, Morehead, and Georgia Southern," he said. "And especially impressive was that forty-three athletes in the decade of the 50s went to college on their football and basketball abilities."

Not Every Fan Came From Corbin

Don Dampier didn't come from Corbin, but his wife Pat knew all about the Birds, at least Jerry and Calvin, because she grew up in nearby Barbourville.

"I first saw Calvin play when he was a Redhound in 1955," offered Dampier, a Carlisle High School graduate the year before, but then a freshman at U.K. "I went over to Mount Sterling to see the Recreation Bowl. It was called the "Granddaddy" of high school bowls since its inaugural game in 1948."

Dampier saw Corbin defeat Newport 27-21, and went back the next year when Dixie Heights bumped off the Hounds 26-7. "I wanted to see Calvin play," continued Dampier. "Being a student at U.K., and with everyone expecting him to be a Wildcat, I wanted to see him play. I remember Ron Zigler was the MVP for Dixie Heights. If that name sounds familiar, it's because he went on to be Richard Nixon's press secretary."

For sure over the years, Dampier and wife Pat were not just average Kentucky fans. Together they attended fifty-four consecutive Kentucky-Tennessee football games in Lexington and Knoxville before pulling the plug in 2008. "We were an annual glutton for punishment," he said.

Nevertheless, Dampier had a favorite Wildcat-Vol game. "The 1958 game in Knoxville," Dampier proclaimed. "That's when Calvin scored every point for both teams when Kentucky won 6-2." It was also there that Dampier, along with a few of his frat brothers and several other delirious Kentucky fans, stormed the Neyland Stadium field to get at the goal post. "I got my share of the goal post," he said years later. "It was a joint that connected the crossbar to the upright, which I still have. Stan Key, Director of the U.K. Alumni Association for years, has been trying to get me to donate it to them."

The Stories They Still Tell

It didn't take long for Gail Phillips to fit in at Corbin High School when he moved there in 1953. A good athlete who played basketball, football and baseball and with an outgoing personality, he soon picked up the nickname "Dago," which he was called throughout his high school career, and still so today by his old classmates. He had spent some time at his uncle's home in Alabama, and at a nearby lake learning to water ski. With black hair and a dark suntan, Gail's first football practice that year led new teammates to believe he was of Italian descent. As a joke he spoke his own made-up language, which some of the guys were sure was Italian, and soon they were calling him "Dago."

There was a time several Redhound football players got together and took a high school home economics cooking class. Of course, some of the class assignments had to be done at home. Phillips was one of those, and he took his class assignment seriously, especially when it came to baking cakes. "My mother could not keep sugar in the house," recalled his sister Jessie. "I loved it, and so did my mother and aunt. They helped him sometime, but mostly they just let him do it."

While the cake baking was supervised, there were times when other extracurricular activities were not. A few of Gail's friends had mixed a large container of grape Kool Aid in the basement. From there they proceeded to the back yard. With all of them wearing white T-shirts, a Kool Aid battle took place to see who could get the most purple on their shirts.

The Phillips' basement was often a gathering place for Gail and his friends. On another occasion, classmate David Miller was at the Phillips' home. The two were "experimenting" with a new chemistry set Gail had received as a birthday gift from an uncle, and like she did lots of times, younger sister Jessie sat on the basement steps taking it all in. Suddenly she heard a loud noise followed by a basement full of smoke. "There was so much smoke I couldn't see them, but I could hear them," Jessie laughed years later.

As smoke filtered through the upstairs, Jessie ran screaming that "Gail and David have set the house on fire." Though the house wasn't on fire, there was enough smoke that it took quite a while to rid the evidence of two Corbin schoolmates' effort to make gun powder.

Like most high school athletes of the 50s, pegged blue jeans and a T-shirt were uniforms of the day. No duck-tail hair styles here. Flat-tops or crew-cuts was the look of the day. For the most part the fun was typically what most young boys enjoyed, even shaving their heads one summer into a Mohawk-style haircut.

All of the fun at Bill White's Pool Room, and those Fox and Hound games on Sunday afternoon after a football film session, were all a part of the Corbin memories. "We'd hitchhike to Cumberland Falls and see who could catch up and get back to Corbin first," David Miller explained.

Under the cover of darkness in September 1954, a couple of Corbin football players slipped in next to the band building with a bucket of black paint. Their intentions, they would say some sixty years later, was to "get even."

The football team in 1953 went 0-10, and according to the footballers, as soon as the band's halftime performance was over, they left the game. Besides that, valuable practice time for football had to be given up in order for the marching band to have their turn on the field.

"We didn't particularly like it back then," one of the painters recalled. "The band had always been with us before, but since we were losing, it seemed they didn't want any part of us." So with that mindset the two proceeded to quickly paint the words

BAND RATS on the building. Through all the years, even though several Corbin students knew who did it, no one ratted them out.

And now after all of this time, David Miller and Winton Boone have admitted to the caper. "It was never our intention to hurt anyone," Miller said. "We were kids and it was our way of getting even, at least we thought. Looking back on it, I wish I had never done it, but it has made for a good story all these years."

The stories are legendary.

One that has been handed down was the night, sometime in the mid-30s, when Corbin was trailing Male 7-0 in Louisville. With a chance to tie the game, quarterback Wes Taylor dropped back to pass. Blondie Hendrickson had drifted out of the backfield into the end zone and seemed to be open. Taylor lofted the pass, and just when it looked like the Redhound receiver would haul it in for a TD, a photographer's flashbulb blinded him, and the ball fell to the ground. Male won 7-0.

Then there's the one about James "Peg" Offutt, a Corbin tackle in the 30s.

Supposedly, just before a big game, as opposing players approached him on the sideline, Offutt took a knife, and hoping to psyche them out, stuck it through his football togs into his wooden leg.

In 1962, when school was over, the senior class took their annual trip to Washington, D.C., except for six who headed for Florida. Russ Willis loaded his 1953 red, 4-door Pontiac he had recently purchased for $50 and pointed south. With him were Gary Holtzclaw, Joe Gambrell, Jerry "Smiley" Martin, Barry Brooks, and Rodger Bird.

"There were bets in Corbin on how far we'd get," laughed Brooks. "Well, it was about midnight when we ran over a rock and it knocked a hole in the gas tank. We weren't sure what to do as the gas was dripping out. We found a service station, and a guy put the car on a rack and rubbed a bar of soap on the tank, and sealed the hole." "It lasted over a year," Willis added. "When we got down there, Rodger and I went on to Miami for the day, because they had been recruiting him and he wanted to look around."

The boys from Corbin knew they couldn't bring the sunshine back with them, but oranges and Spanish Moss, well, that was a different matter. "We climbed a fence at one of those orange groves," said Willis. "I thought we were all going to get shot when the owner fired a couple of rounds."

And what about that Spanish Moss? "We pulled it out of the trees and hung it everywhere on the car," laughed Brooks. "We had it hanging out the windows, from under the hood, out of the trunk…Spanish Moss was everywhere. Suddenly, the car started to overheat plus we had bugs everywhere. The Spanish Moss had to go."

Rodger Bird enjoys telling a couple of stories that involve Dick Vermillion, who was Sheriff in Whitley County and also owned an Army Surplus store in Corbin.

"Dick would hire several people and dress them up in Army-type uniforms to advertise his store. They'd march up and down on the sidewalk with dummy rifles," laughed Rodger. "Well, somebody gave them a folded up piece of paper and told 'em to take it over to the bank and give it to a teller. They didn't read it, but you can guess what it said…'This is a stick-up.' They told them to get out of there."

Then there was the time someone just outside of Corbin was firing shots at people. After several attempts to arrest him, Sheriff Vermillion said he would do it.

"He put on a Santa Claus outfit," said Rodger. "He went up there and arrested him with no problem. Dick reasoned that the man wouldn't shoot Santa Claus."

There were times in the 50s that the Redhound coaches would wear helmets, when Corbin played at Harlan, because of the rocks being thrown at them from the stands.

Back then team benches were placed directly in front of the crowd, and unlike today, any of the players not in the game actually sat on the bench. At Harlan it was so close to the fans that one of them would take a walking cane and rake the back of Redhound substitutes as he walked behind them.

Chapter Six

Another Bird Takes to the Sky

It seemed like there was always a Bird playing football and basketball at Corbin, and from the late 40s to the early 60s there was. Just imagine how Redhound opponents must have felt.

When Billy Bird emerged on the big stage of Corbin football, behind Calvin, he sure did lessen the loss of his older brother, who many said was the best there ever was. Lots had been expected of Billy, but talk was cheap. He had to deliver...and he did. As Nancy said, he was special. Billy's sister, Nancy, says Billy was so kind and gentle. "He never wanted anyone bragging on him," she said. "He was a special kid growing up."

In his early days as a sophomore, Coach Walt Green wasn't always pleased with the way Billy practiced, but come game time it was a different story. "It's hard to keep a boy like him out of the lineup," Green said.

As a freshman he had scored two TD's, both coming in a 19-0 win over Pineville. During that sophomore year, Billy tallied 49 points on seven touchdowns and seven extra points. The 1957 Redhounds wrapped up the season with a 63-7 win over Pikeville to finish the season unbeaten.

Then a disastrous trip to the Exposition Bowl in Louisville led to a 47-0 loss to St. X. *Courier-Journal* sportswriter Earl Cox wrote that it would probably be a long time before Corbin returns.

By Billy Bird's junior year in 1958, great things were anticipated. Corbin football was known throughout Kentucky, and there wasn't a college coach in the southeastern part of the United States who needed a map to get there. They knew Hwy. 25E as well as they knew where they lived.

Some of those coaches would come to Corbin to watch practice, and some would overnight at the Wilbur Hotel or the Yeary Motel. Heck, a few might even have become friends with ole Si, the legendary bellman at the Wilbur, in hopes he'd put in a good word.

Coaches being coaches would stop off at the Dixie or the Lunch Queen, not necessarily to eat, but just to see if some of the local gossip might spill out with a hint of where some of these Redhound stars might be going to college, all in the hopes they had a shot. Some could have lucked into some inside info while gassing up at Colmar McCall's Gulf station on Masters Street. Colmar's son, Mac, played on the football team, and quite often he and his Redhound teammates hung out there.

If they or anyone else was in town, they heard the "shout" of the noon time whistle from Weed's Laundry. You could set your clock by it.

It wasn't just football coaches who came to town. There were plenty of basketball coaches as well.

Harry Taylor's Redhounds were perhaps a year away from being really good. Still they had high hopes. With Harold Queary, Jerry Bible, Terry Smith, Billy Bird, and a rising star in junior Jerry Smith, many of the locals felt like advancing to the regionals was a sure thing.

With the state's basketball season winding down, round ball crazy eastern Kentucky was preparing for tournament time when tragedy struck in a way no one could have imagined.

On March 1, 1958, a Floyd County school bus carrying 39 children and a driver somehow ended up in the rain swollen Big Sandy River just outside of Prestonsburg. By the time passerbyers did their best to pull as many of the kids as they could from the carnage, twenty-three of them along with the driver had died. Sixteen had survived. Word quickly spread, and with it some of the luster of March Madness had vanished.

As soon as the season was over, following Corbin's regional defeat at the hands of Clay County, it was time for spring football practice, and that meant more coaches coming to Corbin.

On April 19, 1958, a large crowd was on hand at Campbell Field to see the annual Varsity-Alumni game. What many had hoped would be a scoring festival turned into a ho-hum defensive struggle as a Ronnie Boone to Keith Hutson pass accounted for the only score in a 6-0 Varsity win.

Although Billy Bird was special, so was lineman Mel Chandler. In August the strapping youngster who had committed to U.K. was selected to play in the All-American High School Grid Classic in Memphis.

Chandler years later recalled how supportive the town was of Corbin youngsters heading to college. "I was getting ready to go to U.K., and Milton Oaks bought me a sports coat," He said. "It came out of nowhere. If a kid needed clothes someone took care of it."

As September rolled around, it quickly became evident that the spring game against the Alumni wasn't an indication of the offensive Redhound firepower that was to come.

In the opening game it didn't take Billy Bird long to leave his calling card. The swift-footed junior scored on runs of 64, 86, 80 and seven in a 26-7 win over Dixie Heights. Dixie Heights coach Bill Shannon said after the game no team that he coached had ever given up a run of more than 40 yards.

Bell County fell next 48-6 with Billy scoring three times on runs of 60, 24 and five. Corbin piled on the points again with a 43-6 win over Pineville. Bird again scored three times, as Keith Hutson and Ronnie Boone had an outstanding game. Pushing their record to 4-0, the Redhounds defeated a good Middlesboro team 25-6. Bird added two more TD's.

On October 3, it took a Boone to Hutson scoring pass to turn back Harlan 7-0. It marked the first game of the year Billy Bird was shutout.

The 5-0 Hounds had a statewide ranking as they headed into the Somerset game. Somerset was always a test, and when it was over the Briar Jumpers had a 7-6 win. The only Corbin score once again came on a Boone to Hutson pass.

Next came Richmond Madison Model, coached by former Corbin star Roy Kidd and quarterbacked by future Kentucky star Jerry Woolum. Bird had a great game, scoring twice and intercepting a pair of Woolum passes. Cruiser Boone rang up four TD passes, two to Bird, in the 26-7 win.

The Redhounds improved their record to 7-1 with a 26-0 shutout win over Williamsburg.

As some 7,000 fans watched at Danville, Corbin failed to convert two extra points in falling to the Admirals 14-12. Billy scored once, and his 201 rushing yards was more than the entire Danville team. This was followed with a 62-0 win over Lynn Camp in the Hounds only day game of the year.

Remember Coach Moon Conde? He was winless as a Corbin coach in his only season at the Redhound helm in 1953. Now coaching at Louisville Manual, he brought his squad to Corbin to play in front of an emotionally charged 4,000 spectators. It was homecoming. Conde's team was loaded and ranked number one in the state. Led by future Michigan State star Sherman Lewis at one halfback and equally talented Paul McPherson at the other, Manual's speed would be one of the few opponents to ever be faster than a Corbin team. Lewis had won the 100 and 220 at the State Track Meet, and Steve Wright, a 6'5", 240-pound tackle, who would later star at Alabama and with the Green Bay Packers, assured Manual of bringing one of the best football teams to Corbin in many a year.

A failed extra point conversion by the Redhounds led to a 21-20 loss to the visitors. Bird, Hutson and Bob Croley each scored a touchdown, and linemen Fred Rader, Jesse Grant, and Eddie "Amos" Miller more than held their own against the Louisville team.

At the conclusion of the season Rader was named Southeast Kentucky Conference Player-of-the Year. However, with a 7-3 record that many schools would only dream of, for the Corbin team, coaches and fans it was "what if?" The three losses were by a total of only four points.

When the following August rolled around it was football time in Corbin, Kentucky, and it looked like the parade of college coaches would continue in hopes of getting a foot in the recruiting door for Billy Bird, Fred Rader, Jesse Grant, and Billy's little brother, Rodger, a sophomore.

In the August heat Coach Walt Green took his squad of forty to a football camp in Due West, South Carolina. Green wrote back to Corbin that his team was practicing twice a day in 106 degree heat. "That's in the shade," he reported. "I don't know what it is on the field."

The Redhounds returned to Corbin and were ready. Right out of the gate they defeated Somerset 7-6, with a point-after kick by sophomore Barry Brooks being the difference.

Next came a 25-0 win over Bell County as Billy scored on a 73-yard punt return and nine yard run.

At Pineville, Corbin won 19-0 with Billy scoring twice. Then Middlesboro fell 26-13. Billy ran for three scores and little brother Rodger added another.

The Redhounds were rolling as they blasted Hall 54-14. Billy scored twice and then added three point-afters.

In a 26-6 win over Richmond Madison at Hanger Stadium on Eastern's campus, Billy scored three times. Madison Model was led by future U.K. star Talbott Todd and running back Freddy Ballou. The Hounds scored in every quarter, and Bird not only ran for three, but passed to Jim Andy Wilder for the fourth.

Harlan refused to wilt against the mighty Hounds and hung in for a 13-13 tie. Billy and Rodger each scored once.

Danville then fell 13-7, with Billy scoring once.

On October 23, 1959, Corbin's Billy Bird was about to make history, and his teammates all wanted to be a part of it. Williamsburg came to town and the fact that the field that night was described as a "sea of mud" mattered little to Billy and his buddies. In the first quarter Billy scored on runs of one, 20 and 19, adding two extra points. It was more of the same in the second with TD runs of 47 and nine yards. With 32 points in the books, Billy had all the points as Corbin led Williamsburg 32-0.

"After Billy had those 32 points in the first half, our boys had a meeting at halftime and agreed to let him go for Calvin's record (49 points)," revealed Walt Green the day after the game. Tackle Fred Rader, a 250-pounder, took it upon himself to set the stage for what was in store for high school football in Kentucky. "We've heard what Calvin had done and what Rodger is going to do. Now let's give Billy his chance," Rader told his teammates. And that's exactly what the Redhounds did.

Billy picked up where he left off when the Hounds took the field. A buzz had been created as just about everyone in the crowd was aware of what was happening and wondering if Calvin Bird's single game record would actually be broken. There was still a lot of football to be played.

Every time quarterback Bill Short pitched the ball to Billy, he was a threat to score. And score he did. A 75-yard punt return gave him touchdown number six. When he added the extra point he had now scored 39 points. It didn't take long for him to find the end zone again with a 21-yard burst. After scoring another extra point, he now had 46 points with plenty of time left in the game.

It was evident that Billy was on the verge of breaking Calvin's record; one that many in Corbin thought would never be broken. The question was no longer "can Billy break the record, but by how many?"

An eight yard scamper and a point-after game him 53 points and the record. But he wasn't finished. An 11-yard run and another from five, with an extra point tacked on, gave Billy Bird an unheard of 66 points on ten touchdowns and six extra points. It was a single game Kentucky high school record for the boy from Corbin, and Walt Green said, "He earned every one of 'em."

Billy's single game mark still ranks third all-time in Kentucky. In 1962, Herbie Phelps scored ten TD's and eight extra points as his Old Kentucky Home High School beat Louisville Catholic Country Day. Then in 1968, Don Gullett tallied 72 points on 11 TD's and six extra points for McKell against Wurtland. Gullett later became a star pitcher for the Cincinnati Reds.

Younger brother Rodger caught a 21-yard scoring pass from Short to give Corbin a 75-0 win over Williamsburg.

The Redhounds still had two games remaining, Jenkins and Manual.

If you can believe it, the Corbin-Jenkins game was moved to November 5, a Thursday night, so Corbin's coaches could travel to Louisville and scout Manual in a Friday night encounter with New Albany, Indiana. That's the importance the Corbin school put on a game with Manual. The fact that Jenkins agreed to the change points out the relationship the mountain schools had with each other.

Corbin disposed of Jenkins 41-6. Billy had three TDs, but had two more on runs of 70 and 87, called back because of penalties.

Heading into the Manual game, Corbin was unbeaten with the 13-13 tie against Harlan as the only blemish on their 7-0-1 record. But Manual was ranked number one in the state.

Remember the school from Louisville had won at Corbin the year before 21-20, and the Hounds wanted revenge. It was not to be. The Hounds lost again, 21-20, in a game many felt they should have won.

The Redhounds received an invitation to play in the Exposition Bowl against a Louisville team, but voted not to participate this year. The Corbin team had played in the Bowl in 1955, 66, and 57, but perhaps the 47-0 thumping they received from Louisville St. X on their last visit still lingered in their minds.

For the season Billy had scored 172 points, and when added to the 115 he had as a junior, 49 as a sophomore, and 12 as a freshman, his four year total was 348 points. Some thought it might be a national record.

Billy became the third Bird brother behind Jerry and Calvin to be recognized with high school All-American honors. At the time it was believed the Bird family was the only one in the country with three All-American sons. And Rodger was still to come.

Coach Walt Green talked about his star: "Billy is the best open field runner I've ever seen. He doesn't have blinding speed, but he's quick, has a good change of pace and good peripheral vision. He can see 'em coming and get away from 'em."

Corbin dominated the All-Conference with Bird, Rader and Grant on the first team. Short, Bobby Croley, Duane Hart, and Jim Andy Wilder also received accolades for their play.

Basketball was on the horizon, and the Hounds in the 1959-60 season were expected to put one of the best teams ever on the Edwards Gym court. With Billy, David Selvy, Jerry Bible, Keith Hutson and Jerry Smith, and a deep bench, Coach Harry Taylor knew he had one of the best teams in Kentucky. After breezing through district play and into the regionals, wouldn't you know it; they ran into Bell County and lost in the finals 49-44 in overtime.

For his Corbin High career Billy had earned twelve letters in four sports, and as expected, every major college in the southeast plus Ohio State and Clemson wanted him for football or basketball. Tennessee even offered him the opportunity to play both sports. It was Kentucky assistant football coach Norm Deeb, however, who signed him. There was really no other school he seriously considered. He was a Bird, and the Birds went to Kentucky.

As Billy prepared for his freshman year at U.K., the 165-pound star knew he would have to use his finesse as a runner and kick return specialist if he was to make his mark in the SEC.

Moving up to the Wildcat varsity in 1961, Coach Blanton Collier used Billy, along with Bill Ransdell, as his top kickoff returners, where he averaged just over 21 yards a return. In the fourth game of the season he sprang loose for a 40-yard touchdown run in a 21-8 win over Kansas State.

"Everyone just knew Billy was going to be good, just like Calvin," offered Ransdell. "He wasn't big, but he had a knack of finding the holes and avoiding the hits."

Billy's future as a Wildcat looked good, but with a season record of 5-5, Collier was suddenly fired with three years remaining on his contract. He left with a 41-36-3 record that included a 5-2-1 mark against U.K.'s biggest rival, Tennessee. Remarkably, Collier would be the last Kentucky coach to depart with a winning record. It was said that Collier had been saddled with some restrictions while coaching at Kentucky.

Rumors were prevalent that before he left U.K. for Texas A & M, Bear Bryant encouraged the administration to implement a football policy of no more than five out-of-state recruits annually, even though his squads were rich with kids from Ohio and Pennsylvania. Nowhere has that policy surfaced in any official document, but if it was true, Collier was certainly at a disadvantage.

To begin with, there were just a few more than one hundred Kentucky high schools playing eleven man football. Tennessee, on the other hand had over 300. Added to Collier's recruiting woes was that the university upped its academic requirements for athletes. If that wasn't bad enough, U.K. school administrators were opposed to "redshirting," a practice that allowed holding athletes out of participation for a year without affecting their eligibility.

With the arrival of Charlie Bradshaw in 1962, it meant that Billy was expendable. The boy from Corbin went from first string to fourth, and during spring drills, on April 22, 1962, it was announced that Billy Bird had left the team.

A teammate and roommate of Billy's was Buddy Bell, a hulk of a man, who was an All-State tackle at Louisville Eastern High School. Buddy was one of those youngsters Blanton Collier knew was going to be a top-notch lineman for the Wildcats. At 6'1", 245-pounds, with quick feet and an explosive charge, he had also been one of the best prep shot putters in the state.

Rooming in Kitten Lodge with Billy, Hugh Sturgeon, the younger brother of former Wildcat Charlie Sturgeon, and another boy from Corbin, Fred Rader, the four of them were confident in their ability to move up to the varsity. "We had all been signed by Collier," said Bell. "It just all changed so quickly when Bradshaw came in. Billy was such a neat guy. I was called the "Whale" and Billy the "Minnow." He was just a good guy to be around."

Bell also remembered how Billy felt about his younger brother Rodger. "Rodger used to come up and sleep on the floor in our room," he said. "He knew Rader from Corbin, and we really enjoyed him. Billy talked all the time about Rodger. You could tell he really loved him."

Looking back on it all, perhaps not realizing it at the time, had Collier stayed, Billy would have too. But on the other hand, had Collier stayed, younger brother Rodger probably would not have gone to U.K. because of the issues older brother Calvin had with the departed coach.

After college, Billy was employed by General Telephone in Lexington. He stayed involved in sports, becoming one of the best amateur basketball players in the city, playing for CWA (Communication Workers Association), "Dad's" team.

He had two children, Bill Jr., born in 1963 and Angela, born in 1965. The boy from Corbin had a virus that affected his heart and died in December 1975.

Chapter Seven

A Smith and Three Selvys

It seemed that everyone growing up in Corbin had to overcome something to be successful. They didn't know it, but that's the way it seemed. For most, they didn't realize the hardships they endured, or did they?

"I didn't know it at the time, but my life growing up in Corbin made me tough and hungry," says Jerry Smith, a former Redhound basketball great.

As one of the boys from Corbin, nothing was ever given to him, and though the 1958 and 1959 Redhound basketball teams never reached the state tournament, they are still considered among the best teams ever. Jerry Smith, like Frank Selvy, was a late bloomer. And wouldn't you know it, he reached All-American status at Furman, too.

"I played basketball to survive," Smith said.

Jerry, brother Terry, sister Brenda, and his mother Dorothy moved to Corbin when Jerry was in the sixth grade. They had lived in the Straight Creek area of Bell County where Jerry's dad, Roscoe, had been involved in a shootout centered around an argument that resulted in the death of four people. With Roscoe Smith in prison and now divorced, Dorothy moved her family to Corbin.

"We had one bedroom at the Brashear Apartments on Fourth Street," recalled Jerry. "Mom was a nurse at the Corbin Hospital."

Jerry and Terry, who was a year older, looked so much alike, that they were often thought to be twins. Terry, too, was a good athlete, playing basketball and football. Like so many kids growing up in eastern Kentucky, they also had to do their share when it came to earning money. "I had two paper routes, and Terry had two," Smith says. "And looking back on it, carrying all those papers on my bicycle up and down those hills made my legs unbelievably strong."

Jerry had something that couldn't be taught or coached...desire. He shot baskets for hours, often by himself, in the rain, mud or snow.

"My freshman and sophomore year, I was 5'7" - 5'8" and Coach Taylor wouldn't let me come out for the team," he said. "I guess I was getting a little rowdy in school, wanting to play and everything, when they let me come out my junior year.

A little bit of the rowdiness might have occurred the night he and three of his friends climbed the fence that surrounded the YMCA pool. "We took off our clothes and went in," he laughed. "But suddenly the police showed up. We got away, but had to leave our clothes. Believe it or not, one of the guys went by the police station a little later, saw our clothes in there, grabbed them and took off. We got 'em back."

It was quickly evident that Jerry was going to be a star. Immediately contributing, his play along with that of brother Terry, Billy Bird, and Harold Queary, helped the Redhounds to the regionals where they lost to Bell County.

By now Smith was a bit over six feet, and possessing the ability to "jump out of the gym," he jumped center for the Hounds. "I could really jump for my size," he says. "I was a jumpin' white boy, and all of that peddling on the bicycle had paid off."

It was the beginning of Jerry's senior year that his game went to another level. "I owe so much to Coach (Bob) Cathers," Jerry said, choking back the emotions. "He's the first person who really believed in me.

"Coach Taylor was okay, but Coach Cathers had come along, and was, what do you call it, head coach in waiting. He was a disciplinarian and was so competitive. He made me out a practice schedule to work on shooting and dribbling that hadn't been done before."

And practice Jerry Smith did. "I had sixth period study hall, and I went to the gym where I shot for an hour to an hour and a half before our team practice ever started. I was dedicated."

Sometime during his senior year, Jerry's dad showed up in Corbin. He had been released from prison. "After I got to know him, we had a good relationship," he said. "He was a professional gambler…card player…and dressed like the head of a big corporation."

On days when Edwards Gym was closed, Smith still found a way to get in and shoot baskets.

"The school's janitor, John Broughton, lived next door to the gym, and I delivered his paper every day," he said. "He'd give me the keys so I could go in and shoot. When I didn't have the key, I'd find a window I could crawl through."

"I remember one day Coach Cathers said, 'Jerry, I don't know how you do it all, delivering those papers in the morning and all of the basketball.' Heck, I knew basketball was my way out." In the meantime Jerry's mother had remarried, and was regularly present at his games.

The 1959 Redhound basketball team was loaded with everything but size. Still they were projected to advance to the Sweet Sixteen in Lexington, but lost to Clay County in Manchester in overtime in the semi-finals after beating Harlan.

"I came down with the flu," recalled Jerry. "Had a fever of 102, but tried to play. Those games with Clay County were something. During the regular season we beat them on their home floor, and when we left they threw rocks at the bus, actually breaking some of the windows."

And like so many Corbin hoop stars, he heard from Adolph Rupp. "Yea, we talked, that's about all. I was 6-feet, but like Selvy, I grew to 6'3" and could play."

Furman and Coach Lyles Alley had gone down this road before, and one of his assistant coaches, Nield Gordon, who had played with Frank, was impressed with the "new" boy from Corbin, Jerry Smith.

At Furman he was immediately being compared to Frank even to the extent of being called "Mr. Corbin Number Two." "I don't like being number two at anything, but if I have to be behind someone, Frank's not bad," he said.

Meanwhile, back in Corbin, his sister Brenda was married to somewhat of a celebrity around town. In 1955, during the filming of the movie "The Kentuckian," a scene called for a boy to leap from high atop a paddle wheeler on the Kentucky River. Her husband, Charles Smith, who went by the nickname "Preacher" was small in stature, and agreed to become a temporary stunt man for the film. "I think he got paid $400 or $500 for doing it," Jerry Smith said years later.

As a sophomore Smith averaged 22.6 per game and was named to the All-Southern Conference team. Two of his teammates that year were Don Fry from Monticello and Gerald Glur from Louisville Manual, and together they helped lead the Palidins to wins over Clemson, South Carolina, Davidson and Florida State. Coach Alley went as far as to say "Smith is every bit as good right now as Frank was during a similar stage in his career."

In 1962, *The Sporting News* wrote that "normally nobody puts a nickel in the slot after the jackpot has been hit, but (Lyles) Alley has gone back to Corbin and found himself another scorer like Selvy. The name…Jerry Smith."

Smith, as a junior upped his scoring to 27 points a game that led the conference and nationally ranked seventh. Along the way he was voted the MVP of the Poinsettia Classic by scoring 28 against Georgia Tech and 33 against Clemson, and the Helms Foundation All-American team had the boy from Corbin on its second team.

"My family would get to Greenville now and then," he said. "And my dad would go up on Clinch Mountain, near Middlesboro, where he could get a good radio signal and listen to my road games. He was in Greenville to see me play just about every game."

By the time Jerry's senior season rolled around he was a marked man. "Al McGuire was coaching at Belmont Abby," Smith said. "And he was the first coach to employ a box and one defense against us. Then some of the other schools used special defenses. Coach Alley said I'd be a decoy. I wasn't very happy about it, because naturally I was getting fewer shots."

Indeed he was. Taking 200 less shots than the year before, his scoring average slipped to 20.2. The gimmick defenses cut down on the scoring average for the entire team, but still they were good enough to defeat South Carolina, Clemson, Davidson, Wake Forest and West Virginia.

"Lefty Driesell was turning out some good teams at Davidson," says Smith. "And West Virginia with all of those great players was one of the top teams in the country. To beat those guys really felt great."

In spite of the lower numbers, the boy from Corbin was named All-Southern Conference for the third consecutive year, and the *Associated Press* named him to their All-American second team.

West Virginia placed him for three years on their all-opponent team, by virtue of his career average against them of just under 29 points a game. Driesell, the Davidson coach, said Smith could play for any team in the country.

When it was all over at Furman, Jerry Smith had scored 1885 points in three years, ranking fifth of all-time, and his 23.3 point average placed him third. An 85.7 percent single season free throw mark was a Furman record, as was his career 82.3 percentage.

"I was one of the original dunkers as a guard, and averaged more than seven rebounds a game," Smith says. "I could drive to the basket and because of that, I'd get fouled and shoot free throws."

Lou Mohs, general manager of the Los Angeles Lakers scouted Smith, and told Greenville sportswriter Dan Foster that the boy from Corbin had a pro-game. "The pro game is essentially a one-on-one game, and that seems to be right down Jerry Smith's alley," Mohs said. "He's a great one-on-one player."

Smith sometimes displayed a fiery temper, especially when things didn't always go his way on the court. It could be an occasional off-shooting night, the lack of hustle of a teammate, or just remembering how hard he had to work to gain respect as a basketball player. So when the Laker's general manager was asked if he thought Smith was mean enough for pro basketball, he chuckled, nodded and said, "I put on my scouting report 'surly'."

It was written that at Furman, Smith might be considered a loner among his teammates. Striving for perfection from not only himself, but from other Palidins as well, this sometimes didn't set well with them. Still, they knew what Smith was all about, and that was winning.

The 1963 NBA draft had Jerry going to the Detroit Pistons in the second round. "There were only nine NBA teams back then, and I was the thirteenth overall pick that year," Jerry said. "But then I also got drafted in the military, and by the time I got out I decided against playing pro ball and went into business in Greenville.

"Ed Jucker, the coach of the Royals (Cincinnati) seemed to have liked my ability too. I should have given that a shot," he said. I sometime regret not playing."

On September 19, 1964, Jerry married Connie Copeland. Connie knew who he was long before he knew her. "My dad was a big Furman basketball fan," she said. "He didn't have any sons and I was a big tomboy, so I'd go to all of the games with him. Later on a mutual friend fixed us up on a date."

In 1968 Jerry said his dad, Roscoe, was traveling back to Middlesboro after playing cards in a surrounding county. "He'd been gambling, and had a car wreck. He died in the hospital at Middlesboro," Smith recalled. "Dad had remarried and had a daughter, Sonya, who is my half-sister." He wanted me to try out for the Kentucky Colonels Basketball team in the ABA, but I didn't and regret it to this day."

Naturally Smith is in the Furman Athletic Hall of Fame, but one of his crowning recognitions was when he became only the sixth men's basketball player to have his number 50 jersey retired on January 16, 2010.

David Selvy

David Selvy, at least across Kentucky, perhaps is the forgotten Selvy when it comes to basketball talent. But make no mistake about it, he could play.

Frank Selvy, far right, lines up with his five younger brothers Edd, David, Donald, Marvin and Charles at halftime of the Furman-Newberry College game. The Selvys played a game at halftime.

Left to right: Frank, Curly (Charles), Dad, Don, David (on floor), Marvin (on floor), Mom, Sarah, Stella, Beverly (Stella's daughter).

Stella Selvy shares some pictures with (left to right) Charles (Curly), Don and Marvin.

Above: *David Selvy*

Left: *Charles Selvy*

Right: *Edd Selvy*

The Selvys. Back row: Frank, Iva, James, Curt. Front row: Sarah, David, Edd, Charles, Marvin, Stella.

Curly Selvy signs with Western Kentucky University in 1966. Next to him is brother Curt. Hilltopper Coach Johnny Oldham (in sportscoat) and Redhound Coach Bill Smith watch.

Curt Selvy

Curt Selvy, Corbin High School, Courier Journal All Kentucky High School Basketball Squad, 1947.

Curt Selvy (far left) during the House of David vs Harlem Globetrotters.

1947 team after WWII. Pictured are Manager Charles Stewart, Dusty Yates, Harold Brooks, Curt Selvy, Max Mobley, Bob Sturgill, Jerry Bryant, Manager Carl Neil, Bill Brown, Bob Selvy, Jack Crabtree, B. Mobley, Dorman Siler, unidentified, Bobby McNeil, Robert Barton, Carl Jones, E. Von Grunigen, Roy Kidd, Bob Cathers, Sylvester Wright, Robert Burch.

Left to right: Curt Selvy, Hand Decker, Jack Garrett, circa 1950.

Curt Selvy (back left) with touring team.

Calvin Bird kneeling far right; Edd Selvy standing second from far right in 1954. Notice the depleted roster.

Ralph Beard, former U.K. great, drives by Edd Selvy in a "business league" in Louisville. Beard played for Dizzy Whiz.

The 1963-64 Furman starters. Kneeling: Frye and Shaffer. Standing: Heicher, Selvy and Peacock.

The 1963-64 Basketball Team. Front row, left to right: Peacock, Shaffer, Haford, Blyler, Frye, Jennings. Second row: Coach Williams, Lee, Selvy, Oelschlager, Feil, Heicher, Turrentine, Coach Alley.

1966-67 Western Kentucky University Scholarship freshmen. Left to right: Curly Selvy, Walker Banks, Wayne Bright, Charles Starbuck and Kenny Davis.

Western Kentucky University 1967-68 Varsity Basketball team. Front row: Butch Kaufman, Charles Selvy, Joe Mac Hill, Johnn Russell, Rich Hendrick, Mike Fawcett. Second row: Wayne Chapman (co-captain), Greg Smith (co-captain), Wayne Bright, Walker Banks, Norm Weaver, Paul Haskins. Third row: Manager Larry Williams, Head Coach John Oldham, Athletic Director Ted Hornback, Team Physician Dr. W.R. McCormack, Manager Robert Walden.

David Selvy

Curly Selvy at Furman.

David Selvy gets a Citadel hand in the face.

Furman Coach Frank Selvy talks to the team. Curly is in the middle.

Curly Selvy gets off a shot at Furman against South Carolina.

Left and below: *Marvin Selvy in action as a starter at the University of Louisville.*

1966-67 University of Louisville "Fighting Cardinals" Missouri Valley Champs of which Marvin Selvy was a regular.

Selvy brothers. Left to right: Charles, Frank, Curt, Edd and Marvin at the dedication of "Frank Selvy Way."

***Left:** Jerry Smith*

***Below:** Three Selvys and Jerry Smith, all of Corbin, were participants in three games at Memorial Auditorium and all did well on "Corbin Night." Left to right: Marvin Selvy, David Selvy, Jerry Smith and Charles Selvy.*

Corbin's Jerry Smith signed a grant-in-aid at Furman. In this photo, Smith talks to Lyles Alley, the coach at Furman.

Left and below: *Jerry Smith in action at Furman.*

Jerry Smith (right, holding jersey) had his number retired in January of 2010 at Furman. With Smith is AD Gary Clarkson, left, and Coach Jeff Jackson.

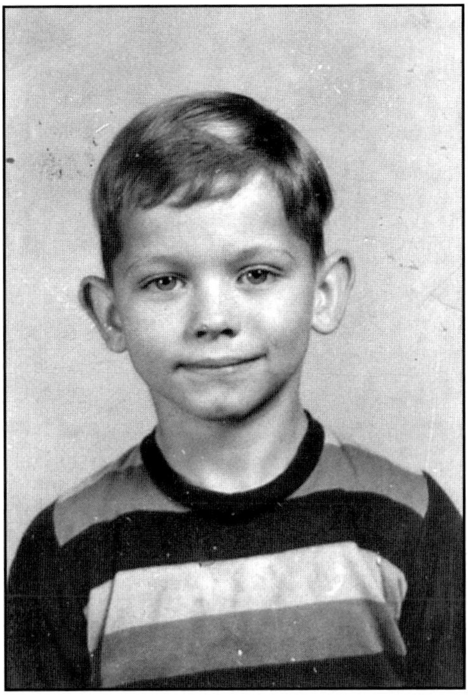

Left: *Rodger Bird*

Below: *Rodger Bird with a puppy at his grandparents house in Pleasant View.*

Right: *Rodger Bird (junior year) and Coach Green, 1960.*

Below: *Florida Spring Break 1962. Rodger Bird, Barry Brooks, Russ Willis, Jerry "Smiley" Martin, Gary Holtzclaw, Joe Gambrell.*

Rodger Bird looks over U.K. scholarship papers with his parents as Wildcat Coach Charlie Bradshaw (left) and Corbin Coach Carl Oakley observe.

Rodger Bird, spring of 1963 with a groundhog kill.

Rodger Bird talks to U.K. quarterback Rick Norton during a game in 1964.

Rodger Bird in his R.O.T.C. uniform walks across U.K. campus with teammates Rick Norton (left) and Rick Kestner.

Playboy's 1965 Preview All-American Offensive Team. Front row: Paul Crane, center (Alabama); Jerry Burns, Coach of the Year (Iowa). Second row: Karl Noonan, end (Iowa); George Rice, tackle (Louisiana State); Stan Hindman, guard (Mississippi); Dick Arrington, guard (Notre Dame); John Niland, tackel (Iowa); Rick Kestner, end (Kentucky). Third row: Nick Eddy, halfback (Notre Dame); Gary Snook, quarterback (Iowa); Floyd Little, halfback (Syracuse). Rear: Jim Grabowski, fullback (Illinois).

Playboy's 1965 Preview All-American Defensive Team. Front row: Jack Shinholser, guard (Florida State). Second row: Casimir Banaszek, end (Northwestern); Stan Dzura, tackle (California); Bill Yearby, tackle (Michigan); Aaron Brown, end (Minnesota). Third row: Bill Cody, linebacker (Auburn); Carl McAdams, linebacker (Oklahoma); Tom Cecchini, linebacker (Michigan). Back row: Rodger Bird, halfback (Kentucky); Bruce Bennett, safety (Florida); Mike Garrett, halfback (Southern California).

Right: *The 1965 University of Kentucky Football Media Guide featured on the cover Rick Kestner (80), Rick Norton (11) and Rodger Bird (21).*

Below: *Barry Brooks (left) and Rodger Bird with hound George in 1961.*

Rodger Bird's 92 yard touchdown.

Rodger Bird shows his leaping ability while catching a pass at U.K.

Rodger Bird stands between Kentucky Governor A.B. "Happy" Chandler and his son Dan at an Oakland Raider game.

1966 Oakland Raiders. Front row: Head Coach John Rauch, Mike Eischeid, Charlie Green, Tom Flores, Jim Otto, Cotton Davidson, Warren Powers, Rodger Bird, Larry Todd, Assistant Coach Ollie Spencer. Second row: Trainer George Anderson, Joe Krakoski, Howie Williams, Roger Hagberg, Richard Jackson, Billy Cannon, Gus Otto, Hewritt Dixon, Clem Daniels, Pervis Atkins, Equipment Manager Dick Romanski. Third row: Assistant Coach Charlie Sumner, Pete Banaszak, Bill Laskey, David Grayson, Kent McCloughan, Bill Budness, Willie Williams, J.R. Williamson, Dan Birdwell, Dan Conners, Assistant Coach Tom Dahms. Fourth row: Ray Schmautz, Wayne Hawkins, Palmer Pyle, James Harvey, Richard Tyson, Greg Kent, Tom Keating, David Daniels, Bob Svihus, Isaac Lassiter. Fifth row: Assistant Coach Bill Walsh, Rex Mirich, Harry Schuh, Tom Mitchell, Ben Davidson, Art Powell, Carleton Oats, Bill Miller, Assistant Coach Clancy Osborne.

Rodger Bird next to his all-terrain vehicle in 2011.

Barry Brooks and Rodger Bird with London's Jim Handy, owner of the Hampton Inn in Corbin and London. Handy played in two memorable games against Corbin in the early 1960s (pictured below in one of those games).

For years, many around Corbin thought the 1959 Redhound team might have been one of the all-time best ever, though it never made it to the state tournament.

"We lost in the regional finals my junior year to Clay County on their floor in overtime," David Selvy recalled. "We were loaded. Billy Bird and Jerry Smith were really good, and then Jerry came down with the flu. We were one of the best four or five schools in the state that year. Then in my senior year Bell County got us in the regionals at their place."

Selvy had several schools with scholarship offers, but it surprised no one when he headed to Furman to play for Lyles Alley and assistant coach Joe Williams, who would later coach those great Jacksonville teams that featured Artis Gilmore.

David Selvy scored 25 in a win over Richmond in early January 1964, and then came back a month later to help Furman with their biggest win of the year.

On February 13, 1964, Furman with an 8-13 record went up against a very good 19-1 Davidson team, coached by Lefty Driesell. David scored 14 key points to lead the Palidins to a win.

"After Furman, I was an assistant coach at Trinity High School in Louisville for W.C. Sergent, who had coached at Corbin," Selvy said. "Coach Williams contacted me and offered me a job with him at Jacksonville, but I had to have a master's degree. So I got a job at a Junior High and worked on my master's degree in Florida. But then in October 1967, I got drafted into the Army. For six months I was in the Pershing's Missile School, and then spent a year in Vietnam assigned to a MP (Military Police) unit."

David Selvy's time away from basketball allowed him to reevaluate his life and the role basketball would play in it. Sports, and particularly basketball, was all he had even known. After all, when you were a boy from Corbin and your last name was Selvy, that's what was expected.

"When I got out of the Army, I was burned out," he offered. "So I moved to California and got into snow skiing and the house painting business."

David is well aware of the doors brother Frank opened for his family as well as other Corbin athletes. As great as Frank was as a player, David says in his opinion one of his other brothers was the best that ever wore a Redhound uniform.

"Marvin was the greatest basketball player to ever play at Corbin," says David. "Just look what he did. Marvin was underrated and overlooked when it came to basketball in Kentucky."

With that said, David once wrote a letter back to Corbin to be read at a basketball celebration:

> *My brother, Frank, has always been an outstanding person. Everyone knows what a great athlete Frank has been in high school, college and professionally. Frank has also been totally dedicated to making life better for his family members. He made it possible for us younger brothers to have privileges and advantages that we never could have dreamed possible.*

David, too, has his thoughts on why his family excelled in basketball. "We had good genes first of all," he said. "And believe it or not we ate organic food before we called it that. None of us had any money for junk food back then. Heck, fifty cents was a lot of money to us. We were all lean and in shape. We ran home for lunch and ran back to school."

David also gives his mother much credit for keeping his large family focused and on track to do the right things. "She was a strong religious person in a good way," he says. "She made sure of two things: We were accountable and we were on time. Back then my dad had been in a miner's hospital for a year, and he drank some. When he got out of the hospital, he worked for the city on the garbage truck and street cleaning. My mother kept an eye on all of us."

Marvin Selvy

"My life was like winning the lottery every day," Marvin Selvy recalled about his Corbin days. "Frank was fourteen years older than me, and he had opened so many doors for all of us brothers that followed him. He was a great basketball player, but let me tell you he was even a greater brother."

It was a severe blow however, when on Labor Day weekend in 1952, while returning from Corbin to Cincinnati, older brother James, known as Babe, was killed in a car wreck just outside of Richmond, Kentucky.

"It was a setback for our whole family when Babe died," Marvin recalled. "I was about six at the time and Babe, I think, was about 24. He worked as a brick layer in Cincinnati and helped look out for our family. I remember when he walked out the door he told mom, 'I'll see you next weekend.' We were living on Maynard Street just before we moved to Earl Street. Babe didn't play sports; he knew he had to earn some money. But believe me he could have."

Marvin was a star player at Corbin High School for three years, and in 1965 he was named to the all-state team. His accomplishments included being a two year team captain, all-district, all-conference, and his single-game 61 points against Lynn Camp tied Calvin Bird's school record. If that wasn't enough, he set a high school record by connecting on 63 consecutive free throws.

"None of us who followed Frank ever thought about being as good as him," he said. "Just being his little brother was an honor, and it still is today."

Marvin was seven years old when he went with his entire family for "Frank Selvy Night" in Greenville, S.C. "That was the night Frank scored 100," Marvin recalled. "I remember all of us staying in the Poinsett Hotel. All of those Corbin people caravanned down there."

By the time Marvin realized he wanted to be a basketball player, and be serious about it, Frank had gotten the other Selvy boys involved in basketball camps throughout the south. "We were around people and met people we would never have been associated with if it wasn't for Frank," he said.

One of those camps was in Walhalla, South Carolina, and it was run by Press

Maravich, the head coach at Clemson University, who also happened to have a young son named Pete. Marvin's memories of that camp came to define who he was, but it also had an impact on quite a few other young boys growing up in Corbin.

"First, let me say that Pete Maravich was a shooter, even back then. As soon as he crossed half-court he would shoot," Marvin laughed. "But it didn't go in very often."

At this particular camp, Marvin, brother Curly, and Corbin boys Gary Fredrickson, and Bill Hoover were driven there by Bill's grandmother, Kathryn Day.

"We all stayed in cabins at the camp," Marvin said. "And the four of us were standing outside of our cabin after the curfew rules. One night we heard a voice come over the speaker for us to report to the gym. Press was there, and he told us we could run all night or go home, we had a choice."

"He stood in that gym with a big plug of tobacco in his mouth while we ran, and every time we ran by him he'd spit in the floor," recalled Marvin. "We ran all night and then he made us clean it up. The next day in between the camp games and during rest periods, he made us run some more. He reminded us we could go home if we wanted to, but we told each other he was not going to run us off."

After running for two days and a night, Maravich realized these boys from Corbin weren't going anywhere. They came to play basketball…not go home. "He came over to us and said, God, I love you guys,'" Marvin said. "We were tough little guys. It was our Corbin mentality."

Marvin had played for longtime coach Harry Taylor until his retirement in 1963, after twenty years at Corbin. W.C. Sargent took over the Redhound program, and along with it came a Selvy or two.

The night Marvin scored his 61 points came in an odd sort of way. He did it and only played three quarters. "Curly and I had missed a practice because we went for a visit at the University of Tennessee," said Selvy. "The coach didn't start me, so when I got in I was really mad. It was just one of those nights. My mom and dad didn't go to the games, but they listened to them on radio. My mom ruled with an iron hand in our family, so she kept up with what was going on. I was exhausted when I got home, but she was waiting for me. 'What did you do to not to get to play in the first quarter?'" She wanted to know.

To further show the concern and control Iva Selvy had for her boys, once Edd's football days were over at U.K., so were the days of any Selvy boys playing football in Corbin. "She put a stop to it," Marvin said. "So David, Curly or I didn't play. I don't know, we might have been pretty good."

Marvin's senior year was plagued by injuries. "I went from one injury to another," he said. "There was a knee, a broken finger, and an ankle sprain, so I didn't get to play in several of the all-star games."

Still he had been impressive enough that lots of colleges wanted him. It was assumed he would be going to Furman. By now Frank had finished his pro career and was an assistant coach there, and brother David was winding up his senior year at the school. There was just one problem, however.

"I really didn't want to go to Furman," he said. "Coach Rupp asked me what I was going to do, even leading me on a little, and Louisville had been after me. But I went ahead and signed with Furman."

Marvin, however, still was not happy with his decision. "David and I talked, and finally I decided to go to Louisville and play for Peck Hickman. I had been hearing a lot from them, and I thought Coach Alley at Furman would give me my release."

Marvin joined the Cardinal freshman team, coached by John Dromo, which included Butch Beard, Jerry King, Dennis Deeken, and Gary Hollard, who later coached Larry Bird in high school. The varsity featured a future all-time great in Westley Unseld, so Marvin would be part of a Cardinal team that would be considered one of the best in the country.

That first year, the frosh lost only one game, and quickly Selvy made his mark as a defensive guy. "I could guard people," Selvy said. "That's what Corbin boys could do, defend."

Marvin was ready now to move up to the varsity. "Things were good," he said. "The only problem was that Coach Dromo had changed the way I shot free throws. I had been a great free throw shooter in high school, but Dromo would not allow me to shoot the way I did. I'd sort of curl my wrist over the ball before I released it, and he wanted no part of that. I became an average shooter."

With excitement and high expectations of moving up to the varsity, Marvin's basketball came to a screeching halt. It seems that the release he thought he had gotten from Furman had not officially been granted, and suddenly his eligibility at U of L was in question.

"It really affected me," Selvy said. "They would not release me, and Louisville was going to redshirt me, but in reality in the end I lost a whole year of basketball. In what should have been my sophomore year turned out to be my junior. I was a starter, but my main role was defense. At 6'4", I could guard people."

"He could definitely guard people," offered former U of L assistant coach, Howard Stacey. "If we needed to lock down an opposing player, we called on Marvin. He could win ballgames for you."

In Selvy's senior season he tore a hamstring in the first game and never fully recovered. "Still bothers me today," he said.

While Marvin played at U of L, the Cardinals played in a couple of NCAA tournaments and an NIT.

Even with the controversy between Marvin and Furman over the release issue, after U of L, he went to the school in Greenville and coached the freshman team for one year to a 17-3 record. "I regret some times that I got out of coaching," he said. "But I had a business opportunity back in Louisville, so I came back."

Marvin enjoys talking as much about his brothers as he does himself.

"My brother Edd was probably the best all-around athlete in the family," he offered. "Everybody in Corbin wanted him to be a quarterback, but he always wanted to play defense. He was built for it, and he was tough…even did some boxing.

"In high school mom put a stop to Edd playing football for a time, but then some of the people came and talked her into letting him play. And in basketball he was on a high school All-American team with Wilt Chamberlain."

The boy from Corbin continued: "When I came along I was like a spoiled brat. I felt like I was rich. Our family had so much love. My dad didn't talk much about it, but he had been a machine-gunner in France in WWI. He and mom didn't marry until he was 30, and he was 52 when I was born.

Marvin had heard the stories about his dad, James, hopping a freight train out of Corbin along with his mom's younger brother, Howard Wilson, and traveling to St. Louis to play a baseball game. "It was like a minor league back then," Marvin said. "The two of them each bought a suit they had made for them and wore it home. But they got rained on, and by the time they arrived back home the coat and pants had shrunk."

Curly Selvy

There were those in Corbin who thought Charles "Curly" Selvy was the best basketball playing Selvy as a high schooler. But they said that at one time or another about them all. It's almost like the last one you saw was the best, and Curly was the last of the Selvys at Corbin High School.

As far back as his memories take him, he has always been called Curly. "I've been Curly all my life," he said. "Don't know who gave it to me."

His scoring and skills as a defensive stopper earned him the coveted Ted Meadors award as well as Player of the Year in the Southeastern Kentucky Conference in 1966.

With his legacy as a Selvy, and the game to back it up, he won high school All-American honors by *Coach and Athlete Magazine*. He was named to the East-West All-Star game, and had a key role in Kentucky's two-game sweep over Indiana, hitting seven of eight field goals and doing a defensive job on Hoosier great, Rick Mount.

"Curly became good friends with Mike Casey (Kentucky's Mr. Basketball) when they played for the Kentucky All-Stars against Indiana," brother Marvin recalled of the 1966 summer game. "And Mike came to visit us during the NIBROC (Corbin spelled backwards) Festival. There was one of those basketball deals where for a quarter, if you hit three straight you can win a teddy bear. Heck, the rim had been cut down to where the ball would barely go thru. Anyway, they started shooting and it didn't take long for them to clean out the teddy bears, and the guy said, 'no more.'"

Sought after by many of the same colleges that tried to recruit those who came before him, he only gave U.K. a passing thought. "They recruited me, but I remembered how they treated Marvin when they talked to him. He got a bad deal, but it worked out okay for him at Louisville," Curly recalled.

"I visited Tennessee, Florida and Ohio State," he continued. "But I fell in love with Western. They had some really good teams with (Clem) Haskins, (Wayne) Chapman, and the Smith brothers (Dwight and Greg)."

Years later Marvin Selvy laughed in telling how Curly ended up at Western.

"Coach Diddle was the one recruiting him, and when he went up to Corbin he took a beautiful Western student with him. Her name was Laura Little, from London. Coach Diddle asked her if she knew the Selvy boy over at Corbin, Curly. She said she had never heard of him. But that didn't stop Coach Diddle taking her with him to visit Curly. He knew what buttons to push with Curly, and I think he rode back to Bowling Green that day with Laura and Diddle."

Marvin continued. "It wasn't that Curly and Laura would be dating or anything like that. I think she was already dating her future husband, Wayne Chapman (and Rex's mother). But Curly was probably thinking, "There's got to be more like her at Western."

"I went down to Western to visit Curly one weekend, and I have never seen so many pretty girls in my life," Marvin recalled. "Heck, I went back to Louisville and told my buddies about it. Half the basketball and football team was ready to transfer to Western."

Colleges still had freshmen teams then, and Curly picked up where he left off in high school, being named Freshman of the Year in the Ohio Valley Conference.

Wallace "Buck" Sydnor coached the freshman team, and Selvy recalled some of the heated practice sessions that took place in the auxiliary gym, not far from the main floor in Diddle Arena. "We'd get into fights, he said. "But Coach Sydnor didn't care. He'd raise his eyebrows and look over the top of his glasses and give a big grin."

During Curly's first year at Western, brother Frank, who had been an assistant under Lyles Alley, became the head coach at Furman. As Curly prepared for his sophomore year, he said things began to get crossways with Hilltopper coach Johnny Oldham, and was taken off scholarship.

"I left school and went back to Corbin," he said. "I got a call from Coach Diddle and he told me to get back down there…said he'd pay for my scholarship." He went back, but it was never the same.

"Rich Hendrick and I alternated at guard, and when Coach Oldham got us ready to go to the Cable Car Classic in San Francisco, I wasn't even on the travel squad," said Curly. "Oldham didn't care if I left or not. He had signed five great high school players for the following year, but I really thought I could play with anybody. But it was best if I left." And leave he did, this time for good.

The course of least resistance always seemed to be Furman University. And with Frank as the head coach there, it was almost a given that if Curly was going to continue his basketball career, that's where he would go.

"I transferred there after the first semester of my sophomore year at Western," he said. "It was hard for me. I sat out a year, and then when I became eligible I didn't want to disappoint Frank."

During the 1969-70 season Curly hit for 34 points in an 87-80 win over West Virginia on 10-19 from the field and 14-15 free throws.

Curly, the boy from Corbin, had an okay career at Furman, but when it was all said and done it was not basketball he was the most proud of. "I graduated on the dean's list at Furman," he offered. "Through it all I learned to study. That's my biggest accomplishment."

Chapter Eight

THE LAST OF THE BIRD BROTHERS

Rodger Bird began his football odyssey in 1953 when he was only a third grader playing for the South Ward Elementary Wildcats. The next season they were city champs.

Any boy with a last name of Bird was automatically marked. And wouldn't you know it, though still eligible to play Little League at South Ward, three years later, he transferred to Central Elementary in order to play on the Corbin "B" team where he was a third string halfback in 1957. Rodger didn't have a choice, he had to be good.

But it wasn't easy. Growing up the youngest of three brothers and two sisters, they lived in a two bedroom house on Sycamore Street. An outhouse in the backyard and a round tub in the kitchen took care of any bathroom needs the family might have. "That situation got better for us when Jerry went away to college," Rodger explained. "My mother said we needed a bathroom in case Jerry brought someone home with him."

Years later sister Nancy remembers the reason for the indoor bathroom a little differently. "It wasn't because Jerry went to college," she laughed. "It was because they finally ran the sewer line to our house. As soon as they did that we added it."

Rodger had grown up with all of the fuss being made over his older brothers. He heard the adults in Corbin tell them how great they were, he heard all of the cheering, shouting their names at all of the football and basketball games, and he, like every little boy growing up in Corbin, wanted to be a Redhound someday.

For the most part, he and his family had a good life in Corbin, with one exception.

"We all came down with the ringworm," said Rodger. "And my mom and dad had to hold us out of school for a year. "I was in the second grade and Billy was in the fourth and we were sent to live with my grandparents in Pleasant View. Believe me, the view wasn't so pleasant. They wouldn't let Calvin go to school either, but they figured he was old enough to stay by himself, so he stayed in Corbin."

Pleasant View was about 25 miles from Corbin, and a mile from the coal camp of Packard, where actress Patricia Neal grew up.

Most of those times for Rodger and Billy were tearful. "My grandmother was good to us," Rodger remembers. "But we really missed our home. We'd go back on weekends. Mom worked at the sewing factory, so they'd take us back for the week. I remember running after their car when they drove away. I'd chase it for a long way and they'd stop, put me in, and take me back to my grandmother. During the week dad would sometimes stop by in his bread truck, and I'd run after him, too."

Rodger also recalled the time U.K. Coach Adolph Rupp and his wife stopped by their house when he was recruiting Jerry. "Rupp said they were just passing through," he said. "My dad had sent me to bed, but I could hear them all talking. Our bedrooms didn't have doors on them, so I just kind of stood next to the door and listened. I'll never forget, he drove a Cadillac that was longer than our house."

As much passion as Rodger had for sports, he had even more for hunting. There were even occasions he would skip a practice to go hunting. Sometimes after his parents had left for work he would stay home from school just to shoot birds in the front yard.

"There'd be snow on the ground, and blackbirds would land in the front yard," recalled Rodger years later. "I'd crack open the door enough to take aim and shoot. Then I'd go out and try to cover the dead birds up with the snow before anyone got home."

Rodger's dad, Ruben, would leave home at 4:30 a.m. six days a week to make his bread deliveries, and in spite of his long days, he and Bonnie were very supportive of their boys. By the time Rodger's athletic career began to take hold, they had already seen that being a good athlete could lead to a college education, something that would have been very difficult, if not impossible, for the Birds. They saw all of their boys' home games and would drive to Lexington to watch Jerry play basketball.

"My parents would keep score for both teams, listening to Jerry's games on radio," Rodger said. "And Billy and I would put up a milk carton in our room and have our own game while it was going on."

Years later Rodger recalled that his dad worked hard, long days, but that he seemed to find time to be there when needed. "I remember, too, that he took his retirement money and built a carport for our green 1957 Ford.

"I remember I had an algebra problem," Rodger laughed. "It might as well have been Greek, but my daddy knew all about it and how to do it. And he only had an eighth grade education."

Jerry, Calvin, and Billy before him, had set a high standard of achievement, and being the last of the Bird brothers, not only did the town expect great things out of him, but also the entire state of Kentucky had the same expectations.

Although no one would admit it, even in those early days on the football field or basketball court, Rodger was a marked youngster. Nothing was given to him. He had to earn his way. The fact that he was a Bird made it a bit satisfying for his teammates in practice when they came up with a good tackle or caught a pass over him. He learned early in his Corbin sports life that's just the way it was.

As a freshman he was dressing for the Redhound varsity, joining brother Billy on the squad, and Coach Walt Green knew he was coaching a special football player.

The 1958 Redhounds ended the season 8-3, but it could have been 11-0. Losses 7-6 to Somerset, 14-12 to Danville, and 21-20 to Manual are all that stood in the way. Four points, three losses.

Corbin's annual spring game in April 1959 featured a good group of returning Redhounds, but believe it or not it was no match for the team the Alumni put on the field.

Coach Walt Green's Varsity had, of course, Billy and Rodger Bird, Fred Rader, Jesse Grant, Johnny Jervis, D.L. Lynch and Jim Andy Wilder. But with Alumni stars Tony Lanham, Mel Chandler, Ronnie Boone, Eddie Miller, Lanny Myers, Bobby Green, Gerald Ellison and Rodney Barton, they overpowered the Varsity 26-6.

To point out the reputation the Birds and Redhound football had earned, in the stands watching the high school spring game, was U.K. Coach Blanton Collier and his assistants Ermal Allen, Bill Arnsparger, Ed Rutledge and Bob Cummins.

When the 1959 season rolled around, Corbin had graduated the likes of speedy quarterback Ronnie "Cruiser" Boone. Boone could not only run, but could also pass, throwing for four TDs against Madison-Model the previous year. He was fast enough to also win the 100 and 220 dashes in the conference track meet. Those youngsters moving in to key positions had created enough stir in Corbin, that maybe, just maybe, a state championship was in the picture, if not this year, possibly next.

Anyone who ever played football in Corbin back in the 50s and 60s remembers when the local fire department would arrive at Campbell Field to hose down the field. "It would be so dry and dusty," Rodger remembered. "And sometimes they'd water it so much it was a mud bath. I think it cost us a game against Danville one year. The school must have had a contract with the city to water it down after four or five games every year."

In Rodger's junior year, though the 1960 Redhounds were expected to be good, even Coach Walt Green could not have predicted his team would run the table and he would see his club ranked number one in Kentucky.

Only two starters, Jesse Grant and Rodger Bird, returned from the previous year, but the Redhounds had enough depth that when it came time for those past reserves to step up, they did. C.S. Frederick, Arthur Morrison, Jim Taylor, O.B. Richardson and Ralph Hodge were anchors in the line, and E.R. Hopper at end joined underclassmen running backs, Bird and Barry Brooks. Senior quarterback Phil Henderlight looked like anything but a big, strapping Redhound football player, but all he did was win. He couldn't throw deep, but deep enough, and he wasn't fast, but he was fast enough.

"Rodger would run 50 yards deep for a pass and run back 45 yards to catch it," Henderlight said years later.

Rodger had come off a great sophomore year, and by now everyone who saw him play said he would be the equal of brothers Calvin and Billy.

Out of the gate the Hounds blanked Evarts 41-0, then Bell County 32-6, Pineville 26-0, Middlesboro 35-6, and Harlan threw up a scare, losing 18-6. Next came always-tough Somerset 34-0.

With a 6-0 record, London was blown out 72-13 as Rodger scored five touchdowns, and E.R. Hopper three. Henderlight threw for two and ran an interception back for another. Bird's came on runs of 57, 26, 70, 54 and one on a 55-yard interception.

London's Jim Handy has memories of two encounters he had with the Redhounds. "Carl Oakley was hired to start football in London in 1958, and he scheduled eight games against "B" teams and junior varsity players," recalled Handy. "One of those games was against Corbin. Rodger Bird scored first for Corbin and they missed the extra point. In the fourth quarter I scored on a 50 yard run in front of hundreds of screaming fans. Tanny Phelps, who later played at Louisville, kicked the extra point and we won 7-6. I was a sophomore and it was unbelievable."

Handy continues, "Coach Oakley left London after one year and Dave Fryrear took over. My senior year he scheduled mighty Corbin, I said, 'Coach they'll kill us,' and they did. I remember it like it was yesterday."

In spite of the 72-13 loss, Handy had a good game scoring in the second quarter on a 64-yard run, and then against Corbin subs in the last minute of the game. "Even after such humiliation, we felt some pride, after we were told that Corbin was disappointed we had scored against their first team. Our team had great respect for Corbin football," he said.

Williamsburg was the next to fall, 45-13, and then Cumberland 67-7. Danville, one of the Redhound's biggest rivals, was shut out 26-0, setting up the last game of the season.

Louisville Manual was all that stood in the way of an unbeaten season for the boys from Corbin. Before the game even started there was controversy. Manual Coach Tom Harper complained that only three referees had been assigned to officiate the game, instead of the customary four they used in Louisville. But at the time this was what all of the mountain schools did. This game was in Corbin.

Jack Dirkin from Lexington; Curt Selvy from Corbin, and the older brother of Frank; and Earl Hill from London were the officials, and they had their hands full in a game that had become a rivalry between two of the state's high school powerhouses. But Selvy now was a referee first and a Redhound second. He wasn't afraid to make a call that night against Corbin and did so when necessary. He spent a lifetime officiating ball games and took great pride in it.

With Campbell Field full to the brim, Corbin fans were lined up as close to the field as they could get. Later several sports writers wrote that Corbin's supporters went overboard in their harassment of Manual players.

When it was all over, Corbin had won 46-34. The final statistics were even more one-sided in the Redhounds favor. Corbin had 27 first downs to Manual's 12; 497 yards rushing to 183; and the Redhounds did not punt the ball one time during the entire game; and an even more double-take stat was only one pass attempt, a 22-yarder from Henderlight to Bird. The Redhound ground game was so impressive there was little need to put it in the air.

But it was Bird in this game against a team from Louisville that solidified his place as one of the all-time greats in Kentucky high school football. With touchdown runs of 11, 7, 21, 3 and 18, plus two extra points, he finished the season with a record setting point total for a junior of 212 points.

Barry Brooks, although not scoring, ripped off runs of 17, 33, 49, 26, 11, and over 200 rushing yards for the game.

There were many Corbin fans who thought that game played on November 11, 1960, was the greatest win in Corbin football history.

In spite of the success of finishing unbeaten, often being ranked number one throughout the season, and defeating two top teams, Somerset and Manual, Corbin did not receive a chance to play for the state title. Because of regional technical complications, the Redhounds were excluded from the state playoffs.

As great as Rodger Bird had been, Jesse Grant, who would often drive his 1953 grey Ford tractor to school, was every bit his equal as a lineman. Grant was not only the Southeastern Kentucky Conference Player of the Year, but also the top vote getter in the Louisville *Courier-Journal*'s All-State team and its honorary captain. Bird was named to second team backfield.

Coach Walt Green received his third Coach of the Year award, having previously won it at Pineville and Middlesboro. Eight Redhounds were named to the All-Conference team: Grant, Bird, Brooks, Sammy Harrell, Jerry Stewart, Jim Taylor, Joe Burton, and Scotty Russell.

As would be expected there was lots of hoopla. Mayor Dick Vermillion proclaimed a Redhound Day. The Redhound Booster Club sponsored a banquet at the Central Elementary School cafeteria. Blanton Collier came calling as the evening speaker. And he didn't come alone. In an effort to stretch his recruiting tentacles and keep the funnel open from Corbin to Lexington, he brought former Redhound stars who were now Kentucky Wildcats. Mel Chandler, Billy Bird, Fred Rader, and Keith Hutson were there. The mere presence of them in the room made a big statement to senior Jesse Grant and junior Rodger Bird. And then for a little more clout, Collier brought Wildcat stars Tommy Simpson, Tom Rodgers and Bob Butler. At some high school banquets it might have been overkill, but not in Corbin. Corbin was a Kentucky Wildcat town, and the more the merrier.

Corbin Times sports writer Jim Lee Crawford wrote in his column that "Collier gave an unusually fine speech." That night the Kentucky coach brought not only his A-team, but also his A-game.

Grant went on to U.K. where he was a member of the infamous Thin Thirty team in 1962. He left the squad in 1963, and never played again.

Before the program concluded, Bird and Brooks were named football captains for the following year.

Before the season began, the 1961 Redhound football program underwent a major head coaching change. Walt Green departed for Hazard, and former Redhound Carl Oakley, who had been an assistant, took over a team that had had one of the most successful seasons in Corbin history. Green however, didn't do Oakley any favors with the schedule, and maybe that's why he left. With perennial powers Manual,

Danville and Somerset always there, two of the previous year's state champions were added, Male, the AAA titlist, and Lynch, Class A winner.

The season got underway in an unusual six team football exhibition extravaganza on the campus of Eastern Kentucky University at Hanger Field. While Danville faced Mt. Sterling and Somerset went up against Shelbyville, Corbin was paired with Madison High, the team from Richmond.

Even though the games didn't count as "real" games, all of the teams, nevertheless, were playing for pride in the 30-minute sessions. Former Redhound star Roy Kidd was coaching against his former teammate, Carl Oakley, for the first time, and Kidd's team won 7-0. Talbott Todd, a future Bird teammate at U.K. was Madison's star player.

Corbin went on the road for their 1961 season opener and blanked Evarts 28-0 behind two TD's each by Bird and Joe Gambrell, and the quarterbacking of Jimmy "Cas" Walker.

The Hounds then measured Bell County 39-7 on the road, before losing 21-7 to Louisville Male. The Hounds jumped out on a Bird touchdown and Brooks' kick to lead 7-0. But that was it, as Male came back with three scores.

Middlesboro was thumped 59-0 the following week, as Rodger ran for four TD's and threw for one to Luther New. Johnny Scalf and Brooks each scored, as did center Russ Willis when he fell on a fumble in the end zone. Then came a 25-0 shutout over Harlan. Rodger Bird did everything but score as he averaged almost nine yards per carry in registering 123 yards.

Next came a 14-12 win over Somerset, and then a 13-0 win over Lynch. In both games Rodger scored a pair of TD's.

Rodger nailed down three more touchdowns in a 40-6 win over Williamsburg, but in an 18-6 victory over Cumberland the following week he failed to score for only the second time that season. Barry Brooks accounted for two of the scores while Scalf added the other. It was a game Gambrell will never forget.

"They tackled Rodger on every play, whether he had the ball or not," he said. "It was total harassment. Then on the second half kick-off, Rodger took the ball and ran over the tackler that had been hounding him, totally flattening him, and it put him out of the game."

At 8-1, the win clinched a district title for the Redhounds in Class AA play, but with it came a problem. Corbin's regular season schedule showed a game in Louisville against Manual. That same night, though, the playoff schedule called for Corbin to host the winner of District 2, Hazard.

The only thing for Corbin to do would be to forfeit to Manual and pay a $500 fee. However, it would still leave Manual without a game unless they could find another opponent. They did, and a Corbin forfeit was not necessary.

A good Danville team came to Corbin, and for the first time since 1957 shut the Hounds out with a 6-0 win. Years later Barry Brooks recalled that night. "The fire department over watered the field," he said, "And then it started to rain on top of that. It turned out to be a mud bowl."

Corbin had advanced in the Kentucky High School Athletic Association's first Class Playoff Championships in hosting the 10-0 Hazard Bulldogs. The winner would move on to play unbeaten Ft. Thomas Highlands.

Hazard and Corbin have quite a football history throughout the years, dating back to 1931. Though the Redhounds had won eight of the previous 12 games, it was a game played way back in 1938 that caused the two teams to quit playing each other for years.

Back then Hazard's Coach, Pat Payne, upset by Corbin's efforts to run out the clock near the end of the first half, loaded his team on the bus at halftime and headed home, thus losing 1-0 on a forfeit.

Here's how it was reported in the local newspaper.

> *In 1931, with Corbin leading 7-0 and Hazard with a first down at the Redhound one-yard line only 15 seconds remained. That's when the Corbin trickery began. Deliberately drawing five straight penalties, three for illegal substitutions, and two off sides. Hazard got off a last play from the six-inch line, but was stopped as time expired. Coach Payne thought his team should have had one more play and accused Corbin's Coach Ted Meadors of un-sportsmanship. It just so happened that referee Clarence "Ossie" Burch, who later coached at Corbin and later was a business partner of Meadors, said the last play was free of any infractions and the half was over.*

With that bit of history behind them, in 1949 Ossie Burch coached the Redhounds to a 54-0 win over Hazard with Carl Oakley kicking six extra points that night.

And now here it was 1961, and another sidebar to the pre-game discussion was that Hazard's assistant coach was none other than former Hound's coach Walt Green. He took the Hazard job with the understanding he would become the Bulldog head man the following year. Posters with Green's picture were tacked up around Corbin a few days before the game, and when Hazard took the field, the Corbin crowd serenaded Green with "Hang Down Your Head Walt Green."

In spite of tickets being priced at an almost unheard of price of $2 to $2.50, some 3,700 fans showed up to see Hazard end Corbin's year with an 18-6 win. "Hazard ran a single wing offense," recalled Gambrell. "It was the first time any of us had ever played against it."

Bird had a six yard touchdown run to close out his high school career. An 8-3 finish hadn't been what Coach Carl Oakley had hoped for, nor was it the way the last of the fabulous Bird brothers wanted to walk away from Campbell Field. A four year career record of 46-9-1 showed just how dominant Bird's Corbin team had been, however.

Jim "Beanie" Taylor was a star on the team, but it's an incident at practice he has memories of. "I was in the huddle laughing," he recalled and Coach Oakley ran over and threw me on the ground. 'Pay attention, he said,' And I did from then on. It was the hardest lick I got all year."

Halfback Joe Gambrell was use to competition. Growing up the youngest of thirteen kids, he had to battle for playing time. "We had some great backs, and I was just glad to play on some great teams," he said.

Rodger, like Calvin and Billy before him, was named to every all-state team from one end of Kentucky to the other, and Sporting News named the boy from Corbin to its National High School All-America Team. It was a given that once again Rodger and most of his Redhound teammates received recognition to the All Conference team.

If you played football at Corbin there's a good chance you also played basketball. And true to form, Rodger had a basketball season left before he was finished.

With so much hoopla created over the Bird brothers' accomplishments, reporters were always looking for a new angle to write about them. One writer asked Bonnie Bird, their mother, about her boys.

"We didn't intend to raise any football players, but when the boys took an interest, we gave them encouragement," she said, seeming to forget the threat her husband had made to Jerry years before if he even thought about playing football.

She went on to say, using their middle names, that "Rodger Paul was probably the best all-around, but then maybe it might be Billy Morris, yes, it might be him." Her uncertainty about it all might be forgiven, because that's exactly how anyone who ever saw a Bird play felt. Ask four different people and you get four different Birds.

College Bound

Initially Rodger had no intentions of going to U.K. In fact there was a point in his earlier years he wasn't even sure about college. Those thoughts quickly changed when he came to his senses and realized that if he was to reach his then long range ambition of working for the Kentucky Fish and Wildlife Department, he needed an education.

There had been a rift between brother Calvin and Collier at U.K. and Rodger was even quoted by several reporters then as saying, "As long as Collier is head coach at Kentucky, I'll never go to school there." A few weeks later Collier was fired and the last three years of his contract were bought out. Some thought, and with good reason, that Bird's statement helped drive the final nail in Collier's coffin.

Rodger Bird was on every football school's "wanted" list. Paul Dietzel at LSU and Bobby Dodd at Georgia Tech were hot after the boy from Corbin. Alabama's Bear Bryant and UT's Bowden Wyatt were trying to do with Rodger what they couldn't do earlier with Calvin—sign him. But now there were two other schools that were in the recruiting mix, Johnny Vaught at Ole Miss, and Bill Yeoman at Houston.

"Coach Bryant told me he could have made Calvin a two time All-American and that he'd do the same for me," Rodger said. "I thought he probably tells that to everybody."

"I asked him if Alabama would ever play Kentucky. 'I don't think so. Their stadium is small, and they wouldn't draw flies here.'"

In talking to Bear, Rodger thought about those suits that his brother Jerry had that once belonged to the legendary Alabama coach. "Jerry had some of those hanging at home and I'd go in the closet just to look at 'em. Inside the coat it said "Made especially for Paul 'Bear' Bryant."

The University of Tennessee never seemed to give up in recruiting a Bird. Their coaches knew the family well. "My junior year at Corbin, Bowden Wyatt invited me, mom and dad up to Lexington to have the pre-game meal with the Tennessee team at the Campbell House before they played Kentucky," Rodger said.

It was no secret of Rodger's love for hunting and he says Tennessee was all over it. "When I went to Knoxville for my visit, they took me hunting. We hunted all night with spotlights," he said. "Back then the football players lived in the stadium and the conditions weren't very good. They offered me an apartment and car. Good summer jobs, though, were their big recruiting tool, plus I would get some season tickets to sell."

"When they came up to Corbin, they brought four or five coaches in a limo that was bigger than our house, and that's the truth," he added.

Rodger's thoughts were playing tricks on him. Early on, before Collier had been fired, he had even told Ole Miss assistant coach Jim Cain that he was going to be a Rebel. There had been some validity to Rodger verbally committing to Ole Miss.

"I told Coach Cain I'd sign with him if he could get David Wells of Madisonville to go there. Wells and I were buddies. But that pressure to sign with Kentucky sure was rough." Bird said.

Like many other 17 year-old youngsters, he just wasn't sure. Heck, he wasn't sure about a lot of things in life. The pressure began to mount, and pretty soon it became an avalanche. He heard from U.K. alums all over the state. Most of all, however, he heard from his friends in Corbin. But what about his own brothers? What had they said?

Calvin told me I should go to Tennessee, but that was while Coach Collier was still there," Rodger said.

In the meantime Kentucky had hired an Alabama assistant coach, 38-year-old Charlie Bradshaw. On the surface he looked like a great hire. He had played for Bryant at Kentucky in the late 40s, and then became a member of his coaching staff. For sure Bryant's methods and ways were deeply entrenched in Bradshaw, a former Marine. If Bear Bryant ever had a disciple it was Kentucky's new coach. So, with the hiring of Bradshaw, it didn't take long before Rodger Bird, like all of the Birds before him, to become a Wildcat.

"Sure enough, a few days after I signed with Kentucky, Wells signed with Ole Miss. I felt a little bad about all that," he said years later.

Even after he had signed with U.K., Rodger still visited a few schools outside of the SEC. As long as it was a non-conference school, he could visit and even sign, and still be within the NCAA rules.

In Corbin, however, in June 1962, it was no secret that Bird was planning to visit Houston. It seemed, however, that everyone was still recruiting for U.K., even two of the town's medical doctors and a local druggist put their two cents into trying to persuade him not to make the Houston trip. Nevertheless, he went to Texas to satisfy himself and to see what their program was all about.

Houston sports columnist Zane Chastain wrote that "Rodger Bird likes Houston and is attracted by the challenge of helping the Cougars in their struggle to regain heights as a football power. Still, the big thing he likes is local opportunity. Only time will tell if he will turn out to be a kid who makes his own decisions, or is pushed into a situation he'll never enjoy. Chances are 50-50 the Cougars will wind up with a "Bird in the hand.'"

Regardless of what was being written or said about where the boy from Corbin might be going to college, no decision would be made without talking to his mom and dad. After all, Rodger and his parents had already inked the papers on a grant-in-aid scholarship at U.K., and the bottom line is that's where he would be playing his football.

But just when Rodger should have been enjoying life, his world was rocked with news that brother Billy had left the Kentucky football team. He had completed a relatively good sophomore year under Collier, but with the arrival of Bradshaw, football life in Lexington began to change. When Collier departed he left a team of 88 players that eventually dwindled to 26, and Billy had been among the ones to leave.

Although grades were said to be part of the problem, it was widely known that Bradshaw's prison camp style spring practices were indeed intended to send those who didn't like it packing. Billy Bird was not the only one who left that spring, there were multitudes.

"I came home after track practice and mom was crying," recalled Rodger. "She said Billy had quit the team at U.K. I didn't have a car, so I went down to the Lunch Queen—ran into Corbin teammate Ralph Hodge, and asked him if he wanted to go to Lexington with me to see Billy. Someone from Catron Motors took us out to the highway where we started hitchhiking. The second car that came by picked us up."

Rodger had to see Billy, had to talk to him face to face. He was confused all of a sudden. Wondering if he had made the right decision to sign with U.K., he had to get to Lexington as soon as he could to talk to his brother.

"When we got there we were dropped off about three miles from the campus. It was raining and Ralph and I ran all the way," he said. "We went to Wildcat Manor (football varsity dorm), and Kitten Lodge (freshman dorm) looking for him. Someone told us he had moved across the street to the Sigma Chi House.

"It was never about Billy not being tough enough," offered Rodger. "He was entering his junior year and Bradshaw demoted most of those guys behind the incoming sophomores. A newspaper release announcing Billy's departure said he was running fourth string. Billy was embarrassed."

Dale Lindsey transferred to Western where he was one of the top players on the school's 1963 Tangerine Bowl champs. Lindsey later played almost ten years as a linebacker for the Cleveland Browns, and went on to coach in the NFL; John Mutchler survived Bradshaw's Thin Thirty days, and then became a part of the championship team at Western; Phil Branson left and went to South Carolina, where he was the team's leading rusher in 1964; Clyde Richardson, a center, was a Thin Thirty member, but the next year decided he had enough of football.

Anyone who was smart enough to know that U.K. was located in Lexington was also wondering if Billy Bird's exit from the Wildcat football team would cause his younger brother to back out of his commitment to Kentucky. "Everyone was asking me if I was still going to U.K." recalled Rodger. "I really thought about it all, thought about Indiana and Houston, but then I decided to stay with U.K."

Years later Rodger brought up another reason he went with the Wildcats.

"I could hitchhike to Lexington in two hours. I didn't have a car, and if I went to Alabama or Ole Miss or Houston, I'm not sure how I would have gotten back and forth to Corbin. Lexington was easy."

Rodger was part of a freshman recruiting class that was hailed as the best crop of talent to ever come from throughout the state to U.K. There was quarterback Rick Norton, Louisville Flaget; Sam Ball, a tackle from Henderson; end Rick Kestner from Stone; Talbott Todd, a quarterback from Richmond; Mike McGraw, a fullback from Ft. Thomas; end Ed Smith from Pineville; lineman Jim Miles from Finley; Basil Mullins, a tackle from Paintsville; and Homer Goins a halfback from Evarts. In all, the 40-player freshmen class included 14 who had been named to various high school All-American teams and 23 who were all-staters.

Kitten Lodge is where the entire Wildcat freshman spent most of their time when not in the classroom or on the football field. It's where they slept, ate and studied in a room off of the main floor dining room. Like any group that lived and played together almost twenty-four hours a day, there had to be some organization to it all. So officers were elected. Teammates elected Norton president, Bird vice-president and Todd secretary-treasurer. If any of the house rules needed to be addressed, this is where it started.

Next door to Kitten Lodge was Wildcat Manor, where the varsity footballers lived. An invitation to a freshman to visit Wildcat Manor usually meant being called to appear before "Kangaroo Court," a mock set up that had become a tradition, or an excuse for upper classmen to harass the freshmen, verbally and occasionally physically with paddling. Though the coaching staff more often than not turned a deaf ear to the "unofficial" goings on, they were aware of it, as it had become a part of Kentucky's tradition, as well as of virtually every football program in America.

Although Kitten Lodge and Wildcat Manor each had a supervising "house mother" who lived on the premises, mischief still happened. It sometime included the freshmen, in the middle of the night, carrying a VW automobile, through the double-wide front door of Wildcat Manor and depositing it in the foyer, or even bringing in livestock. Kangaroo Court was usually pay back time for such shenanigans.

When things got out of hand, coaches would send word to tone it down. "Clarkie Mayfield was really hard on me with the paddle," recalled Rodger. "He told me he was making up for what Calvin did to him when he was a freshman."

Mayfield's career touched both Calvin's and Rodger's, and as good a pressure kicker ever at U.K., his life was a footnote to football history.

Mayfield, in 1974, became the head football coach at Jacksonville State, a Division II college in Alabama. In the spring of 1977, Clarkie had traveled to northern Kentucky for a retirement celebration honoring his mother, Ona Mae, at the Beverly Hills Supper Club. Many recall that on May 28, a fire roared through the 65,000-square foot Campbell County venue, killing 165 people, including Clarkie. Initially he had gotten out, but went back to help others in his group. Mark Story of the *Lexington Herald-Leader* wrote a heart-felt account of the tragedy, and of Mayfield's time at U.K. playing for Bradshaw.

Jerry Woolum told Story, "I can't tell you why—I can't tell you why Bradshaw did most anything he did—but he hated kickers, and Clarkie was our kicker."

Dave Gash, a teammate, said, "At practice Bradshaw would pick Clarkie out as a tackling dummy, where people would run over him. He would pick him out to demonstrate on him. He would run him, criticize him, anything to run him off." Mayfield stayed.

After signing with Blanton Collier, Mayfield came to U.K. as a 200-pound half back, but after one year of Bradshaw he was down to 162. Story wrote that Bradshaw even told Clarkie if he'd leave he'd help him pack his bags. "Clarkie actually went to Bradshaw, Gash said, and told him 'Coach I know you are trying to run me off, but I'm not leaving.'"

The fun-loving, high spirited Clarkie Mayfield hung in there. Knowing he didn't have the speed to be a SEC running back, he was content to just be a kicker. In 1960 his field goal produced a 3-0 win over LSU. Then in 1962, with twenty seconds left and U.T. leading the Wildcats 10-9, Charlie Bradshaw summoned the boy from Harlan County one more time. Clarkie's 26-yarder gave U.K. a 12-10 win. For the Thin Thirty it gave them a 3-5-2 finish.

For the record, Mayfield and Bradshaw actually became friends later in life when Bradshaw became the football coach at Troy in Alabama.

In 1962, the Kittens played a three game schedule under Coach Dave Hart, defeating Vanderbilt 42-28, Cincinnati 37-20, and tying Tennessee 10-10. The Baby Vols had previously won four straight over the Kittens. Bird missed the game with a shoulder injury, but for the season, he had still produced 92 yards on twenty-one carries and four touchdowns.

Kentucky coaches were elated. The Kittens had lived up to their hype and Bird, Norton, Kestner and Ball appeared headed for stardom. Kentucky's football future looked very bright. The media was even calling it a return to Babe Parilli days.

By the time the annual Blue-White spring game rolled around in April 1963, the varsity roster was down to 42 players of which 28 were incoming sophomores.

Already 12 of Rodger's Kitten teammates had departed. With only 16 upperclassmen left over from the rag-tag Thin Thirty team from the year before, it would be up to sophomores to carry much of the load.

In scrimmages and contact drills, as a freshman against the varsity, Bird had quickly earned a reputation as a "hitter," and his all-around skills had labeled him even more than a triple threat football player.

"As football goes, it was fun," Bird recalled. "But there was a lot of unnecessary crap that went on with the way coaches treated you on the practice field. I think I made my first impression when Bob Ford (assistant coach) grabbed me and threw me into a drill against Tommy Simpson, an end. He was a senior and tough. I hit him and got around him because of my quickness. I was never on a second team again. The reputation was I'd hit you."

Bradshaw also talked to the press about Bird, "He has a real fine attitude. He's willing to work and he's coachable. He's ambitious, catches the ball well, and he's a fine kicker."

In the annual spring game Rodger delivered 60 yards on 11 carries and threw a 16 yard pass to Norton in leading his Blue team to a 14-9 win over the Whites.

When picture day rolled around, the Wildcat varsity showed 42 players in uniform, and a coaching staff of eleven that included Bradshaw, Ralph Hawkins, George Sengel, Jim Carmody, Dave Hart, Bud Moore, Matt Lair, Homer Rice, George Boone, Bill Jasper, and Ray Callahan.

For coaches Jasper and Callahan, the Bird name was familiar. Jasper had coached the Morristown, Tennessee team to a 54-0 win over the Moon Conde coached Corbin team in 1953, and then at Louisville Manual for several years, and Callahan had been a successful coach at Danville, annually playing Redhound teams.

Bradshaw, even as his squad numbers began to dwindle, felt like he was keeping those who wanted to be involved in the making of a national championship team. He told the University of Kentucky Alumni Association at a luncheon in Louisville just prior to the first game, "Our aspiration is to have a national champion at U.K. in the next three years."

Are You Ready For Football?

It didn't take long for the boy from Corbin to make the most sensational debut in Wildcat history in the season opener against Virginia Tech on Stoll Field. Standing in his own end zone waiting to receive the opening kick-off, Rodger Bird was prepared to touch the ball for the first time in his varsity career. Perhaps he had a flashback of chasing those rabbits that had escaped from the cage Calvin had built for him when they were young kids. "I raised a few chickens and rabbits," says Rodger. "And those rabbits were out of the cage more than they were in it."

Boom, the game was underway. Bird gathered the ball in at the eight yard line, All-SEC tackle Herschel Turner threw a big block at the 30, and then Bobby Kosid landed another, and Rodger was gone. The play took all of 14 seconds for the Corbin Comet to race 92 yards for a touchdown.

Years later Rodger explained the rabbits. "Those rabbits would never run in a straight line," he said. "It was right, left, right, and back to the left. That's how I once described my running style to someone, right, left, right."

Suddenly Charlie Bradshaw looked like a coaching genius. Several media experts had questioned Bird's presence in the starting lineup ahead of veteran Darrell Cox, but in a matter of seconds it was all forgotten. When Bird had finished, Kentucky had won 33-14. He had carried the ball 19 times for 157 yards and scored another TD. Norton failed to complete a pass. Todd, off the bench, completed the Wildcats' only pass near the end of the game.

Ironically, Kentucky's last opening game win came in 1958 with a 51-0 rout of Hawaii, when Calvin Bird scored a school record 25 points in his debut back then.

But even with all of the anticipation of success on the gridiron, nothing was a sure thing. Bradshaw was relatively new to this head coaching thing, and his own doings, especially those practice sessions, began to once again take its toll.

The 1963 *U.K. Football Press Guide* had been dedicated to Giles Smith, an end who had played at Lexington Lafayette before coming to play at Kentucky. The previous April, Smith had been injured during practice from a blow to the head. On the brink of death, emergency cranial surgery was performed to correct bleeding from a laceration of the brain stem. What caused it was never determined by doctors. It said Smith had received no hard blow to the head according to the coaching staff. A second operation followed in which Smith lapsed into a coma for several days. He never played the game again, but did serve as team manager the following year.

Questions begged to be answered about the incident. When was there ever a Bradshaw practice that no one received a hard blow to the head? Forearm shivers to a helmet and slaps to the face area were common occurrences. And this was from the coaches. Smith's injury was the first of several serious mishaps that took place under the watchful eyes of U.K. coaches. Later, Cecil New, a lineman, was critically injured during practice, and end Greg Page from Middlesboro died as a result of a blocking drill referred to as Bull in the Ring.

Kentucky coaches with bull horns and whistles were perched on watch towers high above the fray, looking for anything and everything that could help turn the Wildcat program into national champs. A coach descending from the tower's platform two steps at a time, sprinting across the field to waylay a unsuspecting player, was a common occurrence.

After the opening game win over Virginia Tech, the Wildcats returned to earth the next week with a thud, falling to Ole Miss 31-7. Then came a 14-13 squeaker loss at Auburn.

The Wildcats were a heavy favorite the following week over non-conference Detroit, but at Kentucky nothing could be taken for granted. The team was only one year removed from suffering perhaps the worst upset in Wildcat history when they fell to Xavier 14-9. That loss was followed by a Sunday morning practice that had included the current crop of sophomores. No one wanted a repeat. Kentucky won 35-18, but Bird limped off the field early with an ankle injury.

Next came back-to-back SEC losses to LSU 28-7 and Georgia 17-14. Then non-conference Miami (Florida) came to Lexington and won 20-14. The Cats self-destructed with four fumbles. The Hurricanes were led by future NFL stars quarterback George Mira and running back Pete Banaszak. Cox's 53-yard run and Bird's 26-yarder accounted for both Wildcat scores. Following the loss to Miami, Bradshaw said his biggest disappointment was the four fumbles. "I'm extremely disappointed for our kids," he said.

Winless Vanderbilt was next, and though the game was played in Nashville, Kentucky, at 2 and 5, was still the favorite. In front of some 18,000 homecoming fans the Commodores slammed the door shut on the Wildcats by recovering two timely fumbles and gained a 0-0 tie. "This is the next thing to winning," said a jubilant Jack Green, the Vandy coach.

It's never a good thing when a team has to punt nine times, but that's what the Wildcats had to do. If one good thing popped up, it was Bird's punting. He averaged 45.7 yards on those nine kicks.

No one in their right mind wanted to be on the plane trip back to Lexington. Once in the air, Bradshaw slowly walked from his seat back down the aisle telling his dejected team, "We'll be in uniform and in our seats at the Sports Center (practice facility) tomorrow morning at 5 o'clock. Lights will be out tonight at 9:30 p.m."

The plane landed in Lexington at 9:15 p.m. A 4:30 a.m. Sunday morning wake-up, sent them scurrying to the Sports Center where not a single light was on. Finding their equipment scattered on the floor, it took matches and cigarette lighters to provide enough light for the team to hurriedly find their uniforms, get dressed and take a seat in the meeting room by 5 o'clock. Sitting in the dark, Herschel Turner cracked a joke, and just as the laughter subsided, the lights were flipped on. There stood Bradshaw.

A five minute warm-up preceded a complete live action replay of the Vandy game, beginning with the opening kick-off. Two hours later a whistle blew, and most of the players thought practice was over as they gathered around Bradshaw, only to learn there would be one hour of running offense, and another hour for defense. Once that was concluded, they again gathered around their coach. They weren't done yet, he told them. Another hour of punt coverage would be added for laughing at Turner's joke in the dark locker room hours earlier. A five hour practice, the Sunday morning following a Saturday tie, had left them physically drained.

The morning had produced several fights among teammates that were only interrupted by Bradshaw telling them to remove their helmets and go at it.

Smiling faces were absent as the Wildcats headed to Waco, Texas, to take on Baylor. With a traveling squad of only 39, and facing the 5-2 Bears, led by quarterback Don Trull and receiver Lawrence Elkins, this would not be a game the Wildcats were expected to win. But win they did.

With Sugar and Gator Bowl scouts among the 18,000 Baylor fans, the Wildcats used a pair of key pass interceptions by Cox and Bird to leave the Lone Star State with a 19-7 win. Kestner was a target for quarterback Norton most of the game, with one covering 73 yards. And Cox's interception was for 42 yards and a TD. Cox had 62 yards receiving, and end Bill Jenkins another 27. The loss to Kentucky doomed Baylor's hopes for a bowl bid.

A picture the next day in the Lexington newspaper showed Bradshaw wearing a ten gallon Texas hat, being hoisted in the air by Jenkins in the locker room, as teammates cheered and toasted with soft drinks. What a difference a week makes!

Perhaps a season ending win over Tennessee could salvage a disastrous season and begin an upward spiral going into next year on their way to the national championship Bradshaw had predicted by 1965.

The temperature was just above freezing when the Vols rolled into Lexington and turned the ice cold Wildcats into a 19-0 win for the Volunteers. The season was over. At 3-6-1 there was much work to be done.

By the time the next spring rolled around, expectations were once again high for football at U.K. With 35 freshmen moving up to varsity, it looked like Bradshaw had put together two of the best back-to-back recruiting years in school history. However, the exodus of players continued.

There was very little fanfare when the *Courier-Journal* reported that "halfback Steve Mott, the first negro to try out for the University of Kentucky football team, has quit the squad." And then in an apparent typo it said, "Smith, a transfer student from Detroit, had practiced two weeks."

Rosters for the annual Blue-White spring game showed 36 sophomores, 16 juniors, and five seniors. As good as the Bird, Norton, Kestner and Ball group had been, the real buzz was about a prized running back and a super-sized tackle.

Frank Antonini, at 6'0", 207-pounds, had broken virtually every Kitten record in leading them to a 4-0 record that included a 70-0 win over UT's Baby Vols in which he ran for six touchdowns. He was so outstanding that when *Playboy Magazine* featured their annual All-American team, Antonini was recognized as the National Freshman of the Year.

Maurice "Moe" Moorman was on everybody's prep All-America team at Louisville St. X, and at 6'4", 246-pounds, he was far and away Kentucky's biggest lineman. To say he was a handful as a freshman in scrimmages against the varsity would be an understatement. His speed, quickness, and desire made him a can't miss collegiate All-American. And he was, albeit, at another school—Texas A & M, after he soon transferred from Kentucky.

Gil Brandt, a scout for the Dallas Cowboys was a regular every spring to see who the hot prospects were for the NFL. He liked what he saw at Kentucky. "That Bird is the complete football player," said Brandt. "He can play for the pros as a ball carrier or a defensive back. He has great balance."

Future Wildcat star and NFL pro Larry Seiple had also turned in a great Kitten season the year before, and the rising of his star was a pleasant surprise. In front of 9,000 fans, the supposedly high-powered offensive minded Kentucky Blue-White teams slow-poked their way to an 8-2 win for the Blues. Bird and Antonini sat out much of the game with minor injuries.

Like many college students at the time, Rodger's personal finances were dire. Though he had joined Pi Kappa Alpha fraternity, money wasn't there, but he still found enough to live a college life. "Governor Happy Chandler paid for my fraternity dues. He wanted me to be a Pike," Rodger says. "I got $30 a month from R.O.T.C., $30 a month for laundry from U.K., I got a few tickets to sell, and $5 from my mom."

And Rodger was in the same boat as several of his teammates when it came to transportation. "There were quite a few of us without cars," he said. "Finally, I bought one from my brother-in-law for $300."

Rodger's Junior Year

It only took one day for Charlie Bradshaw to become out of sorts with his 1964 team. After the opening day of practice he told *Lexington Herald* sports editor Billy Thompson, "It looked like a typical Kentucky football team. The boys get a little hot, get cotton in their mouths and they just won't fight it off. This has been symbolic of Kentucky teams for the past seven or eight years. But they will be in condition. I have faith in these boys, and I know they will quickly get into shape."

Bradshaw, in an unusual player's poll, asked his team, "At this stage, if you could boost one U.K. player for All-American, who would it be?" Twenty-nine of forty-eight players wrote down "Bird."

Rodger Bird had played two years under Bradshaw, and had gone through a lot. Although he was a star, it didn't mean he liked what was going on around him. He had seen teammates that were friends leave during the middle of the night. Several had been injured; others decided they just didn't want to play football anymore. The game was no longer a game; it wasn't fun.

He could not help but think back to when he was a third grader in Corbin. It was then he knew he wanted to be a football player in the local little league. "I wasn't very good at first," he said. "They used to kid me about playing only fifteen seconds a game."

He reflected on the times he would go back to Corbin to visit, and the whole town saw him as one of their sports heroes, and how everyone wanted to ask about the Wildcats. He recalled on those trips back home how he and neighbor Jerry "Smiley" Martin would toss a football around, just having fun like they did in high school.

And here he was now, ready to play his junior year. He had done everything so well he was rarely on the sidelines. As a sophomore he had delivered 85 carries, 382 yards for a 4.4 average, and two TDs. Who would ever forget the first time he touched the ball? He had been labeled everything: Corbin Comet, Rodger the Dodger, Decathlon Man, A Rare Bird, Indeed. And he was already being promoted as the school's first pure All-American halfback.

Still he had thoughts running through his head and they weren't about the upcoming season.

"I thought about quitting at least 100 times, but I was an exception," he said. "It was a hell of a lot harder to stay than leave. At Kentucky we had to prove ourselves every day; there was no let up."

As the Wildcats prepared for their 1964 season opener against Detroit, a team picture in the *Lexington Herald* showed fifty-nine players in uniform.

Preseason ratings had the Cats as high as 20th by *Look Magazine* and as low as 11th in the SEC. Bradshaw, himself, loudly proclaimed "10 or More in '64." But a one-year bowl ban handed down by the NCAA would make that goal impossible. The suspensions came as a result of illegal team practices during certain times of the year. Apparently someone had reported some of those extracurricular indoor sessions that took place in the presence of only the coaches and players.

It wasn't pretty, but it was a 13-6 win over a 22-point underdog Detroit team. Five fumble recoveries kept the Titans in the game, as Bird scored both Wildcat touchdowns.

Heading to Ole Miss and an encounter with the number one ranked team in the nation, Kentucky was a 19-point underdog. A win, or even a competitive game, could go a long way in healing lots of wounds. The school newspaper was once again questioning not just the way Bradshaw conducted his program, but the value of "big time" football in general.

In a game that stunned the college football world, Kentucky defeated Ole Miss 27-21 in Jackson, MS. Rick Kestner had a career game. Three touchdown catches of 32, 60, and 22, from Norton finally showed what could happen. In all, Kestner had nine catches for 175 yards; and Norton threw for 273 yards completing 15 of 31. Bird had run for 69 yards on 12 carries.

In the dressing room following the game, Bradshaw yelled to his team, "Let me ask you…is it worth it?" "Yes, sir," they said in unison.

When the Wildcats landed at Lexington's Bluegrass Field later that night, a crowd estimated at nearly 20,000 was there to greet them. First off the place was Bradshaw, carrying the game ball. Then came team captains Bill Jenkins and Jim Foley, followed by Rodger Bird. All were wearing their dark colored blazers with a U.K. crest on the left side.

The Wildcats couldn't rest long because Auburn was coming to town, and a win at home would add ever more credibility to Bradshaw's prediction of a national title for the Wildcats.

"National ranking here we come" was the battle cry after the Cats disposed of Auburn 20-0 for its second major upset in a row. With it came a number seven national ranking in one poll and number five in another. It marked the first time in thirteen years a Kentucky football team had appeared in the top ten.

Rodger had two TDs, one on a 95-yard pass interception. It was the longest touchdown at U.K. since Bob Davis returned an interception 97 yards in 1937.

Even with the national success for the 3 and 0 Wildcats, still the *Kentucky Kernel*, took Bradshaw's "Is it worth it?" question to task. In part, the paper's editorial asked:

> *"Is this victory worth the heartbreak and anguish suffered by those who found 'total football' too much to endure?*
>
> *"Is it worth the loss of numerous fine athletes who might have profited by attending this university and who might have established proud records as alumni?*
>
> *"Is it worth the embarrassment of censure by the NCAA?*
>
> *"Is it worth not utilizing the talents of Negro athletes in order to be able to play Ole Miss?"*

A trip to Florida State, however, brought every Kentucky football fan in the nation back down to earth as the Seminoles, behind quarterback Steve Tensi and future Hall of Famer Fred Biletnikoff, blistered the Wildcat defense 48-6.

At the time, it was the worst defeat Kentucky had suffered since Alabama won 60-19 in 1945 in a game played in Louisville. A two yard TD run by Frank Antonini was Kentucky's only score. It was a fitting end to a trip to Tallahassee when Florida Highway Patrol's escort car, while leading a Kentucky motorcade from the stadium to the airport, ran out of gas.

Antonini was a gifted runner who eventually left the program, transferring to NAIA Parsons College. Bill Jenkins, years later, had his take on Antonini's departure. "Bradshaw thought you had to treat everybody the same," he said. "What he didn't realize was that you can't do that. Rodger Bird was like a mule. He'd give you a hundred percent every day whether you berated him or not. But Frank was like a thoroughbred. He had to be pampered, told how good he was…that sort of thing. Bradshaw didn't, and he left."

Mighty LSU was now coming to Lexington with a chance for the Cats to get back on track. Bird had suffered a rib injury early in the second half at Florida State, and had been questionable for the Tigers.

However, it didn't take the 38,000 fans long to see that Bird was ready to play. On the first play from scrimmage he took a Norton pitch and raced 76-yards to put Kentucky on top. The game was only 45 seconds old and for Kentucky that was it for the night, as LSU won 27-7.

It didn't get any better the following week as Georgia won 21-7, handing the Wildcats their third straight loss. Bird had the U.K.'s only score on a pass from Norton.

Loss number four came against non-conference West Virginia by a 26-21 margin. Norton opened with a scoring strike to Bill Jenkins that was the Elizabethtown native's first score of the season. Norton threw two more TD passes before he was finished, one to Dan Spanish and the other to Bird.

The loss gave Kentucky the dubious distinction of having the longest losing streak in the SEC.

What had begun so good had now turned so terribly bad for the 3-4 team. With Vandy visiting for homecoming, though, the Wildcats would have a chance to make amends for last season's 0-0 tie. Even though it was a day when all of the alums came back to Lexington, a crowd of only 32,000 was on hand for a nail-biting 22-21 Kentucky win. The Wildcats were 4-4 with two to play.

Bradshaw was very good at giving sound bites to champion his philosophy of winning football. "There's no mystery in it," he would say. "There's only one kind of football. Total football. It's not a game for the faint-hearted. In football you don't compromise with yourself."

Southwest Conference Baylor came to Kentucky with revenge on its mind. They got it with a 17-15 win. It was the season finale at home as Bird scored both Wildcat TDs on runs of 33 and one. A crowd of 28,000 was listed, but several reporters said the real number of fans in attendance was much smaller than that.

The bottom had completely fallen out of a Wildcat team with so much early promise. Remembering the "10 or More In '64" slogan from Bradshaw, fans were beginning to wonder if he could indeed improve on what Collier hadn't done, and that is get the Cats in a bowl game. Bradshaw, for sure, had the pressure on him as he headed to Knoxville to play U.T. A win would at least give him a break-even season, and a loss, well…it was unthinkable.

It was almost unthinkable as Kentucky won 12-7. Bird scored the Wildcats first TD from three yards out, but it was Rick Kestner's 32 yard touchdown catch that sealed the deal. Kestner had 112 yards and Bird's 45 yards made him the top Wildcat ground gainer in history.

Individually Bird, Kestner and Norton had great years. Rodger had 133 carries for 671 yards, which broke Bobby Cravens' 1957 Wildcat rushing record. He did it all. He had run, passed, caught, punted and played defense. Because of it, he had punched his way into the U.K. record books with one year remaining. He was a complete player. Even though slowed by rib and foot injuries, he still managed to make many of the All-America teams, and his 60 points ranked third in the SEC scoring race.

There were a handful of so-called triple threat backs in Bird's collegiate heyday, but none were his equal as a quad threat on offense, running, passing, kicking, and catching. However, it was his defense, many thought, that was where he was at his best. Had U.K. been charting tackles-made as a statistic back then, he might have led the team in that category also.

Kestner broke the school record with 42 catches and yards gained by a receiver. His 185 yards against Ole Miss was a school record. He, like Bird, made All-SEC.

It was difficult to explain Norton's absence from any of the All-SEC teams. He was the conferences' total offense and passing leader with 1,319 yards and 1,512 yards in the air.

Bird's defensive skills, however, would have to be put on hold as college football altered its rules a bit and reverted back to what was called two platoon football. The breathers he missed out on during his junior year from having to play on both sides of the ball would hopefully allow him to concentrate on putting points on the scoreboard.

And as might be expected, there were rumors that Bradshaw would resign, but he would have none of that saying, "We've got too many stakes in Lexington."

It's Now or Never

When *Playboy Magazine*'s September 1965 issue hit the newsstands, there he was, the boy from Corbin, listed as a first team All-American. Rodger had duplicated what brother Calvin had done a few years before. With the two platoon system to be implemented in the 1965 season, Rodger was named to the *Playboy* defensive team, but so was Southern Cal's Mike Garrett, who would go on to win the Heisman Trophy that year. Both went on to become All-American on offense, not defense.

Now, with four potential All-Americans returning, this had to be the national championship team Bradshaw was talking about three years before when he first arrived.

Bird, Kestner and Norton appeared on the cover of the 1965 official *Press Guide*, and Sam Ball just as easily could have been there too. As history would prove, their talents and expectations were not a stretch. Anything less than an SEC title and a major bowl bid would be deemed an unsuccessful season.

In the non-conference season opener, the Wildcats blanked Missouri 7-0 on a 36-yard Norton to junior Larry Seiple touchdown pass. Bird suffered an ankle injury and was pretty much lost for the game. Bradshaw called the win "the greatest effort displayed by a Kentucky team in my four years with the university."

Two platoon football was back, and at last Bird would be able to concentrate on just running, passing, catching and blocking. The Wildcat's shutout road win earned them a number ten national ranking in the *AP*'s first poll of the season. Expectations were high!

Ole Miss came to Lexington, and the Wildcats with their new-found strut were a slight favorite to win. They did not disappoint with a 16-7 victory, and, if you can believe it, a sellout stadium of 38,000 chanting "We're Number One."

Seiple again had a big day, scoring on a 28-yard pass from Norton, and then again on a play for the ages. He was back to punt on fourth and 41, deep in his own end of the field. With his own team running to cover the punt, and Ole Miss running to set up blocking for their punt return, Seiple decided to head in the same direction. His 70 yard jaunt sealed the deal for Kentucky. Still hobbling from the ankle injury, Bird didn't play a single snap during the win.

With a number six national ranking, the Wildcats fell at Auburn 23-18 after falling behind 17-0. Norton, in the loss had a 76-yard scoring pass to Bob Windsor and two more, 74 and 44 yarders to Seiple.

The previous year's 48-6 loss to Florida State was still fresh on the minds of any Wildcat who was involved in a game that many felt the team never recovered from. Rodger Bird, playing like he was supposed to, ran for 83 yards on 29 carries and three TDs as Kentucky won 26-24.

Kentucky's trip to LSU featured a bit of irony in that Bradshaw would be coaching against a former Wildcat teammate, Charlie McClendon, who had just taken over from Paul Deitzel. In fact Bradshaw and McClendon were ends on the 1949 team that was the last Kentucky team to win in Tiger Stadium.

As 68,000 fans watched, LSU won 31-21. Bird scored twice on runs of 18 and 10. Kentucky, now with two SEC losses, had virtually been eliminated from the conference title race.

Georgia brought an undefeated SEC mark and 4-1 overall record to Lexington in a must win game for the Wildcats. And win they did. Scoring four touchdowns in the second quarter, Kentucky routed the Bulldogs 28-10 as Bird scored on a six yard run and a 44-yard pass from Norton.

West Virginia was Kentucky's homecoming foe, and already with wins over two other out of conference teams, they were looking for number three. Kentucky's predictables, Bird, Norton, and Kestner, were living up to their pre-season accolades, but Seiple and junior college transfer Bob Windsor had given the Wildcats a couple of added weapons as well as being two more future pros. Bird scored two more touchdowns in a 28-8 win.

A trip to Vanderbilt was always an adventure, and with a 5-2 record, the Wildcats had to be careful as talk was being heard about a bowl bid with a couple of more wins.

With a 34-0 win in Nashville, it was a record shattering day for the Wildcats, and in particular Rodger Bird. His four touchdowns gave him a season total of 13, the most ever in one year at Kentucky, and his point total for the season of 78, gave him that record, too. The career rushing yardage record became his as well. Some writers called it the finest game of his collegiate career.

It was no surprise that the Wildcats at 6-2, with some impressive wins, were moving up the list of bowl committees. The Cats had taken over 5,000 fans to the Vandy game, and the bowl people really liked schools with fans that followed their team on the road. The Gator Bowl was so impressed with what they had seen out of the Wildcats that an invitation was extended right after the win over Vandy. But Kentucky wanted more than the Gator Bowl. They wanted to be playing on New Year's Day in New Orleans, so they turned it down. The Sugar Bowl was what they had their sights on, and two wins in their two remaining games would do it. Even if they only won just one, they could still manage to step back and take the Gator Bowl invite.

A trip to Houston offered so much promise for a group of seniors that had earlier been labeled as one of Kentucky's best recruiting classes ever. Even as juniors, four of them had been named to at least one All-America team, and here they were, a couple of wins away from fulfilling, not only their dreams, but those of a bowl-starved Kentucky following.

Norton broke three of Babe Parilli's passing marks, but Houston broke Wildcat hearts with a 38-21 come from behind win. Kentucky led at the half 21-16 and trailed only 24-21 early in the fourth quarter, when the Astrodome's roof fell in on the Cats. Norton, through it all, completed 19 of 35 passes for 375 yards. A late fourth quarter knee injury to Norton put his final college game in jeopardy, though.

The Houston loss was called shocking, and the way the Wildcats' high powered offense disappeared in the second half was even more of a mystery. Still there was a chance, and albeit it was against archrival Tennessee, at least the game would be in Lexington.

The Vols came in at 4-1-2, with their only loss 14-13 to Ole Miss the week before. Their chance of a major bowl rested on this game with Kentucky. The bowl situation was hopelessly scrambled. The Orange Bowl had locked up Nebraska and Alabama, and Missouri and Florida would face off in the Sugar. The Cotton wasn't filled and neither was the Bluebonnet. The Liberty had moved to Memphis, and they were still in search of their teams. A Kentucky win over Tennessee would surely make the Cats bowl bound.

Noted *Courier-Journal* sports editor Earl Ruby wrote, even before the Tennessee game, in his column asking a question and then answering it himself in a rambling sort of way. "What about Charlie Bradshaw returning to Alabama?"…"I'd have to see it to believe it. He's set at U.K."…"I don't know. My grandmother could have done more with Kentucky's material than Bradshaw did."…"Well, don't think Bear Bryant is about to hire your grandmother."…"It's a shame that Kentucky, with all its great players and spectacular passing offense, didn't get a bowl bid"…"Don't worry, the Wildcats will get a bowl bid."

Ruby's writing was about as disjointed as the Wildcats season had been.

With Rick Norton out because of the knee injury at Houston, who would Bradshaw turn at quarterback? There were several candidates. Pre-game stories mentioned the likely choices of Roger Walz, a junior, or Terry Beadles, who had become a defensive safety. The names of Joe David Smith and Talbott Todd were thrown into the discussion. Both had been prep All-State quarterbacks. During practice that week, Rodger Bird had even taken some direct snaps from his tailback position.

The Vols, too, had issues at quarterback as Charlie Fulton had been injured in the Ole Miss game. In his place would be redshirt sophomore Dewey Warren. He had been the signal caller for the Baby Vols in the 70-0 loss to the Kittens a couple of years earlier.

It didn't matter. Kentucky lost 19-3, and it was over for the 1965 Wildcat team. Even in defeat, the Wildcats at 6-4 were the school's winningest team in nine years. That statistic, alone, puts Kentucky's football program in perspective.

With no bowl bid, the only thing left now for Rodger Bird was to wait for professional football to get their hands on the graduating talent-rich Wildcats.

Vandy that year would be the only U.K. opponent with a losing record, and Missouri went on to win the Sugar Bowl 20-18 over Florida. Their only loss, other than Kentucky, was 16-14 to Nebraska.

Although labeled the 1966 draft, it actually took place in late November 1965, and the underachieving Wildcats had an almost unbelievable draft, with three first rounders. Sam Ball went to the Colts, Rick Norton to Miami, and Rodger Bird to Oakland.

Rodger and Ball were named to the South team that would play the North in the annual North-South All-Star Game. Finally, the two would be playing in a bowl, the Orange Bowl Stadium on Christmas Day. Ara Parseghian of Notre Dame coached the North and Tulsa's Glenn Dobbs, the South.

Bird and Ball were named to the prestigious College All-Stars in a game that matched the collegiate players against the defending NFL World Champion Green Bay Packers in a game played annually at Chicago's Soldiers Field. The college boys lost 38-0.

"We got beat pretty good," Rodger said. "Most of our team had already been to training camp with the teams that drafted them, and then we went to Chicago to practice for a few days. Donny Anderson was our punter and he got hurt, so I did some punting. I got off one of my best kicks ever, 47 yards from the line of scrimmage. I out kicked the coverage, so they ran it back for a touchdown."

Bird and Ball were in demand for all-star games, and Norton would have been, too, except for his injury in the Houston game.

"I was invited to the East-West Shrine Game in San Francisco, but was able to get out of that one," Bird said. "But I played in the Blue-Gray All-Star game in Mobile. I played defensive back and went up against (Howard) Twilly from Tulsa. He took me to school. He was small, quick, and good…he might have set a record for passes caught, but we still won the game. I really liked our coach, Weeb Eubank."

Years later Rodger still talked about his team's visit to the Children's' Hospital in Mobile. "All those kids there with all those illnesses, it was a very touching experience to go there and try to put some joy in their lives, and just to see them smile was something I'll never forget," he said.

When Rodger departed the University of Kentucky in 1966, it was remarkable that a Bird name had been on a sports roster continually from 1952 through 1966. And equally impressive, in the football "records section" of the media guide, Calvin, Billy, and Rodger have their names listed a total of 76 times (Calvin 32, Billy 1, and Rodger 43).

Drafted in the First Round

For Kentucky the 1966 professional football draft was a bonanza. Rodger went in the first round to the AFL Oakland Raiders and signed a $350,000 five-year contract.

"Calvin was actually working as a scout for the Raiders," recalled Rodger. "So when they made me their number one pick I had to listen. He told me they were going to offer me a quarter of a million dollars. I asked him how much is that? Actually Dallas offered me more money, but Calvin didn't really care much for Ermal Allen (former U.K. assistant). Dallas even offered me a contract that called for me to get $30,000 a year for life when I quit playing."

Teammate Sam Ball was drafted in the first to the Baltimore Colts, Rick Norton, although not named to the first or a second All-SEC team, made several All-America squads, and was drafted in the first round by the Miami Dolphins. Rick Kestner had gone through several injuries his senior year, but was still selected by the Baltimore Colts in the third. Tackle Doug Davis went to the Minnesota Vikings in the fifth. Another tackle, Basil Mullins quickly signed as a free agent with the Cowboys.

Lest anyone forget there were several others on that 1965 team who would later be drafted and go on to have nice pro careers: Larry Seiple, Miami; Bob Windsor, San Francisco; Calvin Withrow, Green Bay; and Jeff VanNote, Atlanta. And remember Maurice "Moe" Moorman? He transferred to Texas A & M, became an All-American, a top draft choice and All-NFL guard for the Kansas City Chiefs. Had he stayed at U.K., unquestionably he would have left as one of the best linemen of all time. A footnote and trivia question: What non-football player at U.K. was drafted by the Cowboys in 1967? The answer: Pat Riley. The former New York all-state quarterback went in the 11th round. Riley was an All-American basketball player at Kentucky.

The Raiders were coached by John Rauch, a former Georgia star quarterback who was the SEC's Most Valuable Player in leading the Bulldogs to the title back in 1949. Al Davis, who would become one of the pro football's legendary figures, was the team's general manager and part owner…at least in title. His fingers were in anything that had to do with Raider football.

"Al Davis was one of those guys who would arrive late to his office, but literally work all night," recalls Rodger. "He was always, and I mean always, trying to figure out how to get an advantage."

Rodger Bird, the boy from Corbin, had been a great offensive player in college, but as an Oakland Raider, the only time he would see the ball was returning kicks and intercepting passes.

Early on, the Raiders, taking on Al Davis' personality, were hard-hitters. Hammers might be a better way to describe their defense, and Rodger fit in perfectly. "Rodger's chief asset is his ability to support against the run. He's our top tackler in the secondary," Rauch said. "He plays the strong safety and draws the tight end… and you need a tough kid to smack those tight ends…and Bird's tough. As for tackling, he is tough enough and big enough to knock the ball carrier backwards."

Although Rauch was the head coach, he was an offense guy. That was his game in college, and it is what he had been as an assistant coach. The Raider's defensive chores fell to Charley Sumptner, who had played for the Chicago Bears.

"He told me, 'Rodger you don't have to hit somebody on every play,' but that's what I usually did. My game was to intimidate those big tight ends. I'd try to knock their ass off when they ran across the middle, whether they had the ball or not. I wanted them to know I was there and they were going to get hit. All those licks probably shortened my career."

Statistics showed the Raiders were the toughest AFL team to complete a pass against.

Rodger Bird was not only good, he was very good, and named as the AFL's Defensive Rookie-of-the-Year.

For three years he was the starting safety for the Raiders, but in a short period of time those high impact collisions with those big tight ends began to quickly take a toll on Bird's shoulders.

Rodger and the Raiders finished the 1967 season with a 13-1 record, and advanced to the World Championship Game, AFL vs. NFL against the Green Bay Packers. It didn't actually become the Super Bowl until later. The game was played in Miami's Orange Bowl on January 14, 1968. The cost of the ticket? Twelve dollars! The actual price on the ticket showed $11.64 price plus 36 cent state tax. The boy from Corbin was playing on football's biggest stage.

Roger had handled a couple of Packer punter Donny Anderson's kicks earlier in the game. And then it happened. With about four minutes left in the first half and the Packers leading 14-0, Rodger retreated back to receive an Anderson punt. "He kicked the ball the highest of all the punters I had received," said Rodger. "Not necessarily long, but high. As the ball turned over in a floating spiral, Bird readied himself to gather it in and set sail from his own 30 yard line.

"We were on our own as far as fair catching it or taking off," he said. "Anderson kicked it so high it was very difficult to get a runback because of their punt coverage. I remember putting my hand up for a fair catch, and the next thing the ball is on the ground and Green Bay had it."

The Packers recovered on Oakland's 30, and moved it a few yards before kicking a field goal to push their halftime lead to 17-0. "I just misjudged it," Bird said years later. "Pure and simple, I should have caught it."

But to Al Davis, who Rodger always called "Coach," it was much more than pure and simple. It was more than just a muffed punt. To Davis there was a reason the sure-fingered Bird had failed to field the punt cleanly, and long after the game was over he was still thinking about it.

"I was living back in Lexington," says Bird. "It had been at least a month since that game, and at 2 a.m. in the morning my phone rings and it's Al Davis. He apologized. Not for calling me at this hour, but for not having had me completely

Left and below: *Steve Bird*

Eastern Coach Roy Kidd talks to Steve Bird.

Steve Bird in action.

Redhounds are the 1976 Class AA State Champs.

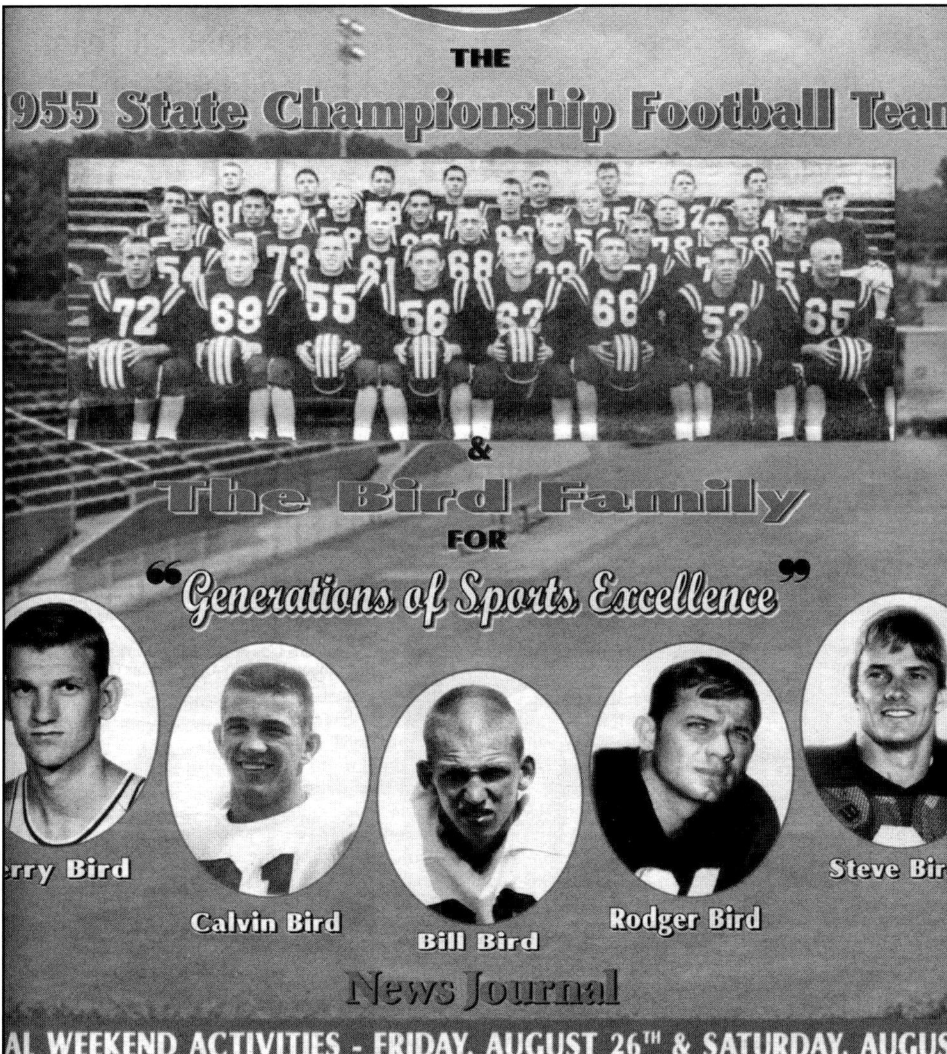

The News Journal published a tabloid recognizing the Birds.

Above and left: *Steve Bird, St. Louis Cardinals Football.*

Steve Bird (#82) and Pat Tilly with the St. Louis Cardinals.

Roy Kidd (left) and Steve Bird hold up the National Championship trophy.

Ruben and Bonnie Bird (right) stand next to twin brother Rufus and wife Billie.

The Bird house on Sycamore Street.

Old Edwards Gym, Corbin

Gary West and Rodger Bird in the Ossie Burch Fieldhouse.

Artwork on the stadium seating.

Campbell Field and Nick Denes Stadium.

The Redhound logo at the popular Dixie Café in downtown Corbin.

Gathering of the Hounds 2005. Front row, left to right: Ralph Wilder, Bill Howard, Ronnie Riley, David Miller, Calvin Bird, John Hoskins, Bill Meadows. Back row: Mel Chandler, William Scalf, Don Turner, Bob Howard, David Chandler, Stan Bunch, Bob Morris, Lonnie Cornelius. Also attending were Carl Bible, Rodger Bird and Lowell Wyatt.

Gathering of the Hounds 2007

The 'Hounds are still "Gathering" 53 years later

Bill Crook
Looking Back

I spent Monday June 23rd, with the wealthiest group of people I know, the members of the 1955 state champions of football in the state of Kentucky.

They are filthy rich in love for each other and they are generous enough to open their arms to others with whom they are willing to share their wealth.

There were many pictures that passed from hand to hand, but the one that captured my attention was a strong young man named Bill "Moon" Conde standing in the center of a rather scruffy looking group of young men who had the looks of having put in a tough day. There was Murrell Barnett with a band aid across his nose, Carl Bible with hair shooting in every direction, and David Chandler and Roy Joiner listening intently as the strong young coach was laying it down.

The picture was taken during the football season of 1953. It was the beginning of an establishment of wealth that no amount of money can buy.

My buddy Bob Watkins was in attendance at this year's gathering of the Redhounds and it was great to see him.

The gathering of the Redhounds is [illegible] great effort by all those who attend but is coordinated primarily by David Chandler and Bill "Yogi" Meadows. As I listened to stories, I marveled at the enjoyment everyone was able to derive from their gathering and I could not help but reflect on each individual and what I remember of them.

David Chandler – I remember a long legged young man racing full throttle toward the end zone on an October evening in 1954 and scoring a huge touchdown against the number one ranked Pineville Mountain Lions. The Redhounds downed the Mountain Lions, 18-6.

Calvin Bird – I remember Calvin as the best all-around athlete, in my opinion, to ever play at Corbin High School.

David Miller – I always thought David would have been an outstanding football coach. David seemed to be ahead of the game as a player, and always made the big play.

Bill Howard – "Piggy Bill" was the ultimate competitor and one tough customer. Bill may have been the Redhounds all-time best punters.

Ronnie Riley – Fiery, mean streak with no regard for rhyme or reason. Riley matured into a good guy.

Lonnie Cornielius – Super great guy who could punt a football a mile and was an excellent baseball pitcher.

Mel Chandler – I will never forget Mel's effort in a loss to Louisville St. Xavier. It was the most courageous effort I have ever seen on a football field.

Bill "Yogi" Meadors – A hard-nosed center on '56 team who went on to distinguish himself in academics as a professor at Western Kentucky University.

Winton Boone – Winton was yet another outstanding all around athlete. Whether it was football, track or basketball, Winton was among the very best.

Don Turner – Still another all-around performer who rattles my memory of a great return of a Danville Admiral pass for a touchdown and that led to the '55 Redhounds' 34-20 win.

Bobby "Puppet" Morris was a punter in football and a very good guard in basketball. He later entered school administration as a principal at Harlan High School.

Morris "Moose" Garrison was very strong from his tackle position on the '55 champions.

Carl Bible – The oldest of three Bible brothers to play football and basketball at Corbin High School.

Ralph Wilder – In my opinion the Redhounds' best quarterback ever. Ralph was also a terrific kick returner.

Rodger Bird – An All-American, Rookie of the Year in the NFL, that I remember most for the most beautiful 12 yard run I have ever seen against Bell County in 1960.

Stanley Bunch, an offensive tackle on the '55 champs.

Johnny Hoskins played football, basketball and baseball as a Redhound, but is better known as the life of the party at the "Gathering of the Redhounds."

There were several guests of the main group, **Sammy Sturgill,** a Redhound of the '54 class, Dallas Hart a Redhound from '59, **Bobby "Muncy" White,** who could best be described as a Redhound for all seasons. **Bill Hoover**, a wide receiver from the class of '65. **Winston Phipps**, a strong Redhound supporter and of course "Mr. Redhound" **Henry Martin** who provided dinner for the group on Monday evening.

There were those unable to attend due to health issues, or prior commitments that were constantly brought up in conversations and stories.

Honorary member of the '55 championship team, Baker Reasor was unable to attend but was mentioned on numerous occasions, as was teammate Bobby "Mo' Green who is experiencing some health issues at this time.

Bob Howard and Gayle "Dago" Phillips were unable to attend as was Bill "Buster" Scalf and Gerald "Curley" Ellison, but if a light came on every time their names were mentioned you could light-up New York City.

As I drove away Monday evening, the thought that went through my mind was "what a family", brothers to the bone.

The 1955 Corbin Redhounds, a team on whom the stars would shine

David Chandler (left) and brother Mel.

Left to right: Rodger Bird, Barry Brooks, Calvin and Jerry Bird chit-chat at the Hampton Inn in Corbin in 2012.

Jesse Grant and Mel Chandler at David's Steak House in Corbin in 2012.

Coaching legend comes home

Monday
Aug. 28, 2000

Corbin's favorite son honored during special football weekend

Roy Kidd and wife Sue in 2000 at Corbin's street dedication.

Curt and Charles (Curly) Selvy celebration reception.

Calvin Bird, Muncy White, David Miller and Rodger Bird at the annual Gathering of the Hounds.

Ossie Burch painting in the Ossie Burch Fieldhouse.

Ossie Burch (with cane) is surrounded by (top left) Carl Bible, Ralph Wilder, David Chandler, Johnny Hoskins, Calvin Bird and Don Turner.

Members of the 1949-50 Corbin High School basketball team. Front row, left to right: Roy Kidd, C.D. Vermillion and Bob Terrell. Second row: Tom Adkins, Jerry Bird, Frank Selvy and Jerry Brooks. February 28, 2004.

Don Estep introduces Frank Selvy to a basketball crowd in Corbin on February 28, 2004.

Gathering of the Hounds 2012

Left to right: Don Turner, Rodger Bird, Bill "Yogi" Meadors and Bobby Morris.

Gathering of the Hounds near Tompkinsville in 2012. Bill Howard and Don Turner.

Left to right: Mel Chandler, David Chandler, Ralph Wilder and Rodger Bird.

Bill Hoover talks with Yogi Meadors and David Miller.

At a Corbin Civic Club luncheon at David's Steak House in 2012. Left to right: Barry Brooks, Corbin native Doug Gibson (from Elizabethtown), Jerry Bird, Gary West, Calvin Bird, Charlie Thurman (from Sonora) and Rodger Bird.

Author Gary West takes notes as News-Journal publisher Don Estep talks.

Columnist/Writer Bill Crook talks about Corbin's sports history.

Left to right: Charlie Thurman, Rodger Bird, Gary West and Doug Gibson in front of the Hall of Fame plaques.

prepared for Anderson's punt. He was a left footed kicker Al told me, and with a left footed kicker, the ball rotates opposite of a right footed kicker. Al was so concerned about me worrying about what some of the reporters had written that he gave me a reason why I dropped the ball."

To Davis, with a call to talk football, the time of day or night was of little concern, after all when it was 2 a.m. in Kentucky; it was only 12 midnight in California. The Oakland head man had been thorough in preparation, but in replaying the loss he had found one area lacking.

On November 17, 1968, Rodger was involved in what was to become the most controversial televised football game in history. Now referred to as the Heidi Game, with the New York Jets leading Oakland 32-29, and only minutes remaining, NBC cut away from the game to broadcast Heidi, a movie that featured child star, Shirley Temple. NBC switchboards were jammed, and it led to public outrage when the Raiders scored two touchdowns in the last minute to win 43-32.

The state of Kentucky was well represented in all facets of that game. With Bird, on the Raider team was former Wildcat George Blanda, and Babe Parilli was a member of the Jets. Julian Goodman, a Glasgow native who had attended Western Kentucky University, was the President of NBC and had the final decision on the switch.

Rodger's shoulder injury became so bad he finally gave way to surgery after the season, and then he reported to Oakland's rookie camp to rehab a bit, and to test his ability to take a hit.

"I hadn't worked out in some time," he said. "They had me on offense, doing some pass blocking. I hadn't done this since U.K. One of the guys I had to block was a linebacker named Carl Withers who had played at San Diego State. Later, he was in the Rocky movie playing Apollo Creed."

Unfortunately, the only taste Rodger had of offense was at that rookie camp. Although the press reported that the Raiders were going to try the boy from Corbin on offense, it never happened. "I would like to have seen what I could have done as a running back," he said years later.

Finally his Oakland days were over. A second shoulder surgery had sealed his fate on the West Coast. But like most great athletes, Rodger held out a glimmer of hope that he could still play. He had been playing football since the third grade, and he wasn't quite ready to exit just yet.

George Boone had been an assistant coach at U.K. and was the player personnel director for the St. Louis Cardinals in the NFL. This connection helped Rodger get a tryout with the Cardinals.

"I worked out with them at their summer camp in northern Illinois," he recalled. "I roomed with Dan Dierdorff who I became good friends with." In the end Rodger failed his team physical because of his shoulder. "Hell, Oakland would have kept me if it had been okay." Rodger Bird was out of football.

"I didn't want to coach," he says. "I wanted to go back to Lexington and get in the car business. I wanted a Volkswagen dealership, but I knew it would take several years to get it going good."

Rodger, on December 30, 1966, had married his college sweetheart, Sally Duncan, a beauty queen from Henderson, Kentucky, in the town's First Christian Church. Standing up with Sally as maid of honor was Lynn Cardwell and matron of honor, Libby Alexander. Although Rick Norton was in Rodger's wedding party, it was an old hunting buddy, Frank Wyatt, who was his best man.

Sally's family wanted to get their daughter and Rodger back home, and Rodger, in 1970, was offered a chance to buy into a Henderson insurance business, and did.

Coming to Henderson allowed Rodger to reunite with his old college buddy, Sam Ball, who grew up there and had returned home after a career with the Baltimore Colts.

"Sam and I ran football camps in Henderson for several years," said Bird.

In 2011 Rodger was honored at the SEC Championship game in Atlanta as an All-Time SEC Legend.

Chapter Nine

One More Bird and Lots of Stories

Steve Bird

As a football player, Steve Bird had a championship career, one that would rival his dad, Jerry's, and Uncles Calvin's, Billy's and Rodger's.

In 1976 his Redhound team captured the state Class 2-A title over Mayfield 6-0. The following year, going for a repeat, lost 14-13 to Mayfield in the championship game. During the season Bird had a five touchdown game in a win over Tates Creek. Archie Powers coached the Hounds in both championship games that were played at Cardinal Stadium in Louisville, and later Powers won another state title in 1980 with a 16-7 win over Fort Campbell.

As all-state and a three sport Redhound letterman, Steve was heavily recruited by almost everyone but the University of Kentucky. Their interest came later, after former Corbin star Roy Kidd had wrapped Steve up with a scholarship to Eastern.

Kidd had been a teammate of Steve's father in high school, and the Bird family knew at Eastern the fleet-footed boy from Corbin would have a chance to develop. And develop he did. Playing as a freshman, his 1979 Colonel team won the National Division 1-AA championship over Lehigh 30-7.

For Steve Bird it was the first of four consecutive national title games. In 1980 and 81 Eastern lost to Boise State 31-29, and Idaho State 34-23, but in 1982 they once again won it all in defeating Delaware 17-14, and with it came All-American honors and a fourth round draft choice of the St. Louis Cardinals where he played two years. His four year record as a player at Eastern was 46-7.

Steve had played in an unbelievable six consecutive championship games in high school and college. His senior year performance was so outstanding with 47 catches that included eight touchdowns and totaled 803 yards that he was named, not only Ohio Valley Conference Offensive Player of the Year, but also the conferences' Male Athlete of the Year. That same year, in a game against Idaho in the playoffs, Bird turned in a game that caused Coach Kidd to say it was perhaps the best individual performance he had ever seen. The boy from Corbin hauled in two TD passes among his seven receptions that accounted for 154 yards. "He was sensational, I'll never forget it," Kidd said years later.

Steve's life revolved around sports in Corbin. How could you be named Bird and it not?

"My father never pushed me into athletics," Steve was quick to tell reporters who asked about the pressure he might have felt. "He let me make choices. Dad always said, 'If you're going to do it, I want you to do it right.' He was always there for me.

He knew quite a bit about every sport I've played, and even if he didn't, he learned and then taught me. He was never too tired to throw a ball around with me."

Though Steve didn't see his dad play basketball at U.K., he does recall his uncles Calvin, Billy and Rodger's playing days. "They were great athletes," he said. "And I can still remember watching them on T.V. and then running out in the yard to imitate their play. We have a strong family of athletic heritage."

Steve made no bones about it several years ago that he had hoped to play at Kentucky. "They were hesitant to sign me," he told one publication. "It didn't work out. But that only drove me to succeed. I had something to prove to them and to myself, and I could have never played for a coach that cared more about me as a person as Coach Kidd."

In a round-about sort of way Bird did in fact end up at U.K. In 1990 and '91 he served as a graduate assistance on the staff of Bill Curry.

Over the years he has served as an assistant at Eastern, Tennessee, Pittsburgh, Kent State, Tulane, Middle Tennessee, West Virginia and South Florida.

Gathering of the Hounds

For those who weren't around when Corbin had what some say is the best high school football team ever, the next best thing is hearing the stories. An annual reunion of the Redhounds' 1955 state championship team takes place down in the remote back woods of Monroe County, a few miles from Tompkinsville, on the Cumberland River.

The rustic lodge-type building called River Breeze is large enough to sleep and feed fourteen or fifteen people, and with zero cell phone service it provides this group of seventy-something year old Hounds nothing to do but tell stories and eat.

There's an old saying, "You can't get here from there," and when it comes to River Breeze it's almost true. Forget the GPS...won't work here. A turn onto a narrow gravel road that quickly becomes dirt, then drops off into a creek bed that continues for some 100 yards in the creek...with water is the route to get there. But suddenly there it is, the place where all of the former Hounds gather to remember THE day.

Over the years the group has expanded to include old Corbin friends, supporters and Redhound stars that came after the '55 team.

David Chandler is there. He's the self-described treasurer, purchasing agent, and most importantly, the chief cook. David, along with Bill "Yogi" Meadors, are the coordinators of the "gathering."

The '55 Hounds were so good that usually their stories didn't have to be embellished. But nevertheless, for three nights and four days they sit around an outdoor fire and talk.

Don't be misled into thinking it's a bunch of senior citizens sitting around reliving their glory days. Its politics, golf, wine making, and chili, the kind you eat.

Not everything is about football or basketball. Each year it gets more and more about family, the teammates that are no longer able to join in, and the genuine love they have for each other. But, also don't think that it is without some serious "ribbing."

There were quiet times, just sitting around recalling how wonderful it was growing up in Corbin. How families didn't lock their doors, and wondering what kids they'd find sleeping on the floor the next morning, and where everybody used to live.

"Everybody looked out after each other. It was a working class town," Mel Chandler said.

The Chandler family, as did others in Corbin, had a charge account over at Tom Smith's Grocery, and the Chandler kids, David, Mel and Betty would stop by there for lunch. "It was about 25-cents for each of us to eat there," Mel said.

Older brother David recalled the J.C. Higgins bicycle they owned. "We'd all ride to school on it," he laughed. "I'd pedal, Mel would be on the back, and Betty on the handlebars."

The Gathering of the Hounds has become a tradition, almost like who will be the last man standing. For sure that 1955 Redhound football team stood tall.

Stan Bunch was a lineman on the '55 team. He told of living in a house provided by the L & N Railroad. "My dad was a welder and mom a bookkeeper for the railroad," he said. "Dad worked for them 55 years."

He spoke with pride that his dad's job allowed him not to serve in the military. "As a welder his job was considered critical to the war effort. He even went to Baltimore for a while to work at the ship yards."

With a tone of respect, these boys from Corbin speak often of the support the youth teams received throughout the years from people like Tom Catron, the Ford dealer; Jack and Kathryn Day at Pepsi; Baker Reasor; and Vernon and Ed Wilder.

Often the stories, which sometimes turn into tales, are told to no one in particular, but rather anyone within hearing distance. And with every passing year, the hearing issue becomes a bit more prevalent.

One of the hounds, Johnny Hoskins, in 2011 started to write a story about his years growing up in Corbin and how it all came together in 1955. "I started it, but stopped with one page," he laughed.

But that one page is powerful stuff that speaks for all of his buddies.

> *"It all started in the early 40s, in a small Southeastern town in Kentucky called Corbin. A bunch of small skinny boys would play football in any yard, or shoot hoops wherever there was a pole with a cordless rim. On Friday nights they would go to the high school field, and watch their heroes play. They would spend most of the game playing tackle in the back of the end zone, dreaming of someday wearing the pads and uniform of the Corbin Redhounds. These young skinny kids would spend days doing whatever they could to be together. You could feel, even back then as young boys, they were forming a special bond. They were separated in grade school; South, East, and Central until the 9th grade when they merged, and it all started to happen. Dating and driving did nothing to*

separate this group of boys, because they now had a youth center, a YMCA gym, and a swimming pool. Now playing high school sports, you could see the cohesion and love that they had for each other. After two or three years of hard knocks, one of them being a winless season, it all came together. In 1955 these young boys won it all–undefeated Kentucky State Champions.

"After leaving school, going to college, entering the military, and getting married; they kept in touch by visits back home, and class reunions. In 2005, they started a Gathering of the Hounds. They meet one week a year, in a large cabin on the river, where they play golf, cook, bunk together, and tell stories. They don't invite wives or children to this special place and no question about it...the skinny little boys from Corbin still act the same. They are hard on each other, but just like in the 40s, they never get angry and have never had a fight. There is only one explanation for that...their love for each other is deep. When a book is written, everyone will read about The Boys of Fall, God bless them all."

Redhound Logo

It is said that the original Redhound logo was from a drawing by Mrs. Harold Gant, an art teacher at Corbin High School. The upright walking Redhound with a determined expression seems to be on a mission. And the white beanie-like cap has a "C" to match the one on the hound's white sweater.

Vicki Gant Kinsel says her mother, Mildred, created the "Redhound" in 1962 for her to wear on a t-shirt to band camp. "I wanted something different," she said. "The original art had a Redhound wearing a band hat, complete with feathers. Everyone liked the new design."

Until then Corbin's symbol had been a greyhound dog stretched out in full-stride.

According to Vicki, the band hat eventually gave way to a beanie to reflect all aspects of the high school.

The Gant's also owned a beagle hound named George that on occasion made appearances at pep rallies in Edwards Gym located just behind the Gant's home. "George would howl loudly on command during the cheers," Vicki said. "He was even known to lead the team on the field at football games until dog napping threats were made by opposing schools."

In July 2010, the Corbin School Board voted unanimously to approve a "Certificate of Service Mark Registration" for the Redhound, which was issued by the Kentucky Secretary of State. The designation allows the school board to control the use of the logo mascot or image, at least in Kentucky.

The board made it clear that it would not restrict the usage by booster clubs when it came to selling T-shirts and other Redhound gear. The fact that the Redhound mascot is painted on the side of a building formerly occupied by the Dixie Café' was not an issue.

A Service Mark is similar to a trademark and must be renewed every five years.

David "Swenney" Farmer

It's amazing what will sometime surface in the research of a book. Filed away among pictures, letters and Corbin memorabilia, Bobby "Puppet" Morris uncovered a series of pencil drawings one of his high school classmates sketched over fifty years ago.

The art work was done by David Farmer, who had been a manager for the Redhound football team, along with Billy Pat Hacker, and his renderings were done in a comic strip style that depicted Morris in various locker room situations involving Coach Taylor, Calvin Bird, Winton Boone, and Harold Queary.

Nowhere is Farmer's name on the work…only Swenney or the "Cog." "My nickname was Swenney," he said, "Has been ever since I was five-years old. When I was little I liked to play one of the comic strip characters from Buzz Sawyer, and his name was Swenney. Most people in high school never knew my real name."

And how did he get all of the inside details for his drawings? "For sure I wasn't in the locker room or anywhere else with them," he laughed years later. "People would say 'Swenney draw this, and then they'd tell me what was said and who all was involved. I thought Puppet or Phillip Tucker (Coach Harry Taylor's son), who was the basketball manager, gave me some of the stories."

It was obvious that Farmer had talent as an artist, and after high school he studied art for two years in Columbus, Ohio. After a career in state government, he retired to devote more time to his oil painting. "I get commissioned for several projects," he offered. "I really enjoy it."

One of his latest paintings appears in this book. It depicts one of the most talked about scenes in Corbin sports history. In 1959 after U.K. defeated Tennessee 20-0, someone painted the words "Bird 20, Tenn 0" across the downtown underpass on Hwy. 25. "I will never forget seeing that," Farmer said. "It was two weeks after that game and I was riding the bus back to Corbin from Columbus. I looked out the window and there it was. I knew I was home."

David "Swenney" Farmer has now recreated that famous scene.

Pepsi Cola

No one in Corbin can remember when the Pepsi Cola Company wasn't involved in sports as a sponsor or cheerleader. In building ball parks and playing fields, not only did Pepsi give of their money, but also their time.

Jack and Kathryn Day in September 1938 opened their Pepsi bottling operation at 1309 South Main. In the beginning their ten-hour days cranked out between 150 to 200 cases to be delivered throughout a ten county area, by a single International truck by one man, Jack Day.

As business accelerated, the Days borrowed a flatbed truck from a friend, Big John Smith, and not long after, drivers were employed who had their own trucks.

Anyone who knows Corbin knows Pepsi Cola. It seems like they have been there forever. Their community involvement in helping to build the Redhound tradition seems on occasion to be taken for granted. The Day family, and now the Hoover family, has always been there for the cause, not just in Corbin but in the entire area. There are very few scoreboards around southeastern Kentucky that do not have a Pepsi logo.

Jack and Kathryn had planned, in the late 50s, to move their original bottling plant to a larger facility. Jack had even purchased some property out on Old Dixie Highway, but before he could get it done, in 1957 he died. Three years later, however, Kathryn made the move.

Over the last several decades Pepsi Cola of Corbin has adapted to the changes in the industry, and has been an area leader with modernization, technology and service to its thousands of customers. With $56 in their pockets to start the business out of a pickup truck, Pepsi has gone from those early day 150 cases to 25,000 cases a day.

The success of Redhound sports and Pepsi Cola seem to have paralleled each other over the last seventy-five years in Corbin. And then in 1982, Bill and Vin Hoover, now operating the Pepsi Cola Company, came forward in helping to establish the Redhound Varsity Club, an organization that pays homage to those men and women who have helped make Corbin athletics the showcase that it is.

Corbin's NASCAR History

It was August 29, 1954 when Lee Petty and twenty other drivers blasted off as Eddie Poynter, a local, waved his green flag at the Corbin Speedway. The race marked the first NASCAR race ever run in Kentucky.

Petty, who had already won at Daytona, was the day's super star and also the father of future racing great Richard. As expected, he won the 200 lap race on the half-mile dirt oval, and with it the $1,000 purse.

Race records show that Petty drove his 1954 Chrysler at a pedestrian-like speed of just over 63 mph average. Four drivers in the race that day, Petty, Hershel McGriff, Buck Baker (Buddy's father), and Herb Thomas wound up listed among the "50 Greatest NASCAR Drivers of All-Time." And, as if on cue, they finished one, two, three, and four.

"It was the real deal for us," recalled Allen Dizney who brought his 1947 Jeep to the track that day. "I volunteered to tow or push cars off the track or out of the pit if need be. I could push them out of the way or throw a chain across their front bumper and pull them."

Dizney, a Corbin resident, later became friends with Lee Petty through the mail, and even though the official NASCAR race results that day show Petty driving a Chrysler, Dizney has his own memories of the historic race. "They said he drove a Chrysler, but I recall him driving a Dodge," says Dizney. "I was in the service station business for twenty years, and I know a Chrysler from a Dodge."

Corbin's Paul Jones was also there. A driver himself at several of the dirt tracks in the area, he drove in the preliminary race that day, not remembering exactly where he finished, but recalling that he always wore his old WWII Navy flight helmet, the one he had used as a pilot. "That helmet was special and I tried to keep it looking good," Jones said. "One of our local boys, Dick Vermillion, won the preliminary and also drove in the big race."

For over thirty years Jones had seven prime seats for the Daytona 500. "Top row on the finish line. They finally kicked me out," he laughed.

Both Dizney and Jones give credit to another local driver, Bub King, for getting NASCAR to Corbin.

"King had run races everywhere, even at Daytona Beach," Dizney said. "He knew some of the NASCAR people, and that was the connection."

Many of the makes of cars on the track that day are no longer manufactured. Petty's Chrysler was the only one in the race, but there were several Hudsons, Oldsmobiles, Plymouths, Dodges, Vermillion's Buick, and King's Lincoln made up the twenty-one car field.

The Famous and the Forgotten

Colonel Sanders

As far as anyone knows, Harland Sanders never ran for a touchdown or scored a basket at Corbin High School, but still he is Corbin's most famous citizen. Known as Colonel Sanders, the fried chicken he developed in the 1940s and 50s at his Highway 25 café, has become a worldwide icon in the food industry. Not only is his original recipe still around, but so is his original restaurant and motel in Corbin.

Stories are plentiful about the Colonel, but there's one in particular that may have fallen through the cracks. Bob Terrell tells it:

"When we were about sixteen, Karl Bays and I were walking along Main Street and our buddy, Norman Berry, was driving his dad's black Dodge past us and we yelled at him to stop and give us a ride. He slammed on the brakes and Colonel Sanders was following him in his new Cadillac and crashed into the back of Norman's car. Karl and I were very upset about the situation, and the police came and questioned witnesses. Finally a police officer went over to the Colonel and said, 'Colonel, I am sorry, but I am going to have to give you a ticket. You were following too close.' The Colonel cussed, stomped his feet, and we stayed away from him for a long time. He finally got over it."

George McAfee

Nicknamed "one-play McAfee," George McAfee was born in Corbin in 1918 and went on to play halfback at Duke, where he was later inducted into the College of Football Hall of Fame.

His eight years with the Chicago Bears, after being picked in the first round of the 1940 NFL draft saw the boy from Corbin, in 1941, lead the league with a 7.3 yards per carry while scoring an NFL high twelve touchdowns in an eleven game schedule.

That same year he led the Bears to their second straight NFL championship over the New York Giants while playing for Papa Bear George Halas. By today's standards those numbers are considered modest, but in that era they were sensational.

From 1942 to 1945, McAfee served his country in the Navy, missing perhaps his best playing days. But still his 234 career points, 5,313 yards, and 25 pass interceptions were good enough numbers to get him into the Pro Football Hall of Fame after retiring in 1950.

Arthur (Dagwood) Lake

Dagwood Bumstead was a central character in the Blondie newspaper comic strip that went on to be developed for radio, movies and television. Dagwood was a Corbin boy. Born Arthur Silverlake, Jr., in 1905, his last name was shortened to Lake by the entertainment business.

As a child actor, appearing with the likes of Gloria Swanson, he advanced to later roles that usually revolved around light comedy.

His Dagwood role began in 1938 with Columbia Pictures, and ended in 1957 with the Blondie TV series. Dagwood earned Lake a star on the Hollywood Walk of Fame.

Arthur Lake was a close friend of newspaper tycoon William Randolph Hearst and his mistress Marion Davies. In 1942, Lake married Patricia Van Cleeve, who later claimed to be the daughter of Hearst and Davies.

In the famous unsolved murder case about the Black Dahlia, Lake was reported to have been questioned as a suspect by the Los Angeles Police because of his acquaintance with the victim.

Debbie Dean

Debbie Dean was born Reba Smith in Corbin in 1928. Her dad, Walter, was an engineer on the railroad and her mother, Alma, was a housewife taking care of their four children.

Debbie became the first white female solo recording artist signed in the early 60s by Berry Gordy at Motown Records. She had moderate success as a singer with "Don't Let Him Shop Around" in 1961. However, later she achieved acclaim in collaborating to write songs for the Supremes, Temptations, Smokey Robinson, and Martha and the Vandellas.

Reasor Brothers

The Reasor brothers, Baker and Bascom, during the 1950s and well into the 60s, are given credit for doing more for Corbin High School student athletes than for perhaps anyone else in the community.

Their efforts and influence with collegiate athletic departments throughout the state opened the door for Corbin kids to go to college on athletic scholarships that might not have otherwise been available.

The support Baker and Bascom gave to Redhound athletics and their aggressiveness in playing an important role in many young men's lives throughout Corbin has never been forgotten.

"The Reasors made sure that if a kid had the desire to continue their athletic career by going to college, they at least got an opportunity," Rodger Bird said.

Karl Bays

Karl Bays grew up in Corbin, and after an outstanding career as a Redhound lineman on the 1950 and '51 football teams went on to star for three years at Eastern Kentucky University where he became the school's first football player to be drafted into the NFL. But instead, he entered the officer's program of the Marine Corp.

It wasn't football, however, where the son of an L & N Railroad conductor made his mark. At the age of 39 he became the president of International Company in Evanston, Illinois, that later merged into American Hospital Supply. Later Bays became CEO of Institutional Industries that eventually became Whitman Corporation.

Along the way Bays was inducted into the Medical Industry Hall of Fame; was the recipient of the Horatio Alger Award; was on the board of directors of American Hospital Supply, the Whitman Corp., AMOCO Oil and Delta Airlines; and won the Wall Street Journal's Medical Industry's CEO of the Year award five times.

Karl Bays died in 1989 at the age of 55.

Mama Bird *(Evelyn Johnson)*

As high as the Bird's flew—Jerry, Calvin, Billy, Rodger and Steve, there was one more that flew even higher.

Known as "Mama Bird," Evelyn Bryan Johnson was a pioneering female pilot and Guinness world record holder.

The Corbin native began flying in 1944 and held the record in "The Guinness Book of World Records" for most hours in the air for a female pilot. She was also one of the first female helicopter pilots.

The girl from Corbin was inducted into the National Aviation Hall of Fame in 2007, after flying for fifty-five years and spending the equivalent of seven years in the air. She had flown 5.5 million miles, equal to twenty-three trips to the moon, and never had a single crash despite several mechanical problems.

She died in May 2012 in Morristown, Tennessee, at the age of 102.

Conclusion

Many consider the 50s the golden era of high school sports in Kentucky, but for Corbin it covered several decades before and after. Not only are the fabulous athletic facilities a bold testimony to the success of past Redhound teams, but it also sends a message to those that follow.

The standard for achievement was established long ago, and the spirit that has evolved from those successes has carried over to young men and women who have only heard the stories. Once it was thought to be a Redhound it was required to play on a Corbin sports team or be in the band, both worthy. But, now to be a Redhound, one only needs to have such a spirit.

The ghosts of those who dashed for touchdowns at Campbell Field or hit layups in Edwards Gym surely return now and then to make sure all is well in Redhound Land.

In Corbin, a presence of the past is very evident. Streets have been named to honor some of the legends. Others have their faces painted in oils surrounded by frames worthy of their accomplishments. Many are members of the school's Hall of Fame that began in 1982.

Edwards Gym still stands. But still it serves as a reminder of what was once there. The standing room only crowds were the first to see what the rest of the basketball world would later experience.

Over at Campbell Field those Corbin football teams were something to behold. Drums beating, horns blaring, crowds screaming, the distinctive thud of a player hitting the rock-hard turf, or the crack of two helmets colliding with the force of a nearby steam engine made it so very real.

Corbin, like so many towns across Kentucky, lived and died with the outcome of basketball and football games played by teenagers. The games were a distraction for many of the hardworking railroaders, timber cutters and coal miners. For a few hours they could forget about their tough, dirty and dangerous jobs and cheer on their Redhounds. It was a chance for Corbin to earn its bragging rights, and the town lived for these games.

Corbin's home crowds were rough. Grown men who had worked ten to twelve hour days, used these games to release tension and frustrations. Often their language, considered salty, would be directed at opposing teams and, of course, referees. Opposing fans didn't always see eye-to-eye either, and their disagreements were known to continue in the parking lot.

Some said Corbin High had evolved into something bigger than life. Players were heroes, and coaches were often viewed as God-like.

The canvas of where these boys performed the art of playing basketball and football still stands, and those who sometime come back home slowly drive by these meccas where it always seemed the crowd was cheering.

Looking back on it, was it really fair? These kids, not just in Corbin, but all across Kentucky, their faces not yet wrinkled by time, stress, or weather were so young. To carry such a burden of hopes and dreams of the entire town was asking a lot. Was it too much?

For these men, though, who are no longer boys, the question is not even for debate. They lived it and loved it. For many it defined who they were and what they would become. And because of it, Corbin became America's Greatest Little Sports Town.

Redhound Varsity Club Hall of Fame

1982

Tommy Adkins, '50
Abie Ayers, '32
Bill Bird, '60
Calvin Bird, '60
Jerry Bird, '52
Rodger Bird, '62
Sam Brasel, '36
Dr. G.W. Campbell, Honorary
Mel Chandler, '58
Marion Cluggish, '36
Jim Cummins, '40
Kathryn Day, Honorary
Nick Denes, Coach
Walt Green, Coach
Alfred Keck, '36
Roy Kidd, '50
Ted Meadors, '30
Rusty Peace, '41
Frank Selvy, '50
Jerry Smith, '59
Margie Smith, '32
Harry Taylor, '28
W.F. Babe Taylor, Honorary
Wes Taylor, '32
Jack Thurston, Honorary
Bill Tucker, Coach
Charles Bill Walker, '40
Edd White, Honorary
Newell Wilder, '26

1983

Bill Asher, '36
Bob Cathers, '49
David Chandler, '56
Bob Coleman, '42
Jesse Grant, '61
Amos Miller, Honorary '59
Carl Oakley, '50
Harold Queary, '58
Fred Rader, '60
Edd Selvy, '55
Dr. Keith Smith, Honorary
Don Turner, '56
1955 Football Team

1984

Odell Byrley, '40
Tom Catron, Honorary
Archie Powers, Coach
Curt Selvy, '47
Dusty Yates, '47
Robert Barton, '50
1936 Basketball Team

1985

Charles Baker, Honorary
Alvah Bible, '67
Willard "Wid" Ellison, '39
Ben Lankster, '73
Bob Terrell, '51
Ralph Wilder, '56
1939 Football Team

1986

Ossie Burch, Coach
Bosco Cummins, '40
Vin Hoover, '70
Princess McBurney, Honorary
Max Mobley, '48
Jim Spicer, '76
1960 Football Team

1987
Susan Wilder Begley, '74
David Burton, '64
Bill Howard, '57
Joe Moore, Honorary
Dennis Myers, '71
Marvin Selvy, '65
1976 Football Team

1988
Garry Grederick, '65
Tony Lanham, '58
Keith Hutson, '59
Charles "Curly" Selvy, '66
1949-50 Basketball Team

1989
Stephen Lee Bird, '79
Winton Boone, '57
Thomas Horvath, '78
Baker Reasor, Honorary
C. Bascom Reasor, Honorary
Clarence L. Smith, '39
1957 Football Team

1990
Greg Briscoe, M.D. '80
Morris "Moose" Garrison, '56
Monte Goins, '50
Bill Hoover, Honorary
David R. Miller, '56
Roy Taylor, '80
1947 Basketball Team

1991
Barry Brooks, '67
Kenny Cox, '64
Ed Dunn, '50
C.D. Vermillion, '52
Jim Lee Crawford, Honorary
Don Estep, Honorary
1980 Football Team

1992
Bruce Carpenter, '72
Dan Chase, '78
Hut Jones
Bobby Sturgill, '47
Greg Taylor, '82
John Bill Black, Honorary
Terry Wyrick, Honorary
1962 Football Team

1993
Harold Brooks, '49
David Goins, '73
Tommy Greer, '83
Carl Lawson Rusty Onkst, '78
Dr. L.U. Gilliam, Honorary
Henry Martin, '54, Honorary
1982 Football Team

1994
Bill Cummins
Steve Jewell
Martin Earl Pennington
Silas Prewitt
Amon Root
Bill Hood
1949 Football Team

1995
Jim Begley, '77
Stan Cluggish, '37
Dr. B.J. Edwards, Honorary
Curley Ellison, '56
Richie Francioni, '80
Lou Meadors, Honorary
Frank Walker, '34
1976-77 Girls Basketball Team

1996
Jennifer Ann Fuson, '86
Charles Blondie Hendrickson, '32
Tim Logan, '74

Harold Nooners Reedy, Jr., '86
Corean Wells Bohnenberger, '84
Dean Eagle, Honorary '31
1948-49 Basketball Team

1997
Larry "Cotton" Adams
Tony Morton, '84
Charles Triplett, '39
Margy Shelton, '82
Harold Reedy, Honorary '57
Mike Driggers, '71
1969-70 Football Team

1998
Darrell Storm
Jeff Parks
David Meador
Roger Rose
Bob Croley
Burley Foley
1977-78 Football Team

1999
Bob Howard
Don House
Jarree Goodin Wiseman
Jayna Farris
Marvin "Red" Cadle
Willard Farris
1982 Girls Basketball Team

2000
William Keith Branaman
Danny Calia
Frank Clabaugh
David Selvy
Darin Robert Steely
Denise Metzger Taylor
1938-39 Basketball Team

2001
Phil Gregory
Jerry "Zeke" Perkins
Jeff Miller
Bo Roaden
Brent Canady
Corey Reeves
1990 Redhounds Football

2002
Bernard Kincaid
Harry Killinger
Coach Billy Hicks
Rick Cobb
Jerry Brooks
Chad Michael Estep
Dale Grant Fox
Jeff Moran
G. Duane Hart
1990-91 Redhounds Basketball

2003
First Lieutenant Patrick Kelly
Larry Joe Burton
Gregory Lee Duncum
Tom Henson
Kenneth W. Cobb
Coach Gerald Foley
Theresa Hammons, Honorary
Ruth Meadors, Honorary
1951 Redhounds Basketball

2004
Matt Church
David Hannah
S.T. "Bitsey" Holman
David N. Huff
Steve Kersey
Steve Lawsson
Randall Sawyers
Donna Willis
1994 Redhound Baseball Team

2005
Alan Sadler
Bill "Big Eye" Hughes
Charles Judd
Tony Pietrowski
Chris Ledington
Jody Mouser
Clyde Burchette
Terry Joe Martin
1973 Redhound Football Team

2006
Richard Alan Sadler
Cecil Herman Meadors
Karen Lynn Evans
Boyce W. Frederick
Ronnie Watkins
Kent Carter
Tommy R. Faulkner
1979-80 Girls Basketball Team

2007
John L. Crawford II, '76
Nolan M. DeVaughn, '97
John C. Fletcher, Coach
Denny L. Jones, '82
Joe H. Lankford, '47
Joellen M. Petrey, '97
Winston Phipps, Honorary
C. Luke Sadler, '89
1979 Football Team

2008
Teddy Trosper, Honorary
John Jones
Tim Dudley (posthumously)
Teresa Hill
Kathryn (Katty) Hoover
Daniel Valentine
Scotty Wilson
1996-97 Boys Basketball Team

2009
Donald Shane Creekmore
Seth Hauser
Vincent Hoover
Terry Jackson
Jason McDaniel
James R. Mobley
Fred Anderson
Curtis Hart

2010
Jeff Adkins
Jerry Baker (posthumously)
C.E. Brittain
Brent Freeman
Patrick McCowan
Leann Schooler Smith
David Myers
Mike Deaton

2011
Cynthia Emrich
Michael S. Frederick
Kenneth Gilbert
Myrvin Grigsby
Jonathan Sizemore
Brian Tankersley
Darrell Tremaine
Luther "Wayne" Willis

2012
B.J. Foley
Jason Estep
Mike Cima
Mike Wilson
Tonya Taylor
Jeff Adams
1952-53 Basketball Team
Coach Armondo Cima
Carol Craig, Honorary

About the Author

Gary P. West has simple criteria when it comes to writing books.

"I only take on a project that I will enjoy writing about and I only write about something I think people will enjoy reading," he says.

West grew up in Elizabethtown, Kentucky and attended Western Kentucky University before graduating from the University of Kentucky in 1967 with a journalism degree. At U.K. he was a daily sports editor for the *Kentucky Kernel.*

Later he served as editor for the nation's largest civilian enterprise military newspaper at Fort Bragg, North Carolina. From there he was employed in the corporate advertising office of one of the country's largest insurance companies, State Farm Insurance in Bloomington, Illinois, where he was a copywriter.

He returned to Kentucky in 1972 where he began an advertising and publishing business.

Along the way, for twelve years, he was the executive director of the Hilltopper Athletic Foundation at Western Kentucky University, and provided color commentary for Wes Strader on the Hilltopper Basketball Network.

In 1993, he became the executive director of the Bowling Green Area Convention and Visitors Bureau. He retired from there in 2006 to devote more time to his writing.

He is a freelance writer for several magazines in addition to writing a syndicated newspaper travel column, *Out & About...Kentucky Style*, for several papers across the state.

Gary is in demand as a speaker and for book signings throughout Kentucky.

This is his sixth book. Previous books are *King Kelley Coleman: Kentucky's Greatest Basketball Legend (2005), Eating Your Way Across Kentucky (2006), Eating Your Way Across Kentucky – The Recipes (2007), Shopping Your Way Across Kentucky (2009), 101 Must Places to Visit in Kentucky Before You Die (2009),* and co-authored *Kentucky Colonels of the American Basketball Association: The Real Story of a Team Left Behind.*

Gary and his wife, Deborah, live in Bowling Green, Kentucky.

INDEX

Q

R

S

T

U

V

W

X

Y

Z

More Sports Books
Published By Acclaim Press

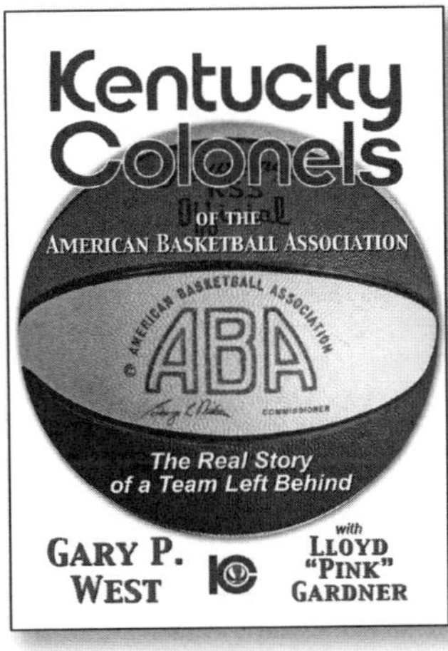

Kentucky Colonels of the American Basketball Association

An inside look at one of the most intriguing times in the history of professional basketball; and the city of Louisville and the state of Kentucky were enjoying every bit of it.

And then as quickly as the Colonels appeared, they were gone. They had been around just long enough to win a world championship and showcase not only some of the best basketball players in the history of the game, but also some of its most colorful characters.

Factors Unknown: The Tragedy that Put a Coach and Football on Trial

As young men across America begin training and conditioning their bodies in summer practice sessions for that ever-demanding, grueling battleground of athleticism known as football, we all know it will happen. Somewhere, somehow, somebody is going to die.

On a sultry August afternoon, it proved too much for a young sophomore at Pleasure Ridge Park High School in Louisville, Ky. He gave his all and then collapsed, never to rise again. But this time was different, very different. Some unknown factors precipitated this tragic outcome. Somebody would pay for this – in prison.

This is that story, the case of Coach David Jason Stinson and, ultimately, the sport of high school football, on trial.

Legacies of Kentucky Mountain Basketball: Champions and Palaces of the Mid-1950s

A look back at what once was the heart and soul of sports in the beautiful, but rugged mountains of Kentucky is what Legacies of Kentucky Mountain Basketball does with photographs from today.

Legacies of Kentucky Mountain Basketball … is about the golden era of high school basketball in Kentucky, high school basketball that was as close to the original game as we will ever see again.

This book features the towns and high schools of the 13th, 14th and 15th Regions of the Commonwealth, including detailed accounts of the 1953-54, 1954-55, and 1955-56 seasons.

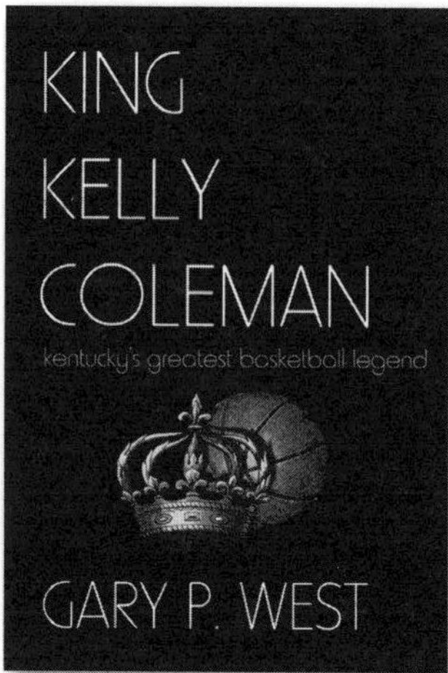

King Kelly Coleman: Kentucky's Greatest Basketball Legend

In a state where the love of basketball itself is legendary, there are its rare heroes who also, through the dispassionate lens of history, rise to legendary status. When that legend rises so far above the others as to acquire mythical or rather, folk hero, proportions – and then enigmatically vanishes- you have King Kelly Coleman.

This shy, humble mountain boy blessed with extraordinary talent and drive captured Kentucky's hearts and its all-time record books with performances that have yet to be equaled – even half a century later. Never before in print, the authorized King Kelly Coleman story, is told by award-winning author Gary P. West, from actual interviews and information from Coleman himself.

Pioneer Spirit: One High School's Rise From Tragedy to Glory

The amazing, true story that will inspire all....

The indomitable spirit of the Simon Kenton Pioneers blazes the trail from horrific devastation and seemingly insurmountable obstacles to basketball supremacy and sports legendry.

Follow the accounts of Simon Kenton High School's devastating explosion and their come-back to win the 1981 Kentucky State Basketball Championship.

Kentucky High School Basketball Records & Facts

Never has there been anything like it: every team, every school, every year from the beginning of high school basketball in Kentucky through 2013!

In cooperation with the Kentucky Association of Basketball Coaches and the Kentucky High School Athletics Association, included are every high school basketball team in the state, boys and girls, from 1906-2013; all postseason scores including district, region and state games; Sweet Sixteen All-Tournament Team members' names and high school team; All-State Teammembers' names and high school team; Coach of the Year winners; Mr. & Miss Basketball; Ted Sanford & Joe Billy Mansfield Award winners; All A State Classic teams and scores; photos of every state championship team; complete roster of current coaches.